I0880391

Intersection of Intensity

Exploring Giftedness and Trauma

By Patricia Gently, MSMHC, Ph.D.

Gifted
UNLIMITED

Edited by: William D. Beuscher and Youssef R. Sleiman
Interior design: The Printed Page
Cover design: The Printed Page

Published by
Gifted Unlimited, LLC
12340 U.S. Highway 42, No. 453
Goshen, KY 40026
www.giftedunlimitedllc.com

© 2024 by Patricia Gently, MSMHC, Ph.D. & Gifted Unlimited LLC

ISBN: 978-1-953360-37-3

All rights reserved under International and Pan-American Copyright Conventions. Unless otherwise noted, no part of this book may be reproduced, stored in a retrieval system, or transmitted in any form or by any means—electronic, mechanical, photocopying, or otherwise—without express written permission of the publisher, except for brief quotations or critical reviews.

Printed and bound in the United States of America.

Gifted Unlimited and associated logos are trademarks and/or registered trademarks of Gifted Unlimited.

At the time of this book's publication, all facts and figures cited are the most current available. All telephone numbers, addresses, and website URLs are accurate and active; all publications, organizations, websites, and other resources exist as described in this book; and all have been verified as of the time this book went to press. The author(s) and Gifted Unlimited make no warranty or guarantee concerning the information and materials given out by organizations or content found at websites, and we are not responsible for any changes that occur after this book's publication. If you find an error or believe that a resource listed here is not as described, please contact Gifted Unlimited.

Dedication

I dedicate this book to my clients and the gifted community. I want you to feel and know that you are not alone as you consider your own intersection of intensity.

Acknowledgment

I would like to acknowledge my daughter, Mikah. She cheered me on through the book-writing process and allowed me grace as an imperfect parent while (and after) raising her. The Chapter 14 section about parenting and trauma is also a love letter to her.

Contents

Foreword and Introduction (Don't Skip This)

A Trauma Therapist First

As the author of this book, I feel it appropriate to share my background. Currently, I hold several titles. I am a mother, daughter, sister, friend, and neighbor. I am also a rescue farmer, professor, researcher, presenter, advocate, therapeutic coach, volunteer, administrator, facilitator, and leader. Most forefront though, I am a trauma therapist who works primarily with gifted, twice-exceptional, neurodivergent, and other marginalized populations.

As a trauma therapist, I use Eye Movement Desensitization and Reprocessing (EMDR), **Neurodiversity-Affirmative** Dialectical Behavior Therapy (NDA-DBT), Internal Family Systems (IFS), and other types of psychoanalytic, solution-focused, and somatic approaches to help individuals process trauma from the top-down (immediate behaviors and cognitions) and from the bottom-up (psychodynamic impact of underlying elements, often held in the body and nervous system). Processing and working on trauma from different perspectives allows clients to not only cope with trauma and **triggers** but also process past experiences and move through trauma to resolve it. Using this process, some clients fully file away and even partially forget the negative impact of traumatic experiences. However, the goal of trauma processing is not to cure trauma but rather to decrease the intensity, duration, and frequency of negative symptoms such that we can *look back but not stare* at past difficulties and events.

It is as an experienced trauma therapist with my master's in clinical mental health counseling and a doctorate in developmental psychology that I approach the topic of trauma. It is as an academic, parent, advocate, and twice-exceptional individual with a history of developmental and complex traumas, though, that I consider the interaction of trauma and **giftedness**. That is, though I can explain this material from a professional perspective, lived experience also informs my understanding.

I was the oldest middle child of four in an initially low-income family. We lived in the poorest and most violent neighborhood in Anchorage, Alaska, where I also attended school and learned to ditch it more often than I showed up, even though I graduated with honors. As a teenager, I also learned to forge my father's signature and found out that if your name is in the computer twice, even if one of you was barred from graduating, the other may still get to walk and even speak on behalf of the student body about making a difference.

Over the years, I saw my parents obtain affluence. Despite this, my siblings and I have had strained relationships with food and weight, criticism, social and employment statuses, substance association, spending and income levels, and even political and parenting philosophies. Some of this is expected in any family. However, I could trace many of these issues from my parents' families, their childhood struggles, and generational traumas from exposure to abuse, war, poverty, immigration, economic depression, racism, mental health difficulties, and more. And while some of my problems growing up as an angsty, demand-avoidant teen could relate to my personality profile and innate expressions, certainly some were due to an integration of ecological systems that lacked support and praise.

Indeed, in addition and intermixed with environment and nurture was a bit of gifted nature seen through the lens of overexcitability (Dąbrowski, 1966). As will be addressed further in the chapters of this book, these overexcitabilities include psychomotor, imaginational, sensual, emotional, and intellectual super-sensitivities along with an existential nature and deep spirituality as a child. When the world is taken in with such deep feeling, thinking, and sensual experiencing, what is not or is minimally traumatic to one person could be super intense to another. This was my world.

Flash-forward to young adulthood, I believed most of my struggles could be blamed on my parents and my developmental trauma, and they may be the first to tell you that they were not perfect. However, as I learned more and more about giftedness, demand avoidance, rejection-sensitive dysphoria, and processing styles, I also learned about how my nature further interacted with my nurture. So, while my parents are not off the proverbial hook, there is undoubtedly more to the story of 'why me.' Part of that story has to do with also being the stereotypical strong-willed daughter, while even more has to do with the twice-exceptionality that masked both my giftedness and my other neurodivergences such as dyslexia, dyscalculia, ADHD, and auditory processing difficulties. Then, throw some complex trauma into the mix, and you get what I got: an intersection of intensity.

What to Expect from This Book

As I finished Chapter 14, an inspirational friend asked me, "So, what would you like someone to get from this book?" It took me absolutely no time to give a succinct and complete answer. To him, I wrote that readers will come away from this book with a deeper understanding of the different ways gifted individuals experience and encounter trauma and post-traumatic growth, and they will have a better understanding of what to do about it while fostering compassion for self and others. I really did not need to say more. This is my ultimate goal for you, dear reader.

A Note About Accessibility, Self-Care, Triggers, and Check-Ins

To write a neurodiversity-affirming and accessible book, I took care to make some modifications that may or may not appeal to **folx**. One of these adaptations involved writing fairly comprehensive introductions and conclusions for each chapter. Please note that some readers will want the recaps offered in the conclusions, and some may find them redundant. Some folx may prefer to jump around and skip the repeated articulations. This is expected.

It is also possible that you, the reader, have an intersection of intensity or giftedness and trauma. Therefore, it is essential to acknowledge how even reading about trauma can evoke strong emotions and possibly distress. There may be stories and information in this book that are relatable and stir up some *stuff*. This is not uncommon and it is not necessarily *bad*. However, awareness of this is wise, as is a gentle plan of action. I purposefully do not go into great detail about triggering topics that are known to cause more visceral reactions, though difficulty is sprinkled throughout the book. We will **titrate** in and out so your mind will not be bombarded with anything heavy. Triggers may still present themselves, so please take care of yourself.

I invite all who enter these pages to engage in self-care inclusive of some solid **grounding**. Check in with yourself and your nervous system as you read through these chapters. And if you need a break, honor that need. To help with this task, I have check-in sections at the end of each chapter such that you can explore the impact this information has on you. Feeling and connecting with this material is valuable, and so is your peace. Be well.

Part One:
Trauma and Giftedness

(1) What is Giftedness?

(2) So Why the Focus on Giftedness?

(3) What is Trauma?

CHAPTER 1: What is Giftedness?

At the core of our exploration exists a common inquiry: *What truly defines* ***giftedness?*** Is it solely a measure of high IQ or developmental **asynchronicity**? Does it encompass acute attunement and intellectual capacity alone? *How complex is it?*

The concept of giftedness extends beyond conventional notions of academic success. Gifted individuals or those who work closely with them recognize that giftedness transcends mere scholastic achievements. In fact, many gifted children grapple with challenges within the educational system, especially when a mismatch exists between their unique qualities, interests, and the learning environment.

In this chapter, I seek to help you consider the actuality of giftedness as we dig into the intricacies of this complex concept and embrace its holistic nature that encompasses intellectual, creative, emotional, and social dimensions. Through careful examination, we aim to move beyond narrow definitions, embracing a broader understanding of giftedness that celebrates diverse strengths, passions, and potential.

By broadening perspectives and concepts of giftedness, we construct a path toward a more inclusive and nurturing environment for gifted individuals. We shed light on the importance of recognizing and supporting their unique needs, creating opportunities that foster growth, validation, self-actualization, and a sense of belonging. Ultimately, our exploration will contribute to a deeper comprehension of giftedness, empowering us further as we consider this **neurodivergence** in relation to **trauma** and its impact in the following chapters.

Defining Giftedness

Though gifted and giftedness are commonly used terms, particularly in education, the definition of giftedness can vary depending on the setting. The Columbus Group (1991) definition cited by Morelock (1992, para. 57) is as follows:

> *Giftedness is* ***asynchronous development*** *in which advanced cognitive abilities and heightened intensity combine to create inner experiences and awareness that are qualitatively different from the norm. This asynchrony increases with higher intellectual capacity. The uniqueness of the gifted renders them particularly vulnerable and requires modifications in parenting, teaching, and counseling in order for them to develop optimally.*

In her book, *Journey Into Your Rainforest Mind*, psychotherapist Paula Prober (2019) uses the metaphor of a rainforest ecosystem to explain one type of gifted manifestation that is complex, creative, sensitive, empathetic, intuitive, and often misunderstood. Other definitions may focus more on IQ cutoffs and the five **levels of giftedness** while some look at how a person is only gifted in certain domains. We see this when people say, "I have an IQ of 135 and am gifted in mathematics and reasoning." However, I tend to look beyond IQ to the Columbus Group's and Prober's conceptualizations of giftedness as starting points.

Considering metaphors like Prober's while expanding on the Columbus Group definition of giftedness can help us address it from a more **whole-person** perspective. With these conceptualizations in mind, I suggest that gifted individuals are complex beings with a distinctly above-average ability and compulsion to develop new understanding, knowledge, behaviors, skills, values, attitudes, and preferences. Expeditious learning can be attributed to a tendency toward rapid pattern-finding and **meaning-making** processes where new (and interesting to them) material is retained after one to two repetitions of exposure. This pattern-finding and meaning-making also lends to the depth and complexity noticed in gifted persons. Along with a rapid ability and drive to learn, and in relation to depth and complexity, it is noted that gifted persons can experience the world with great **intensity** or the **blunting** of intensity in sensual, psychomotor, imaginational, intellectual, and/or emotional domains, and develop in a way that seems initially asynchronous. These categories of intensity, by the way, correlate with Dąbrowski's (1938) **overexcitabilities** or **OEs** within his theory of positive disintegration.

To be considered gifted, individuals are often identified as gifted in grade school, by a psychologist, and/or by a gifted peer group. They could also have an IQ over 130 (this number varies depending on IQ assessments and measures) or be members of groups for gifted individuals, such as Mensa, InterGifted, The Puttyverse, Bloomers, or otherwise. It is understood that many adults do not identify their own giftedness until they have gifted children or gifted peers in adulthood (Kuipers, 2007; Milic & Simeunovic, 2020). Seeing themselves through their later identified children or peers is common and considered reliable in relation to earlier identification efforts (Kuipers, 2007; Milic & Simeunovic, 2020). Self-identification is acknowledged as valid in this context, and individuals exploring their own giftedness are encouraged to consult this or other publications and groups to determine if it resonates with their own experiences.

Asynchronicity and Compensation

Sometimes, and as often recorded and observed in gifted children, development can seem asynchronous. This asynchronous development, where social-emotional, intellectual, creative, and physical skills and abilities develop at significantly different rates, lends to the whole-person profile of giftedness (Blackett & Webb, 2011; The Columbus Group, 1991; Morelock, 1996; NAGC, n.d.). That is "if the gap between cognitive and emotional development is too wide" (Alesi et al., 2015, p.3), it promotes qualities seen in gifted persons. An oh-so-common example of this asynchronicity is seen when a gifted child can comprehend and complete a calculus equation even though they are unable to tie their shoes. This asynchronicity is particularly noticeable and seems limiting when the gap between what a person can and cannot do causes distress. These gaps or struggles, however, are often compensated for.

In her article about gifted **compensation**, Dr. Linda Silverman (2009) shared how gifted individuals excel at problem-solving and present with a capacity for abstract reasoning that is then used to compensate for lack of ability in other areas. That is, there is a tendency for gifted persons to adapt to adversities throughout development by using strengths and creativity. We often call this creative or adaptive problem-solving. Socially, this problem-solving can turn into a **masking** of traits or abilities seen frequently in the gifted population. This may be particularly true if the gifted person also has a second exceptionality or neurodivergence.

Twice-Exceptionality (2e)

The identification of one's own giftedness can be further complicated if there are additional divergences from what is typical, such as developmental or learning differences, or rather, if a person is **twice-exceptional (2e)**. Twice-exceptionality is the presence of intellectual giftedness and what might be defined otherwise as a disability, often specifically a learning difference (Al-Hroub, 2020; Baum et al., 2017; Montgomery, 2015). The concept of twice-exceptionality dates to the 1970s when 2e students and individuals were recognized as "gifted handicapped," as per the so-titled book by Maker (1977). 2e individuals are now distinguished as high potential, talented persons with learning, attention, and/or social "impairments" who, as youth, are reportedly at particular risk of **experiencing** social-emotional difficulties and **underachievement** without appropriate support (Reis et al., 2014). The topic of underachievement, though, is a hairy one and will be discussed further in an upcoming section. Know, however, that it is not a term I appreciate as it can boil the value of a gifted person down to what they can produce rather than who they are.

2e individuals are often unidentified and may be seen as only gifted, only disabled, or **neurotypical** because strengths and/or weaknesses are masked and compensated for within a developmental context (Yssel et al., 2014). 2e children are also often characterized as having a heightened language ability, which can inhibit identification for services (van Viersen et al., 2016) while increasing vulnerability to developing mental health disorders (Alesi et al., 2015). This is particularly true since giftedness can act as a limiting factor when development is asynchronous. Along with enduring and adjusting for asynchronicity, 2e individuals tend to compensate for second exceptionalities, again adding to the masking seen and experienced by many **neurodivergent** persons.

Giftedness and Overexcitability

I attended to the reality that gifted persons often experience the world with intensity in sensual, psychomotor, imaginational, intellectual, and/or emotional domains. These five areas of intensity are known also as Dąbrowski's (1938) overexcitabilities (OEs). According to psychologist Kazimierz Dąbrowski and his theory of positive disintegration, individuals who possess significant potential for growth often exhibit one or more of these five strong manifestations of neurological capacities in their reactions to stimuli. It is now understood that the five OEs are commonly displayed by gifted persons. According to Dąbrowski, and as stated by Dr.

Linda Silverman of The Gifted Development Center (2020, para. 5), these intensities and their brief descriptions can be:

- **psychomotor** – an abundance of physical energy
- **sensual** – heightened responses of the senses and aesthetic appreciation
- **imaginational** – capacity for fantasy
- **intellectual** – curiosity and aliveness of the mind
- **emotional** – sensitivity, intensity, empathy

While one of these OEs may be dominant, they are often combined to form a deep and complex picture of what makes gifted individuals so unique. These OEs will each be considered in relation to trauma in subsequent sections. For now, and to prime our minds, consider how differently such neuro-excitability might impact a person's experiencing of trauma or any phenomena for that matter. Sit with this for a moment before moving on.

Chapter 1 Conclusion

Chapter 1 considered the multifaceted nature of giftedness, expanding beyond traditional measures of academic success. It emphasized the holistic dimensions of giftedness, including intellectual, creative, emotional, and social aspects. By challenging narrow definitions and embracing a broader understanding, the chapter advocated for a more inclusive and nurturing environment for gifted individuals where their depth and complexity can be further understood.

The Columbus Group's definition of giftedness, focusing on asynchronicity and heightened intensity, provided a valuable starting point for comprehending the unique experiences of gifted individuals. The concept of compensation shed light on how gifted individuals adapt and excel in certain areas to compensate for challenges in others. Additionally, the notion of twice-exceptionality introduced the complexity of being gifted while also having a learning difference or other neurodivergence.

Chapter 1 also introduced the concept of overexcitabilities (OEs), which are strong manifestations of neurological capacities often experienced by gifted individuals in psychomotor, sensual, imaginational, intellectual, and emotional domains. These OEs contribute to the depth and complexity observed in gifted persons, shaping their experiences and interactions with the world.

This introductory chapter laid the groundwork for further exploration of giftedness in relation to trauma and its impact in subsequent chapters. By deepening our comprehension of giftedness and its complexities, we hopefully gained valuable insights into the experiences and well-being of gifted individuals, thus enabling us to provide them with the support and opportunities they need to thrive.

Chapter 1 Check-In

Exploration: This chapter was all about giftedness. What is giftedness? How is giftedness present in your life? What are some particulars related to this neurodivergence?

Conclusion: To summarize, characteristics that are unique to gifted persons include:

- advanced cognitive abilities (sometimes seen as creativity or creative problem-solving)
- rapid pattern-finding and meaning-making that lend to depth and complexity
- asynchronous development and compensation (masking)
- overexcitability/heightened intensity (sensual, psychomotor, imaginational, intellectual, and emotional)

Questions to consider include:

1. Do you relate to the characteristics of giftedness?
2. Do your children, friends, coworkers, or family display some of these characteristics?
3. Were you surprised by any of this information?
4. What does this information about giftedness mean to you?

Chapter 1 References

Alesi, M., Rappo, G., & Pepi, A. (2015). Emotional profile and intellectual functioning: A comparison among children with borderline intellectual functioning, average intellectual functioning, and gifted intellectual functioning. *SAGE Open, 5*(3), 1-9. https://doi.org/10.1177/2158244015589995

Al-Hroub, A. (2020). Use of the Jordanian WISC-III for twice-exceptional identification. *International Journal for Talent Development and Creativity, 8*, 121–144. https://doi.org/10.7202/1076752ar

Baum, S., Schader, R., & Owen, S. (2017). *To be gifted and learning disabled: Strength-based strategies for helping twice-exceptional students with LD, ADHD, ASD, and more.* (3rd Ed.). Prufrock Press. https://doi.org/10.4324/9781003239147

Columbus Group. (1991). Unpublished transcript of the meeting of the Columbus Group, Columbus, OH.

Dąbrowski, K. (1938). Typy wzmożonej pobudliwości psychicznej [Types of increased psychic excitability]. *Biuletyn Instytutu Higieny Psychicznej, 1*(3-4), 3-26.

Kuipers, W. (2007). How to charm gifted adults into admitting giftedness: Their own and somebody else's. *Advanced Development, 11*, 9-25. https://www.proquest.com/docview/197463540?

Maker, C.J. (1977). *Providing programs for the gifted handicapped.* Council for Exceptional Children. https://doi.org/10.1093/ptj/58.1.102a

Milic, S., & Simeunovic, V. (2020). Concordance between giftedness assessments by teachers, parents, peers, and the self-assessment using multiple intelligences. *High Ability Studies*, 1-19. https://doi.org/10.1080/13598139.2020.1832445

Montgomery, D. (2015). *Teaching gifted children with special educational needs: Supporting dual and multiple exceptionality.* Routledge. https://doi.org/10.4324/9781315712321

Morelock, M.J. (1992). Giftedness: The view from within. *Understanding Our Gifted, 4*(3), 1, 11-15.

National Association for Gifted Children. (n.d.). *Social & emotional issues.* https://www.nagc.org/resources-publications/resources-parents/social-emotional-issues

Prober, P. (2019). *Journey into your rainforest mind.* Luminare Press.

Reis, S.M., Baum, S.M., & Burke, E. (2014). An operational definition of twice-exceptional learners: Implications and applications. *Gifted Child Quarterly, 58*(3), 217-230. https://doi.org/10.1177/0016986214534976

Silverman, L.K. (2009). The two-edged sword of compensation: How the gifted cope with learning disabilities. *Gifted Education International, 25*(2), 115-130. https://doi.org/10.1177/026142940902500203

Silverman, L.K. (2020). *New Insights into Overexcitability.* Retrieved from https://gifteddevelopment.org/musings/newinsights

van Viersen, S., Kroesbergen, E.H., Slot, E.M., & de Bree, E.H. (2016). High reading skills mask dyslexia in gifted children. *Journal of Learning Disabilities, 49*(2), 189-199. https://doi.org/10.1177/0022219414538517

Yssel, N., Adams, C., Clarke, L.S., & Jones, R. (2014). Applying an RTI model for students with learning disabilities who are gifted. *TEACHING Exceptional Children, 46*(3), 42-52. https://doi.org/10.1177/004005991404600305

Chapter 2:
So Why the Focus on Giftedness?

When I began my journey into researching giftedness, I collected a wealth of information about how gifted individuals face unique challenges that are distinct to this particular group (Alesi et al., 2015; Cross & Cross, 2015; Curtin, 2020; Francis et al., 2016; Guignard et al., 2012; Miron et al., 2019; National Association for Gifted Children, n.d.; Supporting Emotional Needs of the Gifted, 2022). In my presentation of this research, I insist that understanding these struggles and learning about how to navigate them effectively is crucial for the well-being and development of gifted individuals and those who care about them. Though we have some understanding of how to work with this population, it is not always clear how to deviate from research that focuses on neurotypical norms when suggesting interventions. To gain a deeper understanding of this need, it is beneficial to acknowledge research suggesting that gifted individuals utilize their heightened abilities to compensate for difficulties (Gilman et al., 2013; Silverman, 2009; Tan & Chun, 2014; van Viersen et al., 2016). However, it is also important to note that gifted individuals are often more susceptible to experiencing social-emotional challenges (Alesi et al., 2015; Cross & Cross, 2015; Francis et al., 2016; Guignard et al., 2012; National Association for Gifted Children, n.d.; Supporting Emotional Needs of the Gifted, 2022).

By attaining a deeper comprehension of these concepts, professionals, gifted individuals, families, and other concerned parties can recognize shared experiences among the gifted community, such as asynchronous development and compensation, without attaching negative labels or perceiving them as problematic. This understanding holds the potential to foster positive developmental outcomes, encompassing enhanced well-being, boosted self-esteem, reduced suicidality, increased resilience, greater life satisfaction, personal empowerment, integrated identity, and a sense of proficiency. Moreover, while catering to the specific needs of gifted individuals, the best practices employed for their benefit can also serve as a microcosm, offering insights and strategies that have the potential to be applied more universally for the betterment of all individuals.

Struggles With Identifying Gifted Individuals

As again addressed in my research (Williams, 2023), identifying and assessing gifted children and adults can be challenging as there is no universal definition of giftedness. Societal, cultural, or other constructs can also limit our ability to recognize exceptional abilities. For 2e individuals, it can be particularly difficult to identify disabilities that may not be immediately apparent. These "invisible disabilities," such as learning differences or developmental disabilities, are not apparent upon casual observation and can place individuals at a disadvantage when seeking support or recognition (Beer et al., 2022). Similarly, giftedness itself is not readily apparent. Therefore, identifying someone as both gifted and having a learning difference can present difficulties.

While being identified as gifted or twice-exceptional may not appear necessary for navigating life as an exceptional individual, exploring this aspect is relevant as it contributes to the developmental process and aids in understanding the dynamics within this population, which we will later relate to trauma processing and experiencing. And since being 2e entails recognizing both giftedness and what some may consider a functional deficit, it can be challenging to comprehend, especially in cases, for example, where a high school student participates in advanced placement classes while requiring an individualized education program (IEP) or 504 accommodations.

In relation to the difficulty with comprehending twice-exceptionality, Linda Silverman (2009) highlighted how it can be perplexing as it seems contradictory. To further explain this, Silverman wrote in her article about gifted compensation that:

> *There are two basic misunderstandings here: that the learning disabled aren't smart, and that giftedness means high achievement. If someone thinks learning disabled means "dumb," and that the gifted are "smart," you can't be smart and dumb at the same time. However, federal and state definitions of learning disabilities specifically limit the term, "learning disabled," to children of at least average intelligence. So, you have to be smart to be learning disabled! (p. 115)*

Confusion about being both smart and disabled comes partially from a difficulty with detecting learning struggles in gifted individuals. Silverman explained in her article that since gifted persons tend to excel in areas of abstract reasoning and problem-solving, they can use these strengths to compensate for and often conceal such struggles, thus also concealing a need for support. And even when gifted individuals speak up about their struggles or seek support, they are often met with the assertions "but you're so smart," "you are just lazy," and the infamous, "if only they would apply themselves" (Williams, 2023).

To further explore the challenges associated with identifying gifted, Gilman et al. (2013) emphasized in their article the difficulties in recognizing 2e students who were gifted with coexisting disabilities. They highlighted how an emphasis on below-average performance can cause professionals and families to overlook the giftedness of 2e students. In other words, instead of giftedness concealing a learning disability, the disability can conceal giftedness. Gilman et al. also pointed out that learning disabilities and giftedness can mask each other. Through case studies, they found that individuals who are not identified for special education services may perform at grade level by compensating for significant issues using their advanced conceptual abilities while still experiencing struggles.

Assessing 2e individuals for giftedness or the need for other supports can also be problematic since they may not perform as well on IQ tests or other gifted assessments. For instance, if a 2e person is dyslexic, their intelligence may not be fully captured by neurotypical-normed evaluation tools. Aubry and Bourdin (2018) discussed how the commonly used Wechsler Scales for assessing intellectual giftedness may not be suitable for individuals with learning disabilities, further complicating the proper identification of giftedness for 2e individuals.

Another study by Wai and Lovett (2021) emphasized the importance of using multiple and concurrent evaluations to assess for giftedness in order to prevent overlooking 2e students. While there may be concerns about the value of gifted assessment and programming, improving these practices globally and including underrepresented students, as highlighted by Wai and Lovett (2021), can contribute to addressing real-world problems and promoting a higher standard of living for all. However, it is essential to note that placing the burden of improving the world solely on gifted individuals may be misguided. Instead, it is preferable to focus on supporting the well-being and life satisfaction of gifted individuals, as is my common plea. Focusing only on what they produce or offer is unkind at a minimum.

Despite the importance of gifted and 2e identification for various reasons, one might still question why it is challenging to achieve. The underrepresentation of gifted individuals in gifted programming can be attributed to several factors. Knotek et al. (2020)

discussed how a lack of education and awareness regarding behavioral and culturally specific indicators of elevated ability, in the absence of above-average achievement, contributes to the under-identification of 2e and culturally/linguistically diverse children as gifted. Knotek et al. also pointed out a lack of social and cultural capital necessary to navigate American school systems and access better teachers, programs, studios, clubs, and other talent development opportunities. Understanding the privilege of normalcy and how exceptionalities, including multiple exceptionalities, can limit individuals in educational settings is crucial.

While informed parents and teachers can help address the issue of underrepresentation, Livers et al. (2021) highlighted that teaching candidates often feel ill-prepared to develop curriculum modifications and accommodations for students in need, which can affect the development of gifted students. Instead of solely assessing intelligence, there is an increasing focus in the gifted community on identifying gifted individuals by considering non-cognitive characteristics. According to Wai and Lakin (2020), this is especially important for **marginalized populations** who are underrepresented in gifted programs. Non-cognitive characteristics, as explained by Gil-Hernández (2021), encompass thoughts, feelings, and patterns of behavior. Oppong et al. (2019) discussed the connections between giftedness, self-governed learning, self-regulation, and metacognition as non-cognitive traits of gifted individuals. They also noted that social-emotional and motivational aspects of giftedness are often overlooked. Oppong et al. suggested using multiple cognitive and non-cognitive characteristics concurrently to increase the likelihood of detection and reduce false negatives in identification. Similar research by Aubry and Bourdin (2018) and Wai and Lovett (2021) identified the phenomenon of bright students with reading struggles not being appropriately assessed on standard intelligence tests, resulting in placement in learning environments that only address difficulties without acknowledging abilities.

Another potential approach to identifying gifted individuals, including marginalized populations, is to consider Dąbrowski's (1966) concept of overexcitabilities (OEs). OEs, as addressed in the previous chapter, are intensities in individuals that indicate a heightened ability to respond or react to stimuli. These OEs, which are commonly observed in the gifted community, include increased emotional, imaginative, intellectual, psychomotor, and sensual sensitivity and ability. Per Dąbrowski (1972), "One who manifests several forms of **overexcitability**, sees reality in a different, stronger and more multisided manner" (p. 7). Similar to identifying OEs, Büyükkıdık and Şimşek-Batar (2021) shared how other characteristics beyond IQ are identified in gifted persons by their parents. Per these authors,

> *The parents' children put forward dominant characteristics of their gifted children according to the order of importance/priority as strong curiosity, keen powers of observation ability, vivid imagination, high degree of creativity, rapid learning ability, good problem solving/reasoning ability, extensive vocabulary, and perfectionism. (Büyükkıdık & Şimşek-Batar, 2021, p. 448)*

Here, one might notice an overlap between their findings and Dąbrowski's, which is significant when both understanding giftedness and identifying it along with other exceptionalities (Williams, 2023).

Due to issues with the identification of giftedness, particularly if a person is 2e, otherwise neurodivergent, or socially marginalized, an exploration of trauma and giftedness will involve individuals who are self-identified or later-recognized as gifted and/or having a second exceptionality. This openness to self-identification in adulthood seems important and is not readily addressed in the scholarly literature (Williams, 2023).

Risk and Resilience Associated with Giftedness

As further addressed in my dissertation research that resulted in a **gifted/2e identity development theory** (Williams, 2023), a **risk and resilience framework** provides a theoretical foundation for understanding gifted strengths and struggles. According to this framework, there are both risks and protective factors in one's life that can either promote or hinder resilience (Jenson & Fraser, 2016). As mentioned earlier, some risks for gifted individuals may include social-emotional struggles and a lack of support structures while protective factors may include a supportive school or home environment, personal strengths, and innate intelligence. Gifted individuals, and particularly those who are 2e, exhibit high potential and exceptional talent, along with social, attention, and learning difficulties, placing them at risk for social-emotional challenges and underachievement without early professional intervention (Reis et al., 2014). This risk can reportedly be mitigated through the consistent awareness and responsiveness of important leaders and professionals to the needs of twice-exceptional individuals (Reis et al., 2014).

In examining the academic achievement of 2e individuals and their external support systems, such as parents, teachers, and peers, van Viersen et al. (2016) found that these individuals often lack support due to the challenges in identifying their strengths and struggles as a result of compensation, which can act as both a risk and a protective factor for twice-exceptional and gifted individuals (Silverman, 2009). However, the literature on gifted compensation provides varying perspectives with some denying its existence and others offering clear support for it (Silverman, 2009; van Viersen et al., 2015).

Beckmann and Minnaert (2018) acknowledge that gifted and learning-disabled students, who are often at risk of being overlooked for both gifted and special education services, are not typically conceptualized within the context of non-cognitive characteristics. In their analysis of 23 studies on twice-exceptionality, these authors found that 2e individuals reported frequent negative emotions, negative self-perceptions, challenging interpersonal interactions, and frustration with academics. However, they were also found to have higher-than-average levels of motivation, stronger **coping skills**, and perseverance. While a high level of academic frustration was significant, internal protective factors and strengths were found to help mitigate this struggle. This complex interplay is important to note, considering how both internal and external factors impact the development of gifted individuals with high potential (Dąbrowski, 1966). Nonetheless, this duality has not been thoroughly explained in the literature.

Despite the challenges in teaching 2e students, and in line with the risk and resilience framework, there are other protective factors that can help mitigate the associated risks. In an article about effective parenting for gifted and twice-exceptional individuals, Papadopoulos (2021) emphasized that positive parent-child relationships can promote greater academic success, positive self-perceptions, motivation, and overall adjustment. Encouraging talent development was also identified as a positive influence on academic and socio-emotional growth for 2e persons. Positive parenting experiences may act as a safeguard against or reduction of the negative impact of lacking social and cultural capital, as mentioned in Knotek et al.'s (2020) study, while also addressing the lack of teacher preparedness highlighted by Livers et al. (2021).

Another significant risk for gifted and 2e youth is bullying, which can have a major impact on their well-being. Ronksley-Pavia et al. (2019) conducted research on twice-exceptionality and bullying, identifying how 2e children are at an increased risk of bullying due to their multiple differences. The study revealed themes related to bullying by peers and teachers, adult responses to bullying, social isolation, emotional impact, and protective factors such as social support. Winsor and Mueller (2020) explored giftedness in relation to depression and suicide, listing bullying as a major contributing factor to negative mental health outcomes. They also found that 2e students often compensate for learning difficulties, potentially masking mental health challenges associated with these factors.

In the case of gifted individuals with autism, a specific subgroup of twice-exceptionality, researchers Wu et al. (2019) observed that while they exhibit potential for high achievement, they also face an increased risk of mental health and psychosocial concerns, such as negative self-concepts and anxiety disorders. A supportive school context inclusive of a flexible curriculum, strength-based approaches, and a safe environment was found to promote positive development and educational outcomes. It is important to consider these findings as twice-exceptionality is often approached from a deficit perspective, rather than focusing on what works and the strengths of 2e individuals. More research is needed to explore the experiences and needs of 2e learners, including gifted and autistic youth.

When considering academic achievement within the context of the risk and resilience framework, it becomes evident that external support is likely crucial for the positive development of gifted individuals. Wang and Neihart (2015) conducted qualitative research on the impact of support from parents, teachers, and peers on gifted individuals. The study confirmed that external support plays a vital role in their positive development with peer support emerging as the most influential factor in academic achievement. Interestingly, internal motivators were not considered as potential extraneous variables. That contrasts with the earlier article by Casino-García et al. (2021b). Those findings highlight the importance of emotional intelligence and introspection for the positive development of self-esteem and self-concept in 2e adolescents.

If external support plays such a vital role in a gifted individual's positive development, how critical could internal support be? This question pulls into focus a gap in the literature and a need to delve deeper into this question and literary discrepancy. Despite this discrepancy, however, it is clear in existing research that gifted children often face social-emotional difficulties (Cross & Cross, 2015; National Association for Gifted Children, ND; Supporting Emotional Needs of the Gifted, 2022). In fact, Cross and Cross (2015) suggested that the unique experiences and characteristics of gifted individuals contribute to an increased risk of unhealthy perfectionism, anxiety, depression, and even suicidality.

Guénolé et al. (2013) reported that gifted children with a significant verbal-performance discrepancy are more likely to experience social and school maladjustment, along with more serious behavioral symptoms. Given that gifted children, especially when experiencing asynchronous development, may be prone to mental health disorders (Alesi et al., 2015), it is important to strike a balance and develop theories to navigate these challenges while taking into account their strengths and protective factors.

Moving into adulthood, there is a lack of attention given to the adult gifted and 2e population, mainly due to the focus on academic performance and the exclusive identification of giftedness in schools. While research on giftedness and aging is increasing, most accessible studies primarily explore giftedness and emerging adulthood when individuals transition from high school to college or the workforce. Despite a lack of more complete research, it is still valuable to consider the experiences and reflections of emerging gifted adults. For instance, in a review of an exploratory study about how gifted university students with diagnosed learning difficulties maintained motivation, Lo and Yuen (2017) indicated that the support of significant others, such as teachers and parents, is crucial. However, the 2e individuals researched also developed coping strategies to navigate challenging learning environments, which raises the question of whether compensation alone can motivate a gifted university student to overcome adversity in the absence of significant social and academic support.

Similarly, Baum et al. (2014) explored this topic within the context of a strengths-based private school for gifted 2e individuals. The study revealed that those who successfully completed graduation requirements attributed their achievement to factors, such as psychological safety, tolerance for asynchrony, time, positive relationships, and consistent use of a strengths-based, talent-focused approach. So, despite the social-emotional difficulties often experienced by gifted individuals, as highlighted by Cross and Cross (2015) and other sources, the positive experiences identified in Baum et al.'s and Lo and Yuen's studies are significant. Protective factors may extend beyond social support as gifted individuals transition into adulthood, and further exploration is needed in this area.

Studies on gifted adults also often involve reflections on their upbringing and school years. However, existing research focuses more on how individuals felt about their childhood and adolescence and what might have helped them in hindsight. One such study revealed that many gifted and 2e youth struggle with poor self-concepts and strained relationships with their parents, possibly due to perceived underachievement or a discrepancy between their abilities and achievements (Barber & Mueller, 2011). Ronksley-Pavia et al.'s (2019) study, which explored bullying of 2e students by teachers and peers and the lack of support at home, further contributes to these challenges. Another study by Szymanski and Wrenn (2019) found that intense and successful gifted adults often felt misunderstood, unchallenged, and underserved during adolescence, emphasizing the importance of interacting with other gifted and intense individuals to combat feelings of isolation. But, there are also reports of satisfied individuals who lack such support.

The complexity of non-cognitive characteristics in gifted adults necessitates further exploration into this topic.

Seminal Studies About Giftedness

When considering giftedness in preparation for an understanding of how giftedness and trauma interact, it is also worth examining original or seminal studies. For example, Dąbrowski's (1966) article on his positive disintegration theory, discussed earlier, has influenced subsequent studies on gifted development even though his study did not specifically focus on giftedness. It does, however, consider how individuals with greater developmental potential may be better equipped to navigate through the five levels of the positive disintegration process.

The Terman Study of the Gifted, conducted over a span of 70 years, collected longitudinal data on gifted individuals into adulthood (Terman & Oden, 1947). Reviewing this study from a modern perspective, Holahan (2021) acknowledged Terman's unfavorable portrayal of gifted children but also highlighted the study's findings that gifted children fulfilled positive expectations as adults in intellectual, academic, and occupational domains. However, there is some concern that 2e individuals, women, and minorities may have been overlooked in this study, given the ease with which they could have been disregarded in 1921 during its inception. Nevertheless, substantial longitudinal evidence supports the notion that gifted individuals develop into highly accomplished adults. It remains to be seen, though, if this is increasingly true for minorities or women in the modern age and whether it holds true for 2e individuals who not only achieve developmentally but also find satisfaction in their lives.

Chapter 2 Conclusion

In this second chapter, we explored the research on giftedness and how it highlights the unique strengths and challenges associated with this population. It is crucial to understand these struggles and learn how to effectively navigate them for the well-being and development of gifted individuals and those who care about them. It was also considered how the best practices employed for the benefit of gifted individuals can serve as a microcosm, offering insights and strategies that have the potential to be applied more universally.

As we advanced through the chapter, it was explored how the identification of gifted and 2e individuals can be challenging, particularly due to the lack of a universal definition of giftedness and the presence of invisible disabilities. The compensation often exhibited by gifted and 2e individuals can further complicate the identification process. Self-identification is therefore respected here, and associated self-awareness plays a crucial role in gifted development, especially in adulthood.

The underrepresentation of marginalized and 2e individuals in gifted programs was addressed, and we read how it can be attributed to various factors including a lack of education and awareness, social and cultural capital limitations, and teachers' lack of preparedness to support these students. Non-cognitive characteristics and overexcitabilities are starting to be recognized as important aspects of giftedness in literature, and multiple evaluations are recommended to avoid overlooking 2e individuals.

We highlighted how understanding the risks and resilience associated with giftedness is essential for promoting positive developmental outcomes. Gifted individuals may face social-emotional challenges, but they also possess protective factors, such as supportive environments, personal strengths, and innate intelligence. External support from parents, teachers, and peers plays a vital role in their positive development. However, the interplay between risks and protective factors is complex and requires further exploration.

We considered an unfortunate reality of the ways that bullying and mental health challenges are significant risks for gifted and 2e individuals, underlining the need for supportive environments and interventions. Positive parent-child relationships, talent development, and inclusive school contexts can contribute to mitigating these risks. However, there is still more to understand about how, in addition to social supports, non-cognitive factors may also protect gifted individuals and help with identifying them.

Finally, we considered some seminal studies about giftedness. Specifically, Dąbrowski's theory of positive disintegration and the Terman Study of the Gifted provide valuable insights into the developmental potential and long-term outcomes of gifted individuals. These studies suggest that gifted children often fulfill positive expectations and develop into accomplished adults. However, further research is needed to explore the experiences of 2e individuals, women, and diverse gifted populations to ensure a comprehensive understanding of giftedness and its interaction with trauma.

In summary, a comprehensive understanding of giftedness and twice-exceptionality requires considering the unique challenges, protective factors, identification difficulties, and risk-resilience framework associated with this population. Further work is needed to explore the experiences and needs of gifted individuals, as well as the interactions between giftedness and trauma.

Chapter 2 Check-In

Exploration: This chapter considered existing research that suggests a strong need for support of the gifted population due to unique strengths and struggles.

Conclusion: To gain a comprehensive understanding of giftedness and twice-exceptionality, it is essential to take into account the distinct challenges, protective factors, difficulties in identification, and non-cognitive characteristics that help us conceptualize this population's needs.

Questions to consider include:

1. How do you conceptualize giftedness?
2. Does the research about gifted identification align with your own understanding?
3. Are you or someone you know identified as gifted or 2e?
4. Did you learn something new about giftedness?

Nervous system and mental/emotional health:

1. Check in with your understanding of giftedness.
2. Are you feeling triggered or contemplative in relation to this information?
3. Where can you offer compassion to yourself or others in relation to this material?
4. If needed, take a break and tend to your mental and emotional needs as you digest this information.

Chapter 2 References

Alesi, M., Rappo, G., & Pepi, A. (2015). Emotional profile and intellectual functioning: A comparison among children with borderline intellectual functioning, average intellectual functioning, and gifted intellectual functioning. *SAGE Open, 5*(3), 1-9. https://doi.org/10.1177/2158244015589995

Aubry, A., & Bourdin, B. (2018). Short forms of Wechsler scales assessing the intellectually gifted children using simulation data. *Frontiers in Psychology, 9*, 1-12. https://doi.org/10.3389/fpsyg.2018.00830

Barber, C., & Mueller, C.T. (2011). Social and self-perceptions of adolescents identified as gifted, learning disabled, and twice-exceptional. *Roeper Review, 33*(2), 109-120. https://doi.org/10.1080/02783193.2011.554158

Baum, S.M., Schader, R.M., & Hébert, T.P. (2014). Through a different lens: Reflecting on a strengths-based, talent-focused approach for twice-exceptional learners. *Gifted Child Quarterly, 58*(4), 311-327. https://doi.org/10.1177/0016986214547632

Beckmann, E., & Minnaert, A. (2018). Non-cognitive characteristics of gifted students with learning disabilities: An in-depth systematic review. *Frontiers in Psychology, 9*, 1-20. https://doi.org/10.3389/fpsyg.2018.00504

Büyükkıdık, S., & Şimşek-Batar, A. (2021). Scaling gifted children's dominant characteristics using pair-wise comparison method. *Ankara* Üniversitesi *Eğitim Bilimleri Fakültesi Özel Eğitim Dergisi, 22*(2), 439-463. https://doi.org/10.21565/ozelegitimdereisi.695240

Casino-García, A.M., Llopis-Bueno, M.J., & Llinares-Insa, L.I. (2021). Emotional intelligence profiles and self-esteem/self-concept: An analysis of relationships in gifted students. *International Journal of Environmental Research and Public Health, 18*(3), 1-23. https://doi.org/10.3390/ijerph18031006

Cross, J.R., & Cross, T.L. (2015). Clinical and mental health issues in counseling the gifted individual. *Journal of Counseling & Development, 93*(2), 163-172. https://doi.org/10.1002/j.1556-6676.2015.00192.x

Cross, T.L., Cross, J.R., Dudnytska, N., Kim, M., & Vaughn, C.T. (2020). A psychological autopsy of an intellectually gifted student with attention deficit disorder. *Roeper Review, 42*(1), 6-24. https://doi.org/10.1080/02783193.2019.1690081

Curtin, S.C. (2020). State suicide rates among adolescents and young adults aged 10–24: United States, 2000–2018. *National Vital Statistics Report, 69* (11). 1-5. https://stacks.cdc.gov/view/cdc/93667

Dąbrowski, K. (1966). The theory of positive disintegration. *International Journal of Psychiatry, 2*(2), 229-249.

Dąbrowski, K. (1972). *Psychoneurosis is not an illness.* Gryf.

Francis, R., Hawes, D.J., & Abbott, M. (2016). Intellectual giftedness and psychopathology in children and adolescents. *Exceptional Children, 82*(3), 279-302. https://doi.org/10.1177/0014402915598779

Gil-Hernández, C.J. (2021). The (unequal) interplay between cognitive and noncognitive skills in early educational attainment. *The American Behavioral Scientist (Beverly Hills), 65*(11), 1577-1598. https://doi.org/10.1177/0002764221996764

Gilman, B.J., Lovecky, D.V., Kearney, K., Peters, D.B., Wasserman, J.D., Silverman, L.K., Postma, M.G., Robinson, N.M., Amend, E.R., Ryder-Schoeck, M., Curry, P.H., Lyon, S.K., Rogers, K.B., Collins, L.E., Charlebois, G.M., Harsin, C.M., & Rimm, S.B. (2013). Critical issues in the identification of gifted students with co-existing disabilities: The twice-exceptional. *SAGE Open, 3*(3), 1-16. https://doi.org/10.1177/21582440135058

Guénolé, F., Louis, J., Creveuil, C., Baleyte, J., Montlahuc, C., Fourneret, P., & Revol, O. (2013). Behavioral profiles of clinically referred children with intellectual giftedness. *BioMed Research International, 2013*, 1-7. https://doi.org/10.1155/2013/540153

Guignard, J., Jacquet, A., & Lubart, T.I. (2012). Perfectionism and anxiety: A paradox in intellectual giftedness? *PloS One, 7*(7), 1-6. https://doi.org/10.1371/journal.pone.0041043

Holahan, C.K. (2021). Achievement across the life span: Perspectives from the Terman study of the gifted. *The Gifted Child Quarterly, 65*(2), 185-195. https://doi.org/10.1177/0016986220934401

Jenson, J.M., & Fraser, M.W. (2016). *Social policy for children and families: A risk and resilience perspective* (3rd ed.). Sage Publications.

Knotek, S.E., Foley-Nicpon, M., Kozbelt, A., Olszewski-Kubilius, P., Portenga, S., Subotnik, R.F., & Worrell, F.C. (2020). Gatekeeping in high-performance settings. *Review of General Psychology, 24*(3), 254-267. https://doi.org/10.1177/1089268020905578

Livers, S.D., Zhang, S., Davis, T.R., Bolyard, C.S., Daley, S.H., & Sydnor, J. (2021). Examining teacher preparation programs' influence on elementary teacher candidates' sense of preparedness. *Teacher Education Quarterly, 48*(3), 29-52. https://www.jstor.org/stable/27094741

Lo, C.C., & Yuen, M. (2017). Succeeding against the odds: Observations on coping by three intellectually very able university students with specific learning difficulties in Hong Kong. *Gifted Education International, 33*(3), 232-247. https://doi.org/10.1177/0261429415585407

Miron, O., Yu, K., Wilf-Miron, R., & Kohane, I.S. (2019). Suicide rates among adolescents and young adults in the United States, 2000-2017. *JAMA: The Journal of the American Medical Association, 321*(23), 2362-2364. doi:10.1001/jama.2019.5054

National Association for Gifted Children. (n.d.). *Social & emotional issues.* https://www.nagc.org/resources-publications/resources-parents/social-emotional-issues

Oppong, E., Shore, B M., & Muis, K.R. (2019). Clarifying the connections among giftedness, metacognition, self-regulation, and self-regulated learning: Implications for theory and practice. *The Gifted Child Quarterly, 63*(2), 102-119. https://doi.org/10.1177/0016986218814008

Papadopoulos, D. (2021). Parenting the exceptional social-emotional needs of gifted and talented children: What do we know? *Children (Basel), 8*(11), 1-16. https://doi.org/10.3390/children8110953

Reis, S.M., Baum, S.M., & Burke, E. (2014). An operational definition of twice-exceptional learners: Implications and applications. *Gifted Child Quarterly, 58*(3), 217-230. https://doi.org/10.1177/0016986214534976

Ronksley-Pavia, M., Grootenboer, P., & Pendergast, D. (2019). Bullying and the unique experiences of twice exceptional learners: Student perspective narratives. *Gifted Child Today Magazine, 42*(1), 19-35. https://doi.org/10.1177/1076217518804856

Silverman, L.K. (2009). The two-edged sword of compensation: How the gifted cope with learning disabilities. *Gifted Education International, 25*(2), 115-130. https://doi.org/10.1177/026142940902500203

Supporting Emotional Needs of the Gifted. (2022). *About SENG.* https://www.sengifted.org/about

Szymanski, A., & Wrenn, M. (2019). Growing up with intensity: Reflections on the lived experiences of intense, gifted adults. *Roeper Review, 41*(4), 243-257. https://doi.org/10.1080/02783193.2019.1661054

Tan, L.S., & Chun, K.Y.N. (2014). Perfectionism and academic emotions of gifted adolescent girls. *The Asia-Pacific Education Researcher, 23*(3), 389-401. https://doi.org/10.1007/s40299-013-0114-9

Terman, L.M., & Oden, M.H. (1947). *The gifted child grows up. Vol. IV. Genetic studies of genius.* Stanford University Press.

van Viersen, S., de Bree, E.H., Kroesbergen, E.H., Slot, E.M., & de Jong, P.F. (2015). Risk and protective factors in gifted children with dyslexia. *Annals of Dyslexia, 65*(3), 178-198. https://doi.org/10.1007/s11881-015-0106-y

van Viersen, S., Kroesbergen, E.H., Slot, E.M., & de Bree, E.H. (2016). High reading skills mask dyslexia in gifted children. *Journal of Learning Disabilities, 49*(2), 189-199. https://doi.org/10.1177/0022219414538517

Wai, J., & Lovett, B.J. (2021). Improving gifted talent development can help solve multiple consequential real-world problems. *Journal of Intelligence, 9*(2), 1-12. https://doi.org/10.3390/jintelligence9020031

Wang, C.W., & Neihart, M. (2015). How do supports from parents, teachers, and peers influence academic achievement of twice-exceptional students. *Gifted Child Today, 38*(3), 148-159. https://doi.org/10.1177/1076217515583742

Williams, P. (2023). *Understanding how twice-exceptional (2e) individuals navigate adolescence: A grounded theory study.*

Winsor, D.L., & Mueller, C.E. (2020). Depression, suicide, and the gifted student: A primer for the school psychologist. *Psychology in the Schools, 57*(10), 1627-1639. https://doi.org/10.1002/pits.22416

Wu, I., Lo, C.O., & Tsai, K. (2019). Learning experiences of highly able learners with ASD: Using a success case method. *Journal for the Education of the Gifted, 42*(3), 216-242. https://doi.org/10.1177/0162353219855681

CHAPTER 3: What is Trauma?

Trauma, a powerful and dysregulating influence, can cast a disruptive gloom over the human experience. In this chapter, we venture to understand the intricate nature of trauma, examining its various forms and the imprint it can leave on individuals. By deeply exploring this concept, we seek to elucidate the complex ways in which trauma shapes lives, disrupts emotional well-being, and impacts our development. Through this exploration, we aim to foster a deeper comprehension of the complex nature of trauma, laying the groundwork for subsequent discussions on the intersection of giftedness and trauma, followed by topics involving support, healing, and even growth opportunities for those affected by its enduring effects.

Trauma is a common enough term, used in everyday conversation. Calling something traumatic allows us to express intensity such that a person may readily recognize the severity of a situation. What exactly is trauma, though? How do we define this term? How do we apply an understanding of trauma in our daily lives?

There are different types of trauma and different ways to define it. According to the American Psychiatric Association (2013) fifth edition of the *Diagnostic and Statistical Manual of Mental Disorders* (DSM-V), to receive a post-traumatic stress disorder diagnosis, for example, a person must have a history of "exposure to actual or threatened death, serious injury, or sexual violence" (p.271).

However, according to the Center for Health Care Strategies' (2021) Trauma-Informed Care Implementation Resource Center, trauma can result from exposure to a single incident or series of events and can be identified as "emotionally disturbing or life-threatening." It is important to know that not all emotional events are considered traumatic. Significant trauma can impact a person's mental, physical, social, emotional, and spiritual functioning and well-being, though.

Historically, society and the medical profession associated PTSD with soldiers or persons in war-torn communities, later extending the application and understanding of trauma and its impact on first responders and victims of violent crime. However, per the Trauma-Informed Care Implementation Resource Center, other traumatic experiences may include abuse, childhood neglect, having a family member with mental health or substance use disorders, ambiguous separation from loved ones, poverty, racism, discrimination, oppression, community violence, or terrorism. Additionally, according to the International Society for Traumatic Stress Studies (2023), other types of traumas include medical trauma, firearm violence, grief and bereavement (particularly in children and adolescents), refugee trauma, climate change trauma, pandemic (COVID-19) trauma, and traumatic stress related to substance use.

Why We Worry About Trauma

However it is defined, one thing trauma experts and researchers maintain is that exposure to trauma can result in a host of different mental health and medical conditions (Center for Health Care Strategies, 2021; Felitti et al. 1998). Additionally, regardless of a person's motivations and development, trauma can impact their sense of well-being. In relation to **Maslow's (1943) hierarchy of needs** for example, displayed in Figure 1 below, a person could be at a level such that they have physiological, health and safety, and belongingness needs met and are therefore motivated mostly by securing self-esteem. At any point though, significant trauma can cause a person to descend to lower-level motivations to meet lower-level needs when they are seemingly placed at risk. For example, if a person with a strong sense of belongingness was in a destructive earthquake that destroyed their home, they may be motivated rather, by a drive to secure housing, food, health, and safety rather than working on their self-esteem.

Figure 1. Maslow's Hierarchy & Trauma

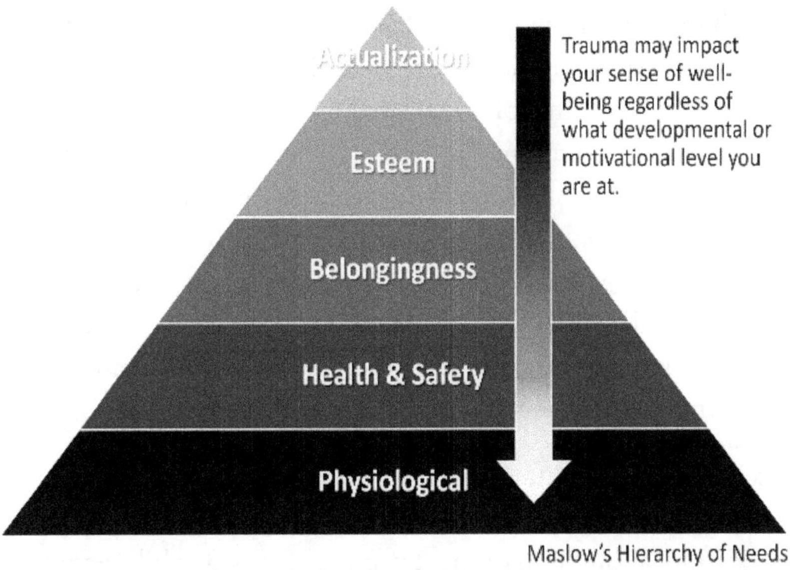

So, any trauma, at any point in a person's life can disrupt how they think, feel, and behave. When trauma happens during development, it can have additional, unfavorable impacts. Specifically, per the hallmark *ACEs Study*, researchers Felitti et al. found a correlation between the number of adverse childhood experiences a person had, identified as their ACE score, and negative mental and physical health outcomes. That is, the higher a person's ACE score, the higher likelihood of certain conditions such as anxiety, depression, suicidality, PTSD, substance use, sexually transmitted disease, COPD, and relationship distress.

As a trauma therapist and individual who also assists clients with chronic health conditions, I can attest I never met a person with fibromyalgia or temporomandibular joint (TMJ) disorder who did not also have a significant trauma history. Particularly, those who seemed to hold trauma in their bodies had generally experienced developmental or complex trauma, types of trauma profiles that will be explored in greater detail in proximate sections.

In addition to identifying ACE scores, it is beneficial to understand how trauma impacts minorities and marginalized populations. Some of this can understandably be related to the identified presence of racial and historical traumas experienced by minorities. However, as documented by the American Psychiatric Association (2023), gender, sexual, racial, and ethnic minorities often endure poor mental health outcomes for a variety of reasons including issues with access to quality mental health care, cultural and social stigmas surrounding mental health support, discrimination and oppression, and a lack of awareness about mental health needs and resources.

Persons with disabilities have also enjoyed a lack of support in society. According to Thomas-Skaf and Jenney (2021) in their publication about remaining trauma-informed while engaging children with disabilities, it was identified that individuals with a divergent ability profile experience trauma differently than those without disabilities. Additionally, while it was recognized how trauma may result in impairment for disabled persons, it was mostly seen in the research findings that those with disabilities are more likely to be exposed to trauma in the form of mistreatment, vulnerability, social stigmas, and discrimination.

When we consider gifted and neurodivergent persons as also a minority group, it allows us to wonder if there has been a lack of attention and resources offered to them as well. Certainly, gifted, twice-exceptional, and neurodivergent peoples have not had their needs fully catered to, as with any marginalized or misunderstood population. The **goodness of fit** mismatch between population needs and environments will be discussed in later chapters. For now, it is helpful to ponder this possibility as we consider different types of trauma that people endure.

Types of Trauma

As attended to earlier, there are different types of trauma as understood by those who work to be trauma-informed, such as educators, therapists, community volunteers, and first responders. For this publication, we will consider three types of trauma: ***big T trauma***, ***little t trauma***, and ***complex trauma***. It should be noted, and reminders will be present, that there is not one trauma that is worse than another and they are not hierarchical in nature. Rather, the terms *big*, *little*, and *complex*, are used to help us conceptualize different occurrences and phenomena. The concepts of big and little traumas are adapted from Dr. Francine Shapiro's primary 2001 text about **Eye Movement Desensitization and Reprocessing (EMDR)** therapy, used to process trauma (Shapiro & Maxfield, 2002).

According to Shapiro, big T traumas are events that are immediately intensive and more singular in nature. For example, war, school shootings, a serious car crash, an injury or attack, being involved in a natural disaster, or experiencing a major loss/death are big T traumas. Big T trauma is often associated with soldiers, victims of violent crime, and those who endured a single event or clustering of events, and they are also most associated with a traditional PTSD diagnosis per the DSM-V. However, any person can experience a big T trauma at any time, and some individuals may be at higher risk of doing so.

Little t traumas are those that can be grouped under the umbrella of adversity although they are not lesser in any way. According to Shapiro, little t trauma refers more to undesirable life experiences, such as chronic criticism, shaming, neglect of emotions or physiological needs, lasting health impairments, frequent discrimination and oppressive actions, chronic harassment or bullying, and so on. Dr. Maggie Crastnopol (2015) refers to some of these experiences as resulting in **cumulative relational trauma** and seemingly minor, inconspicuous psychic wounds that are collected gradually, eroding an individual's self-esteem, distorting their character, and compromising their ability to connect with others. Often, we also refer to little t trauma in childhood as developmental or complex trauma. **Developmental trauma**, according to Abrams (2021) in their American Psychological Association publication, refers to disruptions in development resulting from ongoing trauma during childhood. This trauma is typically classified as little t trauma and typically occurs in the context of relationships.

Complex trauma is often identified as a mix of both big T and little t trauma or different types and combinations of little t trauma, resulting in a complex developmental profile and trauma history. When treating complex trauma with EMDR, I will generally identify developmental trauma with clients that then impacts how more recent big T or little t traumas are affecting them. For example, if a client is enduring workplace harassment and is struggling to set boundaries or assert themselves, it may be because of the impact of earlier, developmental traumas in their childhood home where they learned to avoid conflict as a means of survival. Here, the complexity of developmental trauma impacts current behavior and little t experiences. Any mixture of trauma that adds to the complexity of one's psychological profile can result in complex trauma and therefore complex post-traumatic stress disorder (**cPTSD**).

Developmental trauma disorder (DTD) and complex post-traumatic stress disorder (cPTSD) diagnoses are not in the fifth edition of the DSM even though the World Health Organization added cPTSD to the International Statistical Classification of Diseases and Related Health Problems (ICD-11) in 2019. Professionals such as psychologist Joseph Spinazzola, Ph.D., trauma psychiatrist Bessel van der Kolk, MD, and clinical psychologist Julian Ford, Ph.D., ABPP championed the inclusion of DTD in the DSM, however, it was identified in 2011 as lacking evidential support. In the decade following this finding, these professionals and others have amassed substantial scientific evidence about the occurrence of DTD, further supporting the knowledge of how trauma accounts for developmental disruptions. It is likely that we will see significant changes in the next DSM inclusive of expanded or new trauma diagnoses.

In the following chapter, we will explore giftedness in relation to trauma while referring to terms such as big T trauma, little t trauma, and complex trauma. Despite the type and quality of trauma endured, it is all impactful and important to consider alone and in relation to one's specific brand of neurodivergence. Figure 2, on the following page, acts as a quick reference to remind readers of what the different types of trauma are. You may want to dog-ear that page.

Chapter 3 Conclusion

Chapter 3 provided an in-depth exploration of trauma, its various forms, and its impact on individuals. It identified the complex nature of trauma and its effects on emotional well-being and development. The chapter also sought to foster a deeper understanding of trauma, laying the foundation for subsequent discussions on the intersection of giftedness and trauma, as well as topics related to support, healing, and growth opportunities for those affected by it.

This chapter also acknowledged how trauma can result from a range of experiences, from exposure to life-threatening events to ongoing adversity and discrimination. It emphasized that trauma can affect individuals' mental, physical, social, emotional, and spiritual functioning and well-being. The concept of trauma was not limited to specific populations, though, as it can impact anyone regardless of age, background, or identity. Though the focus of this book is on the gifted population and trauma, we do not compare traumas nor suggest that one group of sufferers are worse off than another.

The significance of trauma was highlighted by its potential to disrupt an individual's hierarchy of needs and motivate them to prioritize lower-level needs for safety and security. Moreover, it was explored how trauma experienced during development can have long-lasting and adverse impacts on individuals' lives. The Adverse Childhood Experiences (ACEs) Study demonstrates the correlation between adverse childhood experiences and negative mental and physical health outcomes.

Chapter 3 also addressed the importance of understanding how trauma impacts marginalized populations, including minorities and individuals with disabilities. It shed light on the barriers they face in accessing mental health support and the increased vulnerability they might experience due to mistreatment, social stigmas, discrimination, and lack of resources. It was also instilled that, though the gifted population is the focus of this book, it is only one minority population that needs consideration.

Figure 2. Types of Trauma

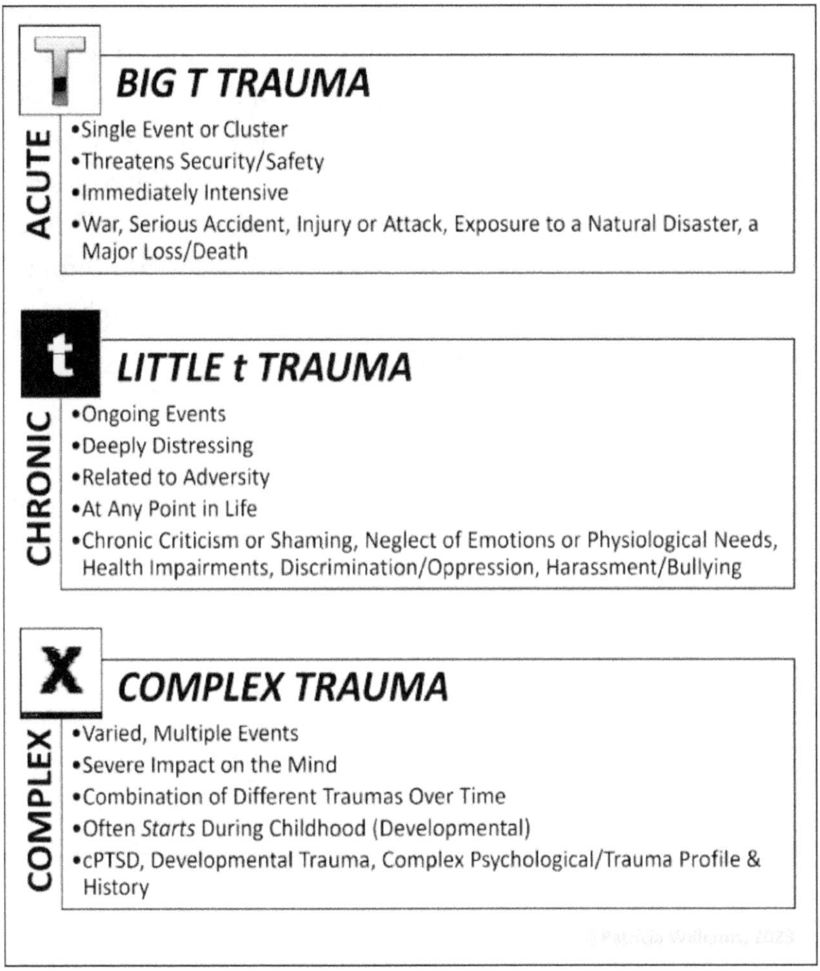

Three types of trauma were discussed: big T trauma, little t trauma, and complex trauma. Big T traumas are intense and often associated with singular events while little t traumas encompass ongoing adversities. Complex trauma refers to a combination of different types of trauma, resulting in a complex developmental profile and trauma history. Although not officially recognized in the DSM, it is identified that complex trauma is acknowledged in the International Statistical Classification of Diseases and Related Health Problems (ICD-11) as complex post-traumatic stress disorder (cPTSD).

By comprehensively exploring trauma, its types, and its impacts, this chapter set the stage for a deeper understanding of the intersection between giftedness and trauma. It provided a solid foundation for subsequent discussions on how trauma affects gifted individuals, the importance of trauma-informed support, and opportunities for healing and growth. Overall, this chapter considered the profound and lasting effects of trauma and the need for comprehensive approaches to address and mitigate its impact.

Chapter 3 Check-In

Exploration: This chapter was all about trauma. What is trauma? How does it present? What are some particulars related to this phenomenon? Why do we worry about trauma? What are the different types of trauma?

Conclusion: A fairly all-inclusive definition of trauma suggests that it is a pervasive problem that results from exposure to an incident or series of events that are emotionally disturbing or life-threatening with lasting adverse effects on the individual's functioning and mental, physical, social, emotional, and/or spiritual well-being (Trauma-Informed Care Implementation Resource Center, 2021).

Questions to consider include:

1. How do you conceptualize trauma?
2. Do big T, little t, and complex categories make sense to you?
3. Can you relate to big T, little t, and complex trauma? How?
4. Did you learn something new about trauma or yourself?

Nervous system and mental/emotional health:

1. Check in with your body. What do you feel?
2. Are you feeling triggered, agitated, tense, heavy, etc.?
3. Where can you offer compassion to yourself or others in relation to this material?
4. If needed, take a break, hydrate, feed yourself, and engage in some **grounding**. (If this term is new to you, you could jump to Chapter 10, which talks about different grounding and coping techniques.)

Chapter 3 References

Abrams, Z. (2021). Improved treatment for developmental trauma. *American Psychological Association, 52*(5), 38. https://www.apa.org/monitor/2021/07/ce-corner-developmental-trauma

American Psychiatric Association. (2013). *Diagnostic and statistical manual of mental disorders* (5th ed.). Arlington, VA: American Psychiatric Association. https://doi-org.library.capella.edu/10.1176/appi.books.9780890425596

American Psychiatric Association. (2023). *Mental Health Disparities: Diverse Populations.* Retrieved from https://www.psychiatry.org/psychiatrists/diversity/education/mental-health-facts

Crastnopol, M. (2015). Micro-trauma: A psychoanalytic understanding of cumulative psychic injury. Routledge. https://doi.org/10.4324/9780203878897

Center for Health Care Strategies. (2021). *Trauma-Informed Care Implementation Resource Center: What is Trauma?* Retrieved from https://www.traumainformedcare.chcs.org/what-is-trauma/

Felitti, V.J., Anda, R.F., Nordenberg, D., Williamson, D.F., Spitz, A.M., Edwards, V., Koss, M.P., & Marks, J.S. (1998). Relationship of childhood abuse and household dysfunction to many of the leading causes of death in adults: The adverse childhood experiences (ACE) study. *American Journal of Preventive Medicine, 14*(4), 245-258. https://doi.org/10.1016/S0749-3797(98)00017-8

International Society for Traumatic Stress Studies. (2023). *Public Resources: Friday Fast Facts.* Retrieved from https://istss.org/public-resources/friday-fast-facts

Maslow, A.H. (1943). A theory of human motivation. *Psychological review, 50*(4), 370.

Shapiro, F., & Maxfield, L. (2002). Eye movement desensitization and reprocessing (EMDR): Information processing in the treatment of trauma. *Journal of clinical psychology, 58*(8), 933-946. https://doi.org/10.1002/jclp.10068

Thomas-Skaf, B.A., & Jenney, A. (2021). Bringing social justice into focus: "trauma-informed" work with children with disabilities. *Child Care in Practice: Northern Ireland Journal of Multi-Disciplinary Child Care Practice, 27*(4), 316-332. https://doi.org/10.1080/13575279.2020.1765146

Part Two:
How Trauma and Giftedness Interact

(4) Trauma and the Gifted Brain

(5) Asynchronicity, Compensation, and Trauma

(6) Heightened Intensity and Trauma

Chapter 4: Trauma and the Gifted Brain

Trauma is a phenomenon that practitioners, educators, community workers, and society should be aware of. This is true for any person or population and is why the world is pushing to be more trauma-informed. Of course, with specific populations, there are different types of trauma or intricacies that are also considered. For example, refugees will have an increased possibility of trauma related to their circumstances surrounding the flight from a country or area because of natural disasters, war, or persecution. Individuals enduring poverty may have trauma related to food insecurity, judgment and discrimination, a lack of access to services, and financial stress. With any marginalized population especially, you will have considerations in relation to that marginalization and circumstantial complications.

There are elements that are consistent enough across the gifted population, too, that they should be considered in relation to trauma. To address this, we will reflect back on Chapter 1 about giftedness and what it is. As a reminder, the elements that may be unique to gifted persons include:

- advanced cognitive abilities (sometimes seen as creativity or creative problem-solving)
- rapid pattern-finding and meaning-making that lends to depth and complexity

- asynchronous development and compensation (masking)
- overexcitability/heightened intensity (sensual, psychomotor, imaginational, intellectual, and emotional)

Obviously, this is not an exhaustive list. However, it is a fine starting place and reference point. In this chapter, we will consider the interaction of trauma and the gifted brain by hitting on the first two categories listed here with greater depth.

While thoroughly exploring giftedness, knowledge of an interesting interplay emerges between advanced cognitive abilities, the process of meaning-making, and the inherent inclination for pattern-finding. This chapter dives into the overlap of these cognitive dimensions and the additional influences of trauma. By examining their complex interrelationships, we can uncover the complexities within the gifted experience where exceptional cognitive capacities encounter the potential disruptions caused by trauma or traumatic contamination. Through this exploration, we aim to more fully comprehend both the vulnerabilities that arise at the convergence of advanced cognitive abilities, meaning-making, pattern-finding, and trauma, offering valuable insights into the challenges faced by gifted individuals and pathways towards growth, healing, and self-realization.

Advanced Cognitive Ability and Trauma

Gifted people are often identified as super intelligent or cognitively capable. And indeed, while gifted people might not excel in all academic domains, they do tend to learn rapidly in areas of interest and ability. They are also often seen as creative or ingenious. For example, many employers and teammates enjoy having gifted people in their industry think tanks as they can have an aptitude for novel problem-solving. Unfortunately, while this advanced ability may seem like an elitist quality with only benefits, it is common for gifted individuals to feel separate from society or peer groups because of this presumed gift. Particularly, gifted individuals identify feeling lonely and ill-supported, often suffering from mental health struggles (Alesi et al., 2015; Cross & Cross, 2015; National Association for Gifted Children, ND; Papadopoulos, 2021; Pfeiffer, 2021; Reis et al., 2014; Winsor & Mueller, 2020; Williams, 2023). They also report feeling misunderstood, unchallenged, and underserved due to a need for more compassion, depth, complexity, and sometimes rigor (Szymanski & Wrenn, 2019; Williams, 2023).

Additionally, a gifted person's brain (and nervous system) is different when compared to the **neuromajority** in several ways. Most physically, there are nearly 40 documented studies as of 2021, finding that intelligence quotient (IQ) is positively correlated with brain volume while several more studies find a higher volume of gray matter in regions related to executive function, intellectual processing, complexity, emotional intelligence, and sensory processing (Tetreault, 2021). Gray matter is crucial in the brain as it contains neurons responsible for processing information and forming memories while playing a vital role in cognition, decision-making, sensory perception, and motor control (Draganski & May, 2008; Fjell & Walhovd, 2010). Due to these roles, an increase in gray matter documented in gifted brains seems significant.

The volume of gray matter in a gifted person's brain may also contribute to increased neuroplasticity, a phenomenon documented in gifted individuals (Tetreault, 2021). Neuroplasticity refers to the brain's ability to change and adapt in response to experiences, learning, and environmental factors. Changes in the structure and connectivity of gray matter can influence the brain's capacity for neuroplasticity (Pascual-Leone, 2005; Tetreault, 2021). Studies have shown that learning new skills or acquiring knowledge can lead to structural changes in gray matter such as increases in synaptic connections and the formation of new neural pathways that enhance neuroplasticity (Draganski & May, 2008; May, 2011).

Gifted persons tend to acquire new skills and knowledge rapidly, lending to this experience.

Intellectually gifted individuals also exhibit larger subcortical structures and stronger white matter microstructural organization in specific brain regions associated with explicit memory (Kuhn et al., 2021). Explicit memory plays a crucial role in learning as it allows individuals to consciously recall and use previously learned information or experiences. By relying on explicit memory, learners can retrieve and apply knowledge, facts, and concepts from their long-term memory, making connections and integrating new information with existing knowledge. This memory system enables the acquisition of new skills, understanding of complex concepts, and problem-solving. Explicit memory significantly impacts learning by facilitating the retention and retrieval of information, enhancing cognitive processes, and supporting the development of expertise in various domains.

When you have documented neurological differences and are identified as *so smart*, you may also start to internalize this, believing that you *should* be able to learn and handle anything. You may even hear comments from others such as "Oh, they will be fine. They are so smart!" And while gifted individuals may be able to problem-solve their way through difficulties, they may also notice more that is judged as wrong or harmful compared to neurotypical peers. Additionally, if someone seemingly over-intellectualizes a situation, they may neglect their emotions. In doing so, trauma may impact a thinker because they think of more ways the difficulty is traumatic. They may also consider more ways in which a traumatic experience is difficult. When considering a tendency to make connections to build neural pathways, it is not a stretch to understand how trauma can be learned more intensely by gifted persons. As such, it is important to remember that, though gifted individuals tend to be resourceful, trauma can still easily contaminate bright minds.

Rapid Pattern-Finding, Meaning-Making, and Trauma

While it is common to associate giftedness with only intellectual aptitude, it is also important to understand other neurological and behavioral differences seen in this population. Gifted individuals often exhibit a notable propensity for pattern recognition (pattern-finding) and the ascription of meaning (meaning-making), setting them apart from others (Williams, 2023). **Pattern-finding**, as it sounds, is when we see repetition and can anticipate outcomes because of it. In relation to learning, a gifted person who is adept at pattern-finding can make connections to seemingly intuit outcomes (Fjell & Walhovd, 2010; Lauer & Yonce, 2017; Winner & Martino, 1993). In situations where gifted persons seem to *just know* something, this may be due to pattern-finding that is either an intentional activity or done even subconsciously. For example, a gifted individual who has never been taught a foreign language may pick it up rapidly because they notice patterns in the foreign lexicon or familiar language roots (Greek, Latin, etc.). This is like how a child may quickly pick up algebra or play the piano by ear by experiencing and recognizing mathematical or musical patterns. When studying new material, pattern-finding helps connect new information to existing data in one's memory to quickly code it in the mind.

On a neurological level, imagine a higher-than-average number of neural pathways being forged and connections made. As is addressed by Dr. Nicole A. Tetreault (2021) in her book about the gifted brain from a neuroscientist's perspective, those with an elevated intellectual capacity and processing ability demonstrate regional expansion and higher-than-average neuroactivity. When more neurons are involved in information coding, processing can happen more rapidly with less exposure. Pattern recognition helps file away, retrieve, and make connections with information.

In addition to pattern-finding, gifted persons tend to engage in meaning-making. Meaning-making, also like it sounds, is when we ascribe a significance or purpose to something. For example, a person might say they graduated college so they could make a difference in the world. For them, completing such a task is meaningful because of what could be done with their sometimes exhausting efforts. The exhaustion was worth it because it meant something. As Victor Frankl (1959) insisted, a search for meaning can reduce suffering.

For gifted persons, meaning-making is often done with greater intensity and frequency because it is craved, and because it connects meaning to behaviors, events, and patterns that then drive development. In research conducted about how twice-exceptional (2e) individuals navigate adolescence, it became apparent that when gifted individuals embraced a belief that their efforts held meaning, they were empowered with motivation and a strong drive to develop (Williams, 2023). As supported by additional research, life purpose acts meaningfully as a guide that directs potential for gifted youth while having a sense of meaning and self-compassion were the greatest predictors of well-being in gifted persons (Moran, 2020; Pollet & Schnell, 2017). Research has revealed that the most effective social-emotional learning programs for gifted youth emphasize the practice of meaning-making, encompassing the attribution of significance to tasks of varying scales (Armstrong et al., 2019). Moreover, when counseling gifted individuals, the collaborative approach to enhancing their overall functioning revolves around tasks including the optimization of **existential** meaning (Pfeiffer, 2021).

Together, pattern-finding and meaning-making help gifted individuals code information into their minds and memories. Meaning-making, in fact, helps individuals group activities, events, and behaviors into categories for more rapid recall such that when a new pattern presents itself, the mind automatically pulls from those stores to categorize by meaning and purpose. For example, suppose a person learns a new skill and readily identifies it as meaningful based on existing values and/or categories. In that case, that skill will be grouped with similar, meaningful skills or activities creating more data to inform an existing pattern. When trauma informs any of these categories, patterns, or meanings, mental coding is at risk of traumatic contamination, or the influence of trauma on the otherwise healthy mental coding process.

With trauma, pattern-finding can plague a sufferer with connections that intensify the traumatic experience in the moment and in concert with complex trauma. In the moment, such as when trauma occurs, a person may see patterns, causing them to immediately analyze an event. Sometimes, such as with little t, complex, or developmental trauma, a gifted individual even immediately creates a mental pattern (aware or not) of events that continue to occur, such as behavioral patterns or patterns of abuse, connecting them to other existing patterns in their minds. When you think of these patterns as worn neuro-pathways, it might become clear how easily these patterns and events are recalled, and how worn and even painful these pathways become, spilling over into the nervous system and body.

Meaning-making, while seemingly positive, can also complicate a gifted person's interaction with trauma, particularly when a person experiences developmental trauma. For example, if someone grows up with a parent that neglects their emotional needs, suggesting that their feelings are *stupid* (an abhorrent word), that individual may grow up believing that all the difficult feelings they have are also *stupid*. Then, when they struggle with emotions in adulthood, the meaning ascribed to sadness or anger for example (because there has to be meaning) is that *they are stupid*. This outcome could happen to any person with developmental trauma. However, for a person who is more prone to ascribing meaning to behaviors or events, an outcome such as this can complicate trauma or make it feel more intense. Also, because some gifted persons tend to intellectualize problems, they may not be fully aware of the negative cognitions and meaning ascription that sits under the surface of their active, conscious minds. Again, this can complicate the experiencing and processing of trauma. How to work through this will be discussed in subsequent sections.

When you add together the traumatic contamination of pattern-finding and meaning-making, both apart and together, along with the interplay of advanced cognitive abilities, it is not difficult to start conceptualizing how very different trauma coding is for gifted persons on neurological and experiential levels. Keep these differences in mind as we consider asynchronous development, gifted compensation, and masking in Chapter 5.

Chapter 4 Conclusion

Chapter 4 explored the intricate interaction between trauma and the gifted brain, focusing on advanced cognitive abilities, pattern-finding, and meaning-making. It addressed how gifted individuals often excel in areas of interest and demonstrate creativity and ingenuity. However, it is also seen how these cognitive strengths can lead to feelings of separateness, loneliness, and being misunderstood as gifted individuals may struggle to find adequate support and understanding from society and peers.

Next, we explored how the gifted brain exhibits neurological differences with documented correlations between intelligence quotient (IQ), brain volume, gray matter, and neuroplasticity. Increased gray matter volume and enhanced white matter microstructural organization in specific brain regions were also identified as associated with the cognitive abilities of gifted individuals, contributing to rapid learning and cognitive processing. However, we also learned how these exceptional cognitive capacities and rapid pattern-finding can make the gifted brain more susceptible to trauma. Gifted individuals may be more attuned to noticing and making connections to traumatic experiences, intensifying their impact. Additionally, their tendency to over-intellectualize situations and neglect emotions can complicate their response to trauma. Despite their resourcefulness, trauma can contaminate the minds of gifted individuals, underscoring the need for understanding and support.

In relation to pattern-finding, Chapter 4 also explored the gifted brain's propensity for meaning-making where gifted individuals ascribe significance and purpose to events and experiences. Meaning-making is an intense and frequent activity for gifted individuals, driving their development and motivation. Finding meaning in the patterns that are identified can further intensify trauma coding. However, meaning-making can also enhance a gifted individual's sense of life purpose and overall well-being.

By more fully examining the intersection of trauma and the gifted brain, this chapter shed light on the vulnerabilities and challenges faced by gifted individuals. It emphasized the importance of recognizing and supporting the unique cognitive characteristics of gifted individuals in trauma-informed approaches. When we understand how trauma can impact the gifted brain, we gain valuable insights into the pathways for growth, healing, and self-realization for gifted individuals affected by trauma.

In subsequent chapters, the discussion will continue about the intersection of trauma and giftedness, addressing topics such as trauma-informed support, healing strategies, and opportunities for growth. The comprehensive understanding of trauma's impact on the gifted brain will contribute to our understanding of how to meet the unique needs of gifted individuals.

Chapter 4 Check-In

Exploration: This chapter was all about trauma and the gifted brain. Specifically, we considered advanced cognitive abilities, pattern-finding, and meaning-making, and we considered how trauma impacts and is impacted by these characteristics.

Conclusion: It was concluded that advanced cognitive abilities related to gifted brain differences can cause people to intellectualize trauma or think about it more deeply and with great complexity. Additionally, trauma can impact pattern-finding and meaning-making in a way that causes the deep coding of traumatic messages and negative cognitions.

Questions to consider include:

1. Can you relate to concepts of advanced cognitive ability, pattern-finding, and/or meaning-making?
2. Does your own unique brand of neurodivergence impact how you experience trauma?
3. Did this chapter make you think of anyone else you know?

Nervous system and mental/emotional health:

1. Check in with your nervous system. What do you feel?
2. Are you feeling activated?
3. Where can you offer compassion to yourself or others in relation to this material?
4. If needed, take a break and engage in some self-care to help with any uncomfortable feelings. Remember laughter can help.

Chapter 4 References

Alesi, M., Rappo, G., & Pepi, A. (2015). Emotional profile and intellectual functioning: A comparison among children with borderline intellectual functioning, average intellectual functioning, and gifted intellectual functioning. *SAGE Open, 5*(3), 1-9. https://doi.org/10.1177/2158244015589995

Armstrong, L.L., Desson, S., St. John, E., & Watt, E. (2019). The D.R.E.A.M. program: Developing resilience through emotions, attitudes, & meaning (gifted edition) - a second wave positive psychology approach. *Counseling Psychology Quarterly, 32*(3-4), 307-332. https://doi.org/10.1080/09515070.2018.1559798

Cross, J.R., & Cross, T.L. (2015). Clinical and mental health issues in counseling the gifted individual. *Journal of Counseling & Development, 93*(2), 163-172. https://doi.org/10.1002/j.1556-6676.2015.00192.x

Draganski, B., & May, A. (2008). Training-induced structural changes in the adult human brain. *Behavioral brain research, 192*(1), 137-142.

Fjell, A.M., & Walhovd, K.B. (2010). Structural brain changes in aging: courses, causes and cognitive consequences. *Reviews in the Neurosciences, 21*(3), 187-221.

Frankl, V.E. (1959). *Man's Search for Meaning*. Boston Press.

Kuhn, T., Blades, R., Gottlieb, L., Knudsen, K., Ashdown, C., Martin-Harris, L.,...& Bookheimer, S.Y. (2021). Neuroanatomical differences in the memory systems of intellectual giftedness and typical development. *Brain and behavior, 11*(11), e2348.

Lauer, T.E., & Yonce, A. (2017). Gifted students' abilities to recognize patterns and relationships in data. *Journal for the Education of the Gifted*, 40(2), 172-199.

National Association for Gifted Children. (n.d.). *Social & emotional issues*. https://www.nagc.org/resources-publications/resources-parents/social-emotional-issues

May, A. (2011). Experience-dependent structural plasticity in the adult human brain. *Trends in Cognitive Sciences, 15*(10), 475-482.

Moran, S. (2020). Life purpose in youth: Turning potential into a lifelong pursuit of prosocial contribution. *Journal for the Education of the Gifted, 43*(1), 38-60. https://doi.org/10.1177/0162353219897844

Pascual-Leone, A., Amedi, A., Fregni, F., & Merabet, L.B. (2005). The plastic human brain cortex. *Annual Review of Neuroscience, 28*, 377-401.

Pfeiffer, S.I. (2021). Optimizing favorable outcomes when counseling the gifted: A best practices approach. *Gifted Education International, 37*(2), 142-157. https://doi.org/10.1177/0261429420969917

Pollet, E., & Schnell, T. (2017). Brilliant: But what for? meaning and subjective well-being in the lives of intellectually gifted and academically high-achieving adults. *Journal of Happiness Studies, 18(*5), 1459-1484. https://doi.org/10.1007/s10902-016-9783-4

Subotnik, R.F., Olszewski-Kubilius, P., & Worrell, F.C. (2011). Rethinking giftedness and gifted education: A proposed direction forward based on psychological science. *Psychological Science in the Public Interest, 12*(1), 3-54.

Szymanski, A., & Wrenn, M. (2019). Growing up with intensity: Reflections on the lived experiences of intense, gifted adults. *Roeper Review, 41*(4), 243-257. https://doi.org/10.1080/02783193.2019.1661054

Tetreault, N. (2021). *Insight Into a Bright Mind: A Neuroscientist's Personal Stories of Unique Thinking*. Gifted Unlimited LLC.

Williams, P. (2023). Understanding how twice-exceptional (2e) individuals navigate adolescence: A grounded theory study.

Winner, E., & Martino, G. (1993). Giftedness in visual arts and music: Giftedness across domains and the relation to IQ. *Journal of Educational Psychology, 85*(3), 403-412.

Winsor, D.L., & Mueller, C.E. (2020). Depression, suicide, and the gifted student: A primer for the school psychologist. *Psychology in the Schools, 57*(10), 1627-1639. https://doi.org/10.1002/pits.22416

CHAPTER 5: Asynchronicity, Compensation, and Trauma

In Chapter 4, we considered trauma and qualities related to giftedness including advanced cognitive abilities and a propensity for rapid pattern-finding and meaning-making. These aspects of giftedness were related to gifted brain differences to help make the topic more tangible. And truly, neurological differences could account for any of these categories. However, I am conceptualizing them all a little differently such that we can understand giftedness and trauma from a whole-person perspective.

Within the realm of giftedness, twice-exceptionality, and neurodivergence, there subsists unique challenges that often mix in unexpected ways. This chapter sets out to explore the intersections of three vital concepts: developmental asynchronicity and underachievement, gifted compensation and masking, and the intensive impact of trauma. By examining the confluence of these factors, we seek to further conceptualize the complex dynamics that shape the lives of gifted individuals, highlighting the intersection of exceptional abilities, coping mechanisms, and traumatic contamination. With a multidimensional lens that is more developmental and social in nature, we aim to gain deeper insights into the intricate connections among these phenomena. Doing so uncovers both the struggles and potential pathways for growth and resilience that emerge at this nexus of development.

Asynchronous Development and Trauma

As a reminder from Chapter 1, asynchronous development is identified when social-emotional, intellectual, creative, and physical skills and abilities develop at significantly different rates, sometimes creating a gap between levels of cognitive and emotional development or other developmental domains (Alesi et al., 2015; Blackett & Webb, 2011; The Columbus Group, 1991; Morelock, 1996; NAGC, n.d.). This gap lends to functional and personality profiles that are often attributed to gifted individuals. For example, gifted kids and adults sometimes identify themselves as socially awkward. In childhood, this awkwardness is demonstrated when a nine-year-old girl will try to talk to other girls in her class excitedly about paleontology while the other girls would rather talk about who got an iPhone for their birthday. Our little paleontology expert may be identified as strange. She may also continue trying to talk about her favorite dinosaur, the armored ankylosaurus, despite social cues that other girls offer. When your social-emotional development pales in comparison to a keen intellect, however, such cues can go unnoticed.

If we consider the previous example of our dinosaur enthusiast in relation to trauma, there are a few topics to consider. First, asynchronicity, particularly in a social context, can lend gifted individuals labels, such as awkward, strange, freak, outcast, misfit, dork, reject, dweeb, or social pariah. These labels themselves are horrifyingly hurtful and can undermine a gifted person's self-esteem and sense of belonging. Receiving such labels can also usher in issues with bullying and self-judgment. Bullying is certainly a well-documented experience amongst gifted individuals and can come from not only other kids but adults as well (Ronksley-Pavia et al., 2019; Williams, 2023; Winsor & Mueller, 2020). It is not a far stretch, and there is little to explain how hurtful labels and bullying lend to complex trauma profiles. That is, asynchronicity may increase a person's exposure to traumatic experiences and needs to be watched for. I don't have to write this but will: it should not have to be this way.

Additionally, when parents, teachers, and mental health workers notice their children struggling with asynchronicity, there is often a desire to help them *fix* what is *wrong*. Well, first of all, I need to interject here by insisting that asynchronous development and social awkwardness *are not wrong*. They are different. The awkwardness exists only because of a mismatch between an individual and their environment. If you put Paleontology Girl in a room with Archaeology Boy and Stratigraphy Kid, well, I think they would get on splendidly. However, if we try to *help fix* our children and adults even, they internalize the message that something is inherently wrong with them. They may also, mistakenly, not accept their quirky, wonderful selves or find peers who *get* them. Rather, it is important to support our gifted children, peers, and selves through a process of collaborative problem-solving while accepting and validating, fervently.

Even if we support individuals' interests, we may end up saying, "But don't talk about that in school" or "Dial it down a notch." Additionally, we may try to help catch kids up by assisting them with age-appropriate skills. And if your ten-year-old cannot tie their shoes, you can help them work on this over time, as agreeable to you both. You can also purchase alternative footwear if you have the means. I guarantee you that regardless of these efforts, a gifted child can grow up to be a successful, happy gifted adult without ever learning to tie their shoes. Often though, we see the frustration in parents, educators, peers, bosses, and other community members, and such frustration ends up presenting to the gifted individual as a wrong they implemented. The message that there is an inherent wrong feeds developmental trauma in an insidious way.

We also need to consider the flip side of asynchrony where gifted children especially have insight beyond their years and understanding that does not seem age appropriate. What then? This can be difficult, particularly when an insightful child asks big questions or understands mature concepts that a parent still believes they need protection from. This is a real and difficult space to be in, particularly since such children lack the perspective of life experience through which they might frame such topics. In these situations, most parents will do what they can to shelter their children while addressing teachable moments as they arise. However, even the most attuned parent may miss opportunities to protect children from their own precocity. What is important is to remain aware and available to our children while validating them, their feelings, and their experiences. The biggest mistake I see here, in relation to trauma, is when we forget our advanced children are still children, leading parents to expect more or expect that which may be developmentally inappropriate for them.

A Note About Underachievement and Trauma

I feel it necessary to mention underachievement here also, in relation to both asynchronous development and trauma. Gifted individuals who do not meet the expected level of accomplishment are considered underachievers, especially when they are twice-exceptional and/or experience asynchronicity (Barber & Mueller, 2011; Reis et al., 2014). This often leads to a notable disparity between their presumed abilities and actual exploits. Individuals in this category will be accused of not applying themselves, being lazy, or not doing their best. Claiming underachievement, however, is a judgment that often bases the value of a gifted person on their ability to produce.

In the face of harsh perfectionistic ideals placed on gifted persons (and that they place on themselves) though, there is also value in learning where to put our energy and when *not* to produce or *not* do our best. There is also a question of *why*. Why might a gifted person be seemingly underachieving, and does using the word "underachieving" fix anything? If a gifted person is not doing well in school or at work, they may be bored, depressed, or struggling with a learning disability. Maybe they just don't want to be there. Regardless, rather than basing change or success on achievement, why not concern ourselves with what is best for the whole person rather than judging if the whole person is doing their best?

The judgment that someone is underachieving orients only to what they can produce to be of value. The message this sends is traumatic in itself. Particularly, if a person internalizes the idea that they are an underachiever that does not do enough, this may feed other issues and traumas. If they are attacked or abused, for example, they may believe they deserve it because they are not good enough. *Not good enough*. That is what underachieving means anyway, doesn't it? Not good enough, not productive enough, not valuable enough, a leech on society. The labels we place on our gifted children, adults, and selves matter. If labels are harmful, they feed trauma and pollute our brains with negative cognitions that are difficult to overcome.

Gifted Compensation and Trauma

Asynchronous development and the asynchronicity of twice-exceptionality can sometimes cause gifted individuals distress. Asynchronicity aside, life can just be distressing at times, even without these phenomena. One notable strength observed in gifted children and adults is their tendency to exhibit compensatory behaviors, often characterized by creative problem-solving and abstract reasoning when confronted with adversity or lack of ability in other areas (Silverman, 2009). This gifted compensation is used in a myriad of ways throughout development when a gifted person's strengths are used to compensate for difficulties.

Gifted compensation may be particularly useful if a gifted person has a disability or second neurodivergence, and research suggests this is common (Gilman et al., 2013; Silverman, 2009; Tan &

Chun, 2014; van Viersen et al., 2016). For example, I am dyslexic *and* I am a published author who did well in her grade-school English classes. Regrettably, however, I struggle with spelling and proofreading eludes me. To my credit, I have a lovely vocabulary cultivated out of need. That is, because of my inability to spell, I grew up substituting difficult words with synonyms, thus expanding my personal lexicon. It may seem that there is no downside to my narrative. However, I did not know I was dyslexic until I was an adult and trained in assessing learning disorders because the world thinks that dyslexics don't write books or ace English exams. Certainly, my teachers and parents did not catch on. When I struggled, though, I was criticized for not trying or applying myself. And as is common, this criticism turned inward. Such is the story for many gifted persons who compensate for difficulties. They end up masking that which is seemingly undesirable, only to welcome further negative judgment.

As is the case for other gifted and twice-exceptional children and adults, compensation results in masking behaviors and difficulties. When behaviors are concealed, a person may struggle to become or present their authentic self, not to mention the energy it takes to conceal what is true. The act of masking is incredibly draining, and frequently, we are not consciously aware that we are engaging in it. When difficulties are concealed, they cannot be attended to. Nobody knew to help me with my dyslexia because nobody knew I struggled with it. This is not an uncommon story. And it is not only disability that is compensated for. Indeed, any difficulty could be veiled by gifted compensation including mental health challenges and suicidality (Winsor & Mueller, 2020). This is why so often when a gifted person is hospitalized or takes their life, we say, "But they seemed so happy." They were compensating. This is why when we find out a gifted child is enduring abuse, we say, "But they seemed OK at school." They were compensating.

Compensation, when acting as a veil, can conceal the trauma that a gifted individual endures. Additionally, a gifted child or adult may feel like they need to compensate for trauma because of a need to appear as perfect or achieving. Even though trauma is not the fault of the survivor, a gifted individual may internalize it as theirs to fix or compensate for alone, thus beginning a snowball effect that feeds and keeps feeding developmental and complex trauma. "But I am strong enough and smart enough to not let this bother me." They were (you may be) compensating.

Chapter 5 Conclusion

Chapter 5 explored the complex interactions between developmental asynchronicity, compensation, and trauma within the context of giftedness, twice-exceptionality, and neurodivergence. By exploring the intricate dynamics and connections among these phenomena, we gained deeper insights into the challenges faced by gifted individuals and the potential pathways for growth and resilience that emerge at their intersection.

The discussion began by highlighting the concept of asynchronous development where various skills and abilities develop at different rates, often leading to what seems like a mismatch between cognitive and emotional development. Asynchronicity can contribute to social difficulties, bullying, and a sense of not belonging, potentially increasing exposure to traumatic experiences. It is crucial to recognize and support the unique developmental trajectory of gifted individuals without labeling them as "awkward" or "disordered" though, as such negative labels can undermine self-esteem and contribute to complex trauma profiles.

Chapter 5 also explored the notion of underachievement and its impact on gifted individuals. The judgment of underachievement is often based on a narrow definition of success tied to productivity and output, disregarding the multifaceted nature of giftedness. The pressure to meet external expectations and the internalization of being an underachiever can perpetuate self-judgment and contribute to trauma. It is essential to shift the focus from achievement to holistic well-being and support the individual's unique strengths and interests.

Moreover, the concept of gifted compensation was examined, highlighting how gifted individuals utilize their strengths to compensate for difficulties or disabilities. While compensation can be a valuable adaptive strategy, it can also lead to masking behaviors and concealing one's authentic self. The act of masking requires significant energy and can hinder the recognition and support of underlying challenges. Recognizing and validating the experiences of gifted individuals, including their struggles and vulnerabilities, is crucial for creating a supportive environment that promotes authenticity and well-being.

Throughout this chapter, the intertwined nature of asynchronicity, compensation, and trauma in the lives of gifted individuals was emphasized. Understanding and addressing these complex dynamics is essential for promoting the mental health, perseverance, and self-realization of gifted individuals. By embracing a holistic and developmental perspective, we can foster a more inclusive and trauma-informed approach to supporting the unique needs and experiences of gifted individuals, ultimately nurturing their growth and well-being.

Chapter 5 Check-In

Exploration: This chapter was all about asynchronicity (also underachievement), gifted compensation (also masking), and trauma. How do asynchronous development and compensation interact with trauma to make trauma experiencing and processing different for gifted people?

Conclusion: It was concluded that asynchronicity or gaps between developmental domains or abilities can inform social and functional differences that cause gifted individuals to experience the world and trauma differently while sometimes also attracting judgment and mistreatment. The compensation for difficulties, disabilities, or developmental differences can mask struggles, lending to and blending with trauma.

Questions to consider include:

1. Do you have any examples of asynchronicity or compensation?
2. Do you have examples of masking or how the concept of underachievement impacted you or others you know?
3. Did any of your own trauma or struggles come to the surface for you while reading this chapter?

Nervous system and mental/emotional health:

1. Check in with your inner child. What are they saying?
2. Are they sad, happy, angry, confused, or scared?
3. Where can you offer compassion to yourself, your child self, or to others in relation to this material?
4. If needed, take a break and consider engaging in some playful, childlike self-care.

Chapter 5 References

Alesi, M., Rappo, G., & Pepi, A. (2015). Emotional profile and intellectual functioning: A comparison among children with borderline intellectual functioning, average intellectual functioning, and gifted intellectual functioning. *SAGE Open, 5*(3), 1-9. https://doi.org/10.1177/2158244015589995

Barber, C., & Mueller, C.T. (2011). Social and self-perceptions of adolescents identified as gifted, learning disabled, and twice-exceptional. *Roeper Review, 33*(2), 109-120. https://doi.org/10.1080/02783193.2011.554158

Blackett, R., & Webb, J.T. (2011). The social-emotional dimension of giftedness: The SENG support model. *Australasian Journal of Gifted Education, 20*(1), 5-13. https://search.informit.org/doi/pdf/10.3316/informit.063962285753287?download=true

Columbus Group. (1991). Unpublished transcript of the meeting of the Columbus Group, Columbus, OH.

Gilman, B.J., Lovecky, D.V., Kearney, K., Peters, D.B., Wasserman, J.D., Silverman, L.K., Postma, M.G., Robinson, N.M., Amend, E.R., Ryder-Schoeck, M., Curry, P.H., Lyon, S.K., Rogers, K.B., Collins, L.E., Charlebois, G.M., Harsin, C.M., & Rimm, S.B. (2013). Critical issues in the identification of gifted students with co-existing disabilities: The twice-exceptional. *SAGE Open, 3*(3), 1-16. https://doi.org/10.1177/2158244013505 8

Morelock, M.J. (1992). Giftedness: The view from within. *Understanding Our Gifted, 4*(3), 1, 11-15.

National Association for Gifted Children. (n.d.). *Social & emotional issues.* https://www.nagc.org/resources-publications/resources-parents/social-emotional-issues

Reis, S.M., Baum, S.M., & Burke, E. (2014). An operational definition of twice-exceptional learners: Implications and applications. *Gifted Child Quarterly, 58*(3), 217-230. https://doi.org/10.1177/0016986214534976

Ronksley-Pavia, M., Grootenboer, P., & Pendergast, D. (2019). Bullying and the unique experiences of twice exceptional learners: Student perspective narratives. *Gifted Child Today Magazine, 42*(1), 19-35. https://doi.org/10.1177/1076217518804856

Silverman, L.K. (2009). The two-edged sword of compensation: How the gifted cope with learning disabilities. *Gifted Education International, 25*(2), 115-130. https://doi.org/10.1177/026142940902500203

Tan, L.S., & Chun, K.Y.N. (2014). Perfectionism and academic emotions of gifted adolescent girls. *The Asia-Pacific Education Researcher, 23*(3), 389-401. https://doi.org/10.1007/s40299-013-0114-9

van Viersen, S., Kroesbergen, E. ., Slot, E.M., & de Bree, E.H. (2016). High reading skills mask dyslexia in gifted children. *Journal of Learning Disabilities, 49*(2), 189-199. https://doi.org/10.1177/0022219414538517

Williams, P. (2023). Understanding how twice-exceptional (2e) individuals navigate adolescence: A grounded theory study.

Winsor, D.L., & Mueller, C.E. (2020). Depression, suicide, and the gifted student: A primer for the school psychologist. *Psychology in the Schools, 57*(10), 1627-1639. https://doi.org/10.1002/pits.22416

CHAPTER 6:
Heightened Intensity and Trauma

Central to the human experience exists interconnections between innate qualities and the impact of life's adversities. In relation to giftedness specifically, this chapter takes a more in-depth look at Kazimierz Dąbrowski's concept of overexcitabilities and how they intersect with the also intensive influence of trauma. By examining the convergence of these two domains, we aim to decode the complex dynamics that unfold when heightened sensitivities and traumatic experiences converge, shedding light on the potential implications for development and well-being.

Defining Overexcitability

As we plunge into the exploration of the interplay between overexcitabilities and trauma, it is crucial to revisit the definition of overexcitability before more deeply examining the five types that prominently manifest within the gifted population. By establishing this foundation, we lay the groundwork for a comprehensive understanding of how OEs intersect with the impact of experiencing trauma.

According to Dąbrowski (1937), there are five forms or distinct types of overexcitability, sometimes referred to as increased psychic excitability, intensity, or superstimulatability. The term overexcitability has since been shortened at times, particularly within gifted communities, to OE. For example, a person might say, "Oh no! I think I have all five OEs!" The five OEs per Dąbrowski include psychomotor, sensual, intellectual, imaginational, and emotional types. Before I go into detail about these five dimensions of overexcitability, I would like to pick apart the word because there can be a lot of misunderstanding surrounding it.

Overexcitability is translated from Dąbrowski's original Polish assertion that people with high developmental potential have *nadpobudliwość*, made up of the words *nad* meaning *above* or *over*, and *pobudliwość*, meaning *excitability*. However, our Western social understanding of the word overexcitability can make it seem to have negative connotations. Often, gifted children and adults are accused of being too much: too loud, too shy, too emotional, too peculiar, too talkative, or too in their heads. As such, being *over-excitable* can sound like a judgment of *too much* excitability, though this is not what Dąbrowski meant by this term. Rather, think of the word or root *over-* as *more*, *above*, or *greater than average*. That is, an overexcitable person appears to have intensified mental activity manifested in one to five overexcitabilities. This mental activity, you guessed it, is neurologically different and exists at an increased level when compared to the neuromajority. That is, overexcitability is a biological difference that manifests first through the nervous system.

One of my favorite explanations of overexcitability comes from the book *Living with Intensity* by Dr. Susan Daniel and Dr. Michael Piechowski. In this book, the authors explain how OEs are also sometimes called *original equipment*, meaning they are innate. That is, like with a child's temperament, OEs can be seen early in a person's life. For example, parents will often report their children looking around or responding more to stimuli in their environments in infancy. In research that examined the developmental experiences of twice-exceptional individuals, all participants shared experiences of qualities that *just were*, ranging from an acute emotional attunement, connectedness with others, intensive passion for life or specific topics, or extreme energy and drive (Williams, 2023).

Gifted individuals often possess an early awareness of differences related to their intensities (Williams, 2023). Similar to asynchronous development or social awkwardness discussed in Chapter 5, OE is not inherently negative—it simply exists. Concerns may arise, however, when our gifted children exhibit traits of highly sensitive people (HSP), leading to worries of excessive emotionality, fragility, being labeled as tattletales or crybabies (more harmful labels…gross) and potentially facing difficulties as a result. The labels assigned to individuals with OE, based on their innate qualities, can be both harmful and inaccurate. While we may not have complete control over shielding those with OE from the world, it remains crucial to recognize the impact such intensity has on intense individuals' experiences. This awareness empowers us to adapt and devise strategies that promote neurodiversity affirmation. Furthermore, by fostering awareness and exploring the interactions between psychomotor, sensual, intellectual, imaginational, and emotional OEs with trauma, we can better prepare ourselves to address trauma and OE in actionable ways in subsequent chapters.

Before diving into each OE separately, I would like to share my favorite OE chart that seems to succinctly encapsulate these five areas of intensity. I have not found or created a better one than what was first presented in a book chapter by Piechowski (1979) about developmental potential in relation to counseling the gifted. Piechowski's chart made later appearances in his chapter about Overexcitability in the *Encyclopedia of Creativity* (1999), in Piechowski and Daniels' (2008) book, *Living with Intensity*, again in Piechowski's (2014) book, *Mellow Out, If I Only Could*, and most recently in Piechowski and Wells' (2021) chapter about reexamining overexcitability in the *Handbook for Counselors Serving Students With Gifts and Talents*. This comprehensive chart remains applicable and relatively unchanged and is presented in Table 1 above. I have several friends, clients, colleagues, and advocacy beneficiaries who dog-eared pages 10 to 11 in *Living with Intensity* for this reason. Do the same here and take this chart with you to IEP meetings, doctor appointments, family reunions, and wherever you can find someone willing to read it!

Table 1. Forms and Expressions of Overexcitability (Piechowski, 1979)

Psychomotor Overexcitability (PmOE)
• *Surplus of Energy: rapid speech, marked excitation, intense physical activity (e.g., fast games and sports), pressure for action (e.g., organizing), marked competitiveness* • *Psychomotor Expression of Emotional Tension: compulsive talking and chattering, impulsive actions, nervous habits (e.g., tics, nail biting), workaholism, acting out*
Sensual Overexcitability (SOE)
• *Enhanced Sensory and Aesthetic Pleasure: seeing, smelling, tasting, touching, hearing, and sex; delight in beautiful objects, sounds of words, music, form, color, balance* • *Sensual Expression of Emotional Tension: overeating, sexual outlets, buying sprees, desire for the limelight*
Intellectual Overexcitability (InOE)
• *Intensified Activity of the Mind: curiosity, concentration, capacity for sustained intellectual effort, avid reading; keen observation, detailed visual recall, detailed planning; passion for precision* • *Passion for Probing Questions and Problem-Solving: search for truth and understanding; forming new concepts; tenacity in problem-solving; passion for precision* • *Reflective Thought: thinking about thinking, love of theory and analysis, preoccupation with logic, moral thinking, introspection (but without self-judgment), conceptual and intuitive integration; independence of thought (sometimes very critical)*

Imaginational Overexcitability (ImOE)
• *Free Play of the Imagination: frequent use of image and metaphor, facility for invention and fantasy, facility for detailed visualization, poetic and dramatic perception, animistic and magical thinking* • *Capacity for Living in a World of Fantasy: predilection for magic and fairy tales, creation of private worlds, imaginary companions, dramatization* • *Spontaneous Imagery as an Expression of Emotional Tension: animistic imagery, mixing truth and fiction, elaborate dreams, illusions* • *Low Tolerance of Boredom: need for novelty and variety*
Emotional Overexcitability (EOE)
• *Feelings and Emotions Intensified: extremes of emotion and of positive and negative feelings, complex emotions, identification with others' feelings, awareness of a whole range of feelings* • *Strong Somatic Expressions: tense stomach, sinking heart, blushing, flushing, pounding heart, sweaty palms* • *Strong Affective Expressions: inhibition (timidity, shyness); enthusiasm, euphoria, pride; strong affective memory; feelings of unreality, fears and anxieties, feelings of shame and guilt, concern with death, depressive and suicidal moods* • *Capacity for Strong Attachments, Deep Relationships: strong emotional ties and attachments to persons, living things, places; attachments to animals; difficulty adjusting to new environments; compassion, responsiveness to others, sensitivity in relationships; loneliness* • *Well-Differentiated Feelings Toward Self: inner dialogue and self-judgment*

Psychomotor Overexcitability and Trauma

Psychomotor overexcitability, or ***PmOE***, involves a notable surplus of energy and the physical expression of emotional tension. It is often associated with hyperactivity, which is commonly observed in individuals with ADHD or those identified as super busy or active. Additionally, *Pm*OE can be readily identified in gifted athletes or those engaged in fast-paced and high-intensity sports and games. However, there are lesser-considered aspects of *Pm*OE, such as rapid speech and heightened excitement, a strong drive for action or organization, significant competitiveness, compulsive talking or interruption, impulsivity, or nervous habits such as **stimming**. During their school years, individuals with *Pm*OE may be accused of disruptive behavior or causing disturbances in the classroom. In adulthood, they may be characterized as workaholics or professionals with an intense level of focus and drive. In either case, presentations of *Pm*OE extend beyond "the wiggles" as we like to identify them in public classroom settings.

Psychomotor overexcitability is an interesting phenomenon that is not always seen as socially acceptable. Certainly, while a champion athlete may be an accepted overexcitable type, there are other *Pm*OEs that receive less grace, particularly when they carry with them a less socially acceptable level of risk. For example, when a child swings around a jump rope on the playground without immediately considering who they might hit, adults can get concerned and frustrated. And we can acknowledge that putting others in danger of harm is never OK. However, we need to also remember that OEs are innate characteristics and not behaviors that children and adults engage in because they are naughty. When *Pm*OE individuals are labeled as such, they can internalize this label, which can later manifest as low self-esteem, negative self-concepts, and/or **rejection-sensitive dysphoria**.

All the manifestations of *Pm*OE and associated judgments impact the interplay of trauma regardless of the level of acceptance a *Pm*OE person has. What we must remember, however, is that when there is a negative judgment assigned to a characteristic that is innate, this feeds trauma coding in the brain because of the aforementioned pattern-finding and meaning-making that gifted persons engage in readily. So, for the child or adult who is judged negatively for their innate *Pm*OE, that judgment may become part of their complex or developmental trauma. So, when parenting, educating, counseling, or otherwise engaging with individuals who have *Pm*OE, it is helpful to start with acceptance and unconditional positive regard. We will talk about how to do this in Chapter 12.

In addition to a sometimes increased enduring of adversity due to judgment or risk-taking behavior, persons with *Pm*OE also experience trauma differently than those without this innate intensity. That is, when a traumatic event occurs, there may be coding that is physical in nature and is therefore stored in the body more intensely. A *Pm*OE person may also respond to the trauma differently, by vocalizing or physically placing energy to expel the tension and distress experienced. For example, if a person with *Pm*OE is in a car accident where they injure their leg, they may try to run on it, yell, or talk rapidly to the paramedics. Additionally, the physicality of the pain and experience will potentially be remembered more intensely and thus coded as an intense experience. And though an accident and injury may feel intense for any person, the increased intensity of a person with *Pm*OE codes it differently in their brain and body. We will discuss the impact of trauma coding on the body to a further extent in Chapter 7. For now, know that trauma impacts and is impacted by the body and the brain with recall often happening because of communication between both.

Sensual Overexcitability and Trauma

In alignment with Piechowski's chart, **sensual overexcitability** or **SOE** encompasses a heightened experiencing of sensory and aesthetic pleasure. It also involves a deep appreciation for various senses, such as sight, smell, taste, touch, hearing, and even sexuality. SOE may manifest while finding delight in beautiful objects, the melodic sounds of words, music that resonates, captivating forms, vibrant colors, and harmonious balance. Furthermore, sensual overexcitability manifests through the sensual expression of emotional tension. For some, this can take the form of overeating or withholding food, seeking sexual outlets, engaging in buying sprees, and having a strong desire to be at the center of attention.

Often, individuals with SOE use creative expression to explore this intensity. For example, it would not surprise me if artists such as Georgia O'Keeffe, Mozart, Ansel Adams, or John Lennon were found to be sensually overexcitable. And when I have clients make comments such as, "I saw a beautiful sunset and cried. What is wrong with me?", I generally insist that SOE and emotional OE may be to blame (or celebrate). That is, keeping in mind that OEs are innate, it would be erroneous to suggest that they point to something wrong. However, society misunderstands the SOE horribly. For example, when a child sucks their thumb or seems drawn to certain textures, we often label them as odd or obsessive. If someone reports urgently removing a bothersome tag from their T-shirt, unable to tolerate its itchiness any longer, they may find themselves met with confused gazes until a kindred spirit softly utters, "I understand completely!" Despite occasional mirroring, the label of odd or overly intense lends to a judgment that, in turn, lends to the trauma coding affecting our brains.

Besides worrying about judgment and misunderstanding, it is again important to identify how SOEs may intensify a person's experience of daily life and trauma differently. That is, when a person with heightened sensual intensity encounters a difficulty, the acutely endured sensory aspects of the encounter are also experienced, remembered, and coded with great intensity. Considering the earlier example of a car accident where the victim injures their leg, let us contemplate how an individual with heightened sensual sensitivity may intensely detect the scent of smoke, gasoline, and burnt rubber that lingers in the air. The *S*OE individual might vividly recall the taste and feel of salty sweat and tears that rest on the edge of their mouth. What's more, every screech, crash, shattering of glass, siren, and shout is potentially etched in the *S*OE person's memory, along with any associated pain, tension, or intensity of other physical sensations. The visual aspects of the accident, too, are imprinted in the *S*OE mind, likely intertwined with varying degrees and layers of other intensities. Thus, a car accident is not merely a fleeting memory but rather a multisensory experience that can appear all the more terrifying to a gifted *S*OE. When considering how an *S*OE individual experiences trauma, therefore, we must also consider how they remember it later, with layers upon layers of sensual stimuli. And when the *S*OE is reminded of these stimuli later, the traumatic memory can again present.

Intellectual Overexcitability and Trauma

Intellectual overexcitability or *In*OE is characterized by a heightened activity of the mind and displaying intensified intellectual engagement. This OE may include a natural curiosity, deep concentration, an increased capacity for sustained intellectual effort, and sometimes a voracious appetite for reading. Additionally, individuals with *In*OE generally possess keen observational skills and a detailed visual recall ability. They may also exhibit meticulous planning tendencies and a passion for precision that drives their pursuits. Furthermore, *In*OE manifests through a fervent passion for probing questions and problem-solving. *In*OE individuals often have an insatiable thirst for truth and understanding, constantly seeking to form new concepts. They exhibit tenacity when faced with problems, showing unwavering determination in finding solutions while also displaying a keen eye for precision in their analyses. Reflective thought is another aspect of *In*OE where individuals engage in metacognitive practice or *thinking about thinking*. Reflective thought and metacognition further demonstrate an *In*OE love for theory and analysis. They tend to be deeply interested in logic and moral thinking, and they may have an adept ability to engage in introspection without self-judgment. *In*OE frequently possesses the ability to integrate conceptual and intuitive ideas and exhibit independence of thought, often displaying a critical mindset.

Often, individuals with great intellectual capacity are recognized by their vast knowledge of seemingly random subjects. An instance of this occurred proximal to the rendering of this chapter when my daughter and I were waiting for our dinner at an English pub. We were astounded and exchanged wide-eyed glances as a young adult sitting at the adjacent table passionately discussed dolphins. His expertise extended far beyond the mere facts; he delved into intricate socio-political topics surrounding these creatures. Although his loud and enthusiastic delivery may have irritated some, I swiftly adjusted my mental lens, allowing myself to savor my meal while appreciating his remarkable knowledge (and likely *PM*OE related to the volume and veracity of his speech). Often, however, onlookers are not accepting of such intense passion. And while we tend to appreciate the *In*OE for what they can contribute to society or our group efforts, they are frequently labeled as oddballs or know-it-alls. Again, such labeling and perspectives can accompany judgment and social struggles. When an individual with *In*OE feels socially alienated, they may lack the social support often needed to thrive while also being exposed to bullying or other social stigmatization.

While the social alienation that accompanies any OE can be difficult, the *In*OE individual's brain and means of processing traumatic stimuli also differs from the norm. More specifically, when a person intensely intellectualizes a traumatic event, it is stored differently in memory networks. Additionally, an *In*OE may think about all the different intellectual elements related to trauma. Taking the example of a car crash, an *In*OE individual could analyze the logistics of the incident and response of emergency crews while simultaneously strategizing the most effective approach to address needs and challenges. While this heightened attentiveness may offer certain advantages, it can also lead the intellectual to overlook or neglect emotional or physical aspects of the event that require appropriate processing. Additionally, the intensity of the intellectual information and all its details add to the intensity of the entire event. When there is an abundance of information accompanying an event, it is not easily reworked or filed away. Rather, any stimuli that are experienced later that are similar to the stimuli experienced during the accident can cause a recall that may be unwanted.

Imaginational Overexcitability and Trauma

Imaginational overexcitability or *Im*OE is evident through the seemingly unrestricted play of the imagination. It involves the frequent utilization of vivid imagery and metaphor, an innate ability for invention and fantasy, and a remarkable talent for detailed visualization. Those with *Im*OE may possess a poetic and dramatic perception of the world, often engaging in animistic and magical thinking. Furthermore, individuals with this trait demonstrate a capacity for immersing themselves in a world of fantasy. They may have a strong inclination towards magic and fairy tales, frequently creating their own private paracosms and welcoming imaginary companions. An *Im*OE may also exhibit a propensity for dramatization, breathing life into imaginative narratives. As such, spontaneous imagery becomes an avenue for expressing emotional tension in the case of *Im*OE. This is characterized by the emergence of animistic imagery, where truth and fiction intertwine, giving rise to elaborate dreams and illusions. Moreover, individuals with imaginational overexcitability have a low tolerance for boredom and seek novelty and variety in their experiences. They actively crave new and stimulating situations, constantly seeking to engage their imagination in fresh and exciting ways.

Those with an intensely imaginative and creative nature often exhibit early signs through their inclination towards having imaginary friends or assigning names and personalities to their stuffed animals. These *Im*OE individuals possess a natural ability to weave fantastical stories but, unfortunately, are sometimes misunderstood and labeled as dishonest or daydreamers with their heads in the clouds. In the realm of play, other children may find themselves perplexed by the intricate rules and elaborate scenarios involved in *Im*OE-led games such as "house." As *Im*OE individuals grow into adulthood, their wild ideas and plans may either be celebrated or dismissed by society. When they find themselves in environments that embrace and nurture their creative spirit, a person with *Im*OE can achieve rapid progress and exceptional success. However, if they are confined to mundane and non-creative tasks, they are prone to experiencing distress and disillusionment.

While the *Im*OE person's unconventional thinking and imaginative outlook can bring fresh perspectives and innovative solutions to various challenges, their ability to think beyond the boundaries of convention can also lend to catastrophizing or imagining the worst. Individuals with an intensely imaginative and creative nature often face the challenge of envisioning the various ways in which a difficulty or traumatic event could worsen or impact different aspects of their lives. Using the example of a car crash, an *Im*OE individual might imagine the struggles of another victim or contemplate the cascading chain of causes and effects that unfold in the aftermath of the incident. It is important to note that the traumatic information encoded in an *Im*OE brain extends beyond the boundaries of what actually transpired and may encompass potential scenarios that could have occurred or may still occur in the future. The *Im*OE imaginative capacity enables them to explore different angles and possibilities, both real and imagined, which can provide valuable insights but may also contribute to heightened emotional responses and anxieties. As such, trauma can be experienced and imagined as intensified for the *Im*OE individual. And when trauma is experienced and/or imagined with great imaginational intensity, it can also be remembered and recalled intensely.

Emotional Overexcitability and Trauma

Lastly, though not least by a long shot, **emotional overexcitability**, or *E*OE, manifests through heightened intensities of feelings and emotions. Individuals with *E*OE often experience extremes of both desired and difficult emotions, displaying a rich and complex emotional landscape. Such individuals are often identified as empaths who possess a deep capacity for aligning with and understanding the feelings of others while also being acutely aware of the wide range of emotions that exist. This is why they are often identified as highly sensitive persons (HSPs) or emotionally intelligent, though sometimes they are judged for lacking emotional intelligence when their emoting is seemingly unharnessed.

Individuals with *E*OEs also tend to have a profound capacity for forming strong attachments and developing deep relationships. They form intense emotional bonds with people, living beings, and places. They may exhibit strong attachments to animals while engaging with compassion, responsiveness, and sensitivity in their relationships. However, feelings of loneliness can be prevalent. Furthermore, the *E*OE mind possesses a well-differentiated range of feelings toward themselves. They engage in inner dialogues and self-judgment, often introspecting and reflecting on their own emotions and experiences.

Physical sensations play a significant role in the expression of *E*OE. Strong somatic expressions are common, such as experiencing a tense stomach, a sinking heart, blushing or flushing, palpitations, or sweaty palms. Affective expressions are equally potent in individuals with *E*OE. They may exhibit inhibitions, including timidity and shyness, alongside bursts of enthusiasm, euphoria, and pride. An *E*OE person's affective memory can be especially strong, often retaining vivid recollections of emotional experiences. However, feelings of unreality, fears and anxieties, shame and guilt, preoccupations with death, and even occasional depressive and suicidal moods can arise.

The perceived moodiness and intense emotional expression of *E*OE and HSP individuals can open them up to harsh judgment from others. For example, *E*OE and HSP persons are often accused of over-exaggerating their emotions, overreacting, or being overly emotional or dramatic. The judgment that accompanies these labels can be harsh and harshly internalized while contributing to an unkind self-image. Additionally, when *E*OE are labeled as crybabies, for example, they can become the target of harsh parenting or bullying.

Because of the emotional and affective intensity through which the *E*OE experiences the world, these individuals can also experience and code trauma in an emotionally intense way. For example, when they experience a traumatic event that puts their stomach in knots and sends intense fear through their nervous system, those knots and trepidation are coded and remembered. As such, when there is any scary or stomach-scrunching event experienced in the future, this can cause the recall of the trauma that was endured earlier. Additionally, the intensity of emotion experienced during a traumatic event can increase the overall intensity of it. When trauma is experienced with emotional intensity, it is remembered more intensely.

What About the Blunting of Overexcitability?

In Chapter 1, we briefly discussed how gifted persons experience the world with great intensity or the *blunting* of intensity in sensual, psychomotor, imaginational, intellectual, and/or emotional domains. This blunting was not addressed in each section about the different OEs so it could be addressed all at once here. Psychological blunting refers to a phenomenon where individuals experience a reduction in their emotional responses or a dulled affective experience. It involves a diminished range and intensity of emotions, resulting in a decreased ability to feel and express emotions compared to what would be considered typical or expected. Psychological blunting can manifest as a decreased capacity for joy, sadness, empathy, or other emotional states. It can also present as physical in nature where people feel disconnected from their bodies or experiences. Blunting may be a symptom of various mental health conditions, such as depression, post-traumatic stress disorder (PTSD), or certain medications or substance use. Psychological blunting can impact an individual's overall emotional well-being and their ability to connect or communicate with others.

The blunting of overexcitability can cause a dulling or complete numbing in emotional, behavioral, and even biological functions. As an example, if an *E*OE child gets yelled at by parents or teased by classmates about being overly emotional, they may blunt emotions such that they are protected from criticism. Similarly, if a person is physically reprimanded for talking too much, they may choose not to speak as a means of self-preservation. This blunting can happen with any one of the OEs and can be perceived as a clipping of wings (ouch). It is important to remember, also, that blunting for any person, especially a gifted person, can be an all-or-nothing event, such that the OE individual shows nothing or everything when pushed past a threshold of tolerance.

On a biological level, post-traumatic stress disorder (PTSD) is linked to a diminished response or blunting in the **hypothalamic-pituitary-adrenocortical (HPA) axis** and reduced cortisol levels (de Kloet et al., 2006; Heim and Nemeroff, 2009; Yehuda and LeDoux, 2007). The HPA axis is a system in the body that helps regulate the response to stress. The hypothalamus releases corticotropin-releasing hormone (CRH), which stimulates the pituitary gland to release adrenocorticotropic hormone (ACTH). ACTH then triggers the adrenal glands to release cortisol, the "stress hormone." Cortisol helps the body cope with stress and returns to normal levels once the stress is resolved. Chronic activation of the HPA axis can have negative health effects. This alteration in the HPA axis occurs due to the repetitive activation of the negative feedback loop as a result of chronic stress (Gjerstad et al., 2018). Such blunting and associated dysregulation contribute to the development and persistence of PTSD symptoms, which can be heightened in gifted individuals (de Voogd et al., 2022). Furthermore, there is evidence suggesting that blunted cardiovascular reactions to stress, as observed in a collection of 23 studies, can serve as a screening tool for identifying a heightened risk of adverse motivational and behavioral dysregulation (O'Riordan et al., 2022).

Several different biological and neurological loops lend to trauma coding and the blunting of intensity. As such, it can be perceived how a person who seems emotionless may explode with an intense emotional response when they push through their window of tolerance. It can also be imagined, therefore, how a gifted person with innate intensity presents as having no overexcitability at all. When this happens, it is wise to look deeper for historical, biological, and ecological reasons for the blunting of OEs such that this can be attended to.

Even when an individual's blunting seems set in place, it should not be ignored. That is, if a person is blunting their anger, there may be intense anger under the surface of their experience or awareness that impacts their health and well-being. If a person is blunting the intensity of sensation, they may not know how tight or nervous their body is when they deal with the sound of a fan or a person chewing. They may not feel emotional or physical pain. That is, some stimuli that they are not aware of or do not readily feel due to psychological blunting still impact an overexcitable person. Additionally, more intensive blunting may manifest in gifted individuals and others as a sort of psychoneurosis that needs attending to rather than pathologizing of. In an age of ableism where the pathologizing of difference seems commonplace, awareness of this experiential and neurological difference is beyond imperative.

The Big Picture of OEs and Trauma

Altogether, an intermixing of the different overexcitabilities with each gifted person's unique personality, experiences, and trauma builds a unique psychological profile for them. To fully consider this, we will look at how trauma is maybe experienced by a person with all five OEs as it adds layers of trauma processing that also need to be regarded.

Using the example of a car accident, consider first how a person with psychomotor OE experiences the physicality of the event while also responding to and mentally coding it physically. Now, add in an overlay of intellectualizing, imagination, and emotionality, along with sensory elements. Contemplate how a person might intellectualize their emotions or sensations while imagining what certain symptoms and sensations may mean. Add in the response from bystanders or first responders to what might be a less-than-typical reaction to trauma. Now contemplate the possible blunting of expression that perceivably does not suit a person, and you begin to conceptualize the gestalt of the event without yet accounting for other unique elements such as personality and prior experiences.

Figure 3. Overexcitability and Trauma

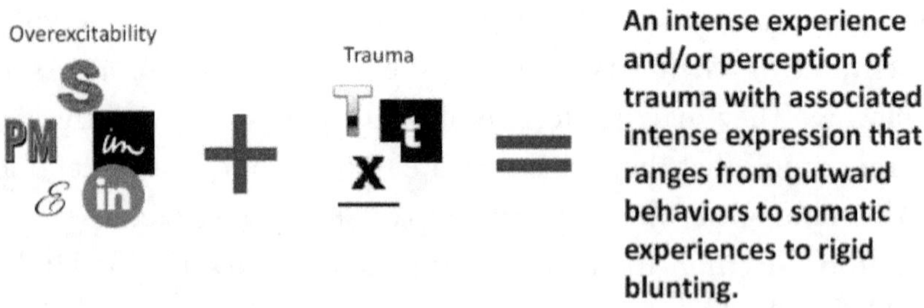

In simplified terms, as presented in Figure 3 above, overexcitabilities plus different types and degrees of trauma combine to form an intense experience and/or perception of trauma with an associated intense expression that ranges from outward behaviors to somatic experiences to rigid blunting that is qualitatively different from the norm.

Additionally, when you consider how different OEs might each impact the other, you might also imagine a cycle of intensity that loops as presented in Figure 4. In this illustration, you can see how each OE may in turn feed another and perpetuate a triggering experience. You might also imagine here how the blunting of OEs could be used to interrupt this cycle, only to leave processing stuck for later. Concepts of stuck processing and somatic experiencing will be discussed in subsequent chapters.

Figure 4. Overexcitability Loop

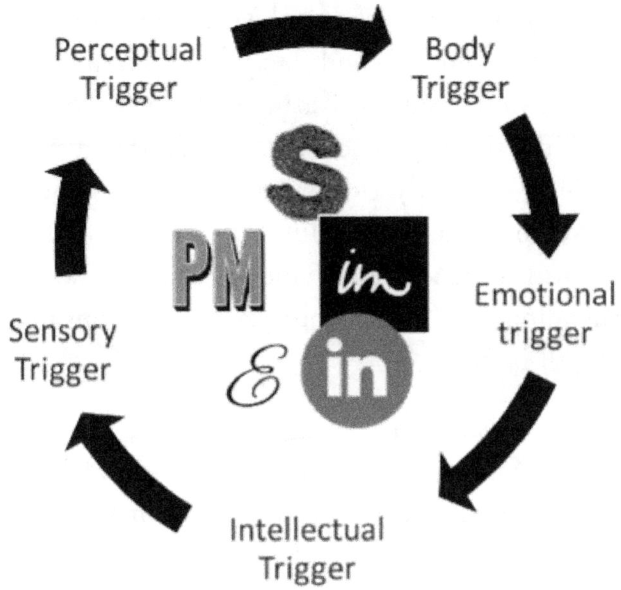

In various combinations, including dyads, triads, and groups of four or five, the different OEs can interact with one another in multiple ways. It is crucial to recognize, however, that while this knowledge applies to all gifted individuals, each person's experience with overexcitability and trauma remains distinct and unique. With this in mind, we will venture into Part Three and Chapter 7 where we expand on topics of gifted learning and memory as it relates to OEs, other aspects of giftedness, and trauma.

Chapter 6 Conclusion

Central to the gifted experience is the complex interplay between our heightened sensitivities and the influence of life's adversities. In Chapter 6, we considered Kazimierz Dąbrowski's concept of overexcitabilities (OEs) and how they intersect with the profound influence of trauma. By exploring the convergence of these domains, we continued unraveling the complex dynamics that unfold when heightened sensitivities and traumatic experiences collide, shedding light on the potential implications for development and well-being.

To begin, we revisited the definition of overexcitability, recognizing its innate nature and its manifestation in five distinct types: psychomotor, sensual, intellectual, imaginational, and emotional. We emphasized the importance of understanding overexcitability as a biological difference, rather than labeling it as negative or excessive. By acknowledging and accepting these intensities, we empower ourselves to adapt and devise strategies that promote neurodiversity affirmation.

Next, we explored each OE and how it might specifically impact or be impacted by trauma. Psychomotor overexcitability (*Pm*OE) is characterized by excess energy and the expression of emotional tension. It is often associated with hyperactivity and can be observed in individuals who engage in intense physical activities or those identified as talkative or energetic. *Pm*OE individuals may face negative judgments and labels, impacting their self-esteem and contributing to complex trauma. When experiencing trauma, *Pm*OE individuals may respond differently, storing events in their bodies more intensely.

Sensual overexcitability (*S*OE) involves heightened sensory and aesthetic pleasure although it is often misunderstood and judged by society, leading to unique trauma coding. *S*OE individuals also experience and remember the sensory aspects of trauma intensely. As such, their memories are often intertwined with various intensities, making the recall of the traumatic event multisensory and potentially more terrifying. The impact of trauma on *S*OE individuals is influenced by the layers of sensual stimuli involved, and reminders of these stimuli can trigger the traumatic memory again.

Intellectual overexcitability (*In*OE) is characterized by heightened mental activity and critical thinking. *In*OE individuals may process and intellectualize traumatic events differently, analyzing them from various perspectives. They may think about various intellectual elements related to the trauma, analyzing and dissecting the event from multiple perspectives. This intellectual processing of trauma adds complexity to the *In*OE's experience and may influence how they recall and respond to traumatic memories.

Imaginational overexcitability (*Im*OE) is characterized in this chapter as unrestricted imagination, vivid imagery, and a talent for detailed visualization. *Im*OE individuals may face misconceptions and their imaginative thinking can also contribute to catastrophizing and envisioning worst-case scenarios, intensifying their emotional responses and anxieties. Traumatic events may encode in the *Im*OE individual's brain beyond what actually transpired, encompassing potential scenarios and imagined outcomes. The imaginative capacity of *Im*OE individuals allows for exploring different angles and possibilities, providing insights but also leading to intense memories and recall.

Emotional overexcitability (*E*OE) manifests through heightened intensity of emotions and a rich emotional landscape. *E*OE individuals often exhibit empathy, deep attachments, and sensitivity. However, they may also face judgment and labeling. Physical and affective expressions play a significant role in the manifestation of *E*OE. Persons with *E*OEs can experience trauma with heightened emotional intensity, encoding the associated feelings and sensations deeply. Labels and judgments can contribute to internalized negativity and self-image, further impacting their emotional experiences with the emotional and affective intensity of *E*OEs impacting the overall experience and recall of trauma.

The blunting of intensity may play a significant role in the experience of gifted individuals with OEs and trauma. Psychological blunting refers to a reduction in emotional or other responses and can manifest as a diminished range and intensity of emotions or a disconnect from one's body and experiences. Biologically, blunting is linked to alterations in the stress response and cortisol levels, particularly in the context of post-traumatic stress disorder (PTSD). Understanding and addressing blunting is crucial for emotional well-being and interpersonal connections.

Throughout this chapter, we gained insights into the multiplex connections between OEs and trauma and how the interplay between them can create an intricate psychological profile with each OE adding layers to the experience and perception of trauma. The interaction between OEs and trauma can perpetuate intensity in a cycle. It is important to recognize that the interaction between OEs and trauma is unique for each gifted individual with various combinations and interactions possible. Part Three and Chapter 7 will delve into gifted learning and memory as they relate to OEs, other aspects of giftedness, and trauma to provide further insight into how these factors shape the experiences of gifted individuals and their processing of trauma.

Chapter 6 Check-In

Exploration: This chapter explored the five overexcitabilities or OEs and considered how they impact and are impacted by trauma.

Conclusion: Psychomotor, intellectual, sensual, imaginational, and emotional overexcitabilities all impact how trauma is experienced and mentally coded. Additionally, it is identified that a combination of OEs and OE blunting can drastically shape traumatic experiences for gifted individuals.

Questions to consider include:

1. Do you have examples of how OEs impact you or others?
2. Have you seen examples of how trauma and OEs interact?
3. Did any of your own trauma or struggles come to the surface for you while reading this chapter?

Nervous system and mental/emotional health:

1. Check in with your body, your breathing, and your experiencing of this chapter.
2. Are there any triggers, images, cognitions, emotions, or sensations that need attending to?
3. What kind of self-care do you need to engage in given this experiencing?
4. If needed, take a break for self-care that settles or engages your specific OEs.

Chapter 6 References

Dąbrowski, K. (1938). Typy wzmożonej pobudliwości psychicznej [Types of increased psychic excitability]. *Biuletyn Instytutu Higieny Psychicznej, 1*(3-4), 3-26.

Daniels, S., & Piechowski, M.M. (2009). *Living with intensity: Understanding the sensitivity, excitability, and emotional development of gifted children, adolescents, and adults.* Great Potential Press, Inc..

De Kloet, C.S., Vermetten, E., Geuze, E., Kavelaars, A.M.A.A., Heijnen, C.J., & Westenberg, H.G. M. (2006). Assessment of HPA-axis function in posttraumatic stress disorder: pharmacological and non-pharmacological challenge tests, a review. *Journal of psychiatric research, 40*(6), 550-567.

de Voogd, L.D., Kampen, R.A., Kaldewaij, R., Zhang, W., Hashemi, M.M., Koch, S.B.,…& Roelofs, K. (2022). Trauma-induced human glucocorticoid receptor expression increases predict subsequent HPA-axis blunting in a prospective longitudinal design. *Psychoneuroendocrinology, 146*, 105909.

Gjerstad, J.K., Lightman, S.L., & Spiga, F. (2018). Role of glucocorticoid negative feedback in the regulation of HPA axis pulsatility. *Stress, 21*(5), 403-416.

Heim, C., & Nemeroff, C.B. (2009). Neurobiology of posttraumatic stress disorder. *CNS spectrums, 14*(1 Suppl 1), 13-24.

O'Riordan, A., Howard, S., & Gallagher, S. (2022). Blunted cardiovascular reactivity to psychological stress and prospective health: a systematic review. *Health Psychology Review*, 1-27.

Piechowski, M.M. (1979). Developmental potential. In N. Colangelo & R. T. Zaffrann (Eds.), *New voices in counseling the gifted* (pp. 25–57). Kendall/Hunt Publishing Company.

Piechowski, M.M. (1999). Overexcitabilities. In M. Runko & S. Pritzker (Eds.). *Encyclopedia of Creativity*. (vol. 2. pp. 325-334). Academic Press.

Piechowski, M.M. (2014). *"Mellow out," they say. If I only could: Intensities and sensitivities of the young and brigh*t (2nd ed.). Royal Fireworks Press.

Piechowski, M.M., & Wells, C. (2021). Reexamining overexcitability: A framework for understanding intense experience. In *Handbook for Counselors Serving Students with Gifts & Talents* (pp. 63-83). Routledge.

Yehuda, R., & LeDoux, J. (2007). Response variation following trauma: a translational neuroscience approach to understanding PTSD. *Neuron, 56*(1), 19-32.

Part Three:
Trauma, Giftedness, and EMDR

Chapter 7:
What is EMDR and How Does It Relate to Giftedness?

While crafting this deeply personal book, I found myself compelled to interject my own narrative. I attended to this desire with caution, carefully considering the opportune moments to do so. Similar to my approach in therapy, I disclose personal details when I perceive a clear advantage for my clients. In this context, I sensed a potential benefit in revealing fragments of my story although I did not wish it to be a full autobiography. Nevertheless, I am eager to impart some insights about Eye Movement Desensitization and Reprocessing (EMDR) therapy and explain my motivation for embracing this approach while working with other gifted, 2e, and neurodivergent individuals. Therefore, this chapter will explore what EMDR is, why I got into it, and what this has to do with giftedness. I assure you, this chapter has meaning even if you never intend to engage in EMDR therapy yourself.

EMDR Overview

EMDR is a therapy modality initially associated with trauma processing. I find it is also excellent to use with any anxiety-driven struggle, and the EMDR International Association identifies it as beneficial in treating depression (EMDRIA, 2023). Though it is called Eye Movement Desensitization and Reprocessing therapy, it has less to do with eye movement and more to do with any sort of **bilateral stimulation**, the associated process of desensitizing a person and their connection to traumatic stimuli, and reprocessing that information in a way that the trauma and associated stimuli no longer limit a person emotionally and functionally. The *why* behind how it works may seem mysterious to some; however, I find (and will explain how) it is biological, neurological, and scientific in nature.

The process of engaging with bilateral stimulation is often achieved through methods like watching a moving light on a light bar, experiencing alternating tactile sensations, and/or listening to alternating tones or music. This engagement serves to occupy parts of the brain that would otherwise impede trauma processing. That is, our brains sometimes meaningfully avoid difficulties and will seek to avoid traumatic thoughts. Other times, we might obsess with intrusive memories. Distracting from these tendencies can help sufferers access natural healing processes. Moreover, bilateral stimulation has a dearousing effect that helps individuals feel a sense of calm while processing challenging material. The dearousal is so potent that many of my clients yawn while engaging in EMDR, and I use bilateral stimulation to fall asleep at night when battling a chattering monkey mind.

It is worth noting that EMDR developer Dr. Francine Shapiro made a serendipitous discovery of this natural process while taking a stroll in a park in 1987. She observed that her alternating feet and saccadic eye movements reduced the intensity of distressing thoughts, leading her to explore eye movements and other forms of bilateral stimulation as a means to assist people in processing traumatic memories. This led to the development and research of EMDR therapy, which has gained international recognition as an evidence-based treatment for trauma. In 1990, Shapiro established the EMDR Institute, which not only trains new EMDR therapists but also supports and conducts empirical studies to substantiate its efficacy. Sadly, Francine Shapiro passed away in 2019. I consider myself fortunate to have received my EMDR training under her guidance while she was still with us.

Francine Shapiro, developer of EMDR (1948-2019)

The Neurobiology of Memory and EMDR

My earlier assertion that EMDR is fully biological, neurological, and scientific in nature deserves some further explanation. Ultimately, the **neurobiology** of EMDR effectiveness relates to the neurobiology of memory. As it is currently understood, memory can be described as a residue of experience in the brain that influences future behavior. Two key regions involved in creating and storing memory are the brain's hippocampal complex and neocortex, which are required for memory consolidation or the process of transforming an initially unstable memory into a more enduring form (Nadel et al., 2003; Squire et al., 2015). This process involves storing the memory in a different part of the brain than where it was initially encoded (Byrne, 2017; Squire et al., 2015). Explicit memory, also known as declarative memory, was previously thought to consist of episodic memory and semantic memory (McClelland et al., 1995; Squire, 1992). However, further research has shown that the hippocampal complex has different roles for episodic and semantic experiences (Nadel & Moscovitch, 1998).

Episodic memory involves storing contextual information about specific events while semantic memory involves knowledge and factual information. Both episodic and semantic processes can be enhanced in gifted persons while data from the senses and associated stimuli can be more intense. Psychiatrist, sleep researcher, and professor of psychiatry at the Harvard Medical School Robert Stickgold (2002) maintains that contextual and qualitative information in episodic memories diminishes and only the significant content or generalities of the memory are remembered. Stickgold's research revealed that older memories are not actually degraded but stored separately and gradually abstracted from the original episodic memory. Sensory images are temporarily metabolized through various brain systems and then encoded in the hippocampal complex where they can be readily accessed during recall.

According to Dr. Shapiro (2017) and later confirmed by researcher and co-director of Saint Louis University's Neuroscience Program Dr. Tony Buchanan (2007), new memories are assimilated into preexisting memory networks, which form the basis of human behavior, attitudes, beliefs, and perceptions. Information is stored in these networks based on similarities in subjects and life experiences, which is where gifted pattern-finding and meaning-making again come into play. New sensory experiences are metabolized and connected to previously stored information, allowing for contextual understanding, learning, and guiding future choices and experiences. However, traumatic memories and their associated emotions can remain unprocessed and trapped in the brain's right hemisphere, blocking learning and preventing them from connecting to preestablished memory networks (Stickgold, 2008). This inadequate processing of distressing experiences results in current psychological and somatic symptoms (Shapiro, 2007). We will discuss somatic symptoms more specifically in upcoming chapters. For now, know that somatic memory is stored in the body and can influence physical sensations, emotions, and behaviors.

EMDR aims to transmute dysfunctionally stored traumatic experiences into adaptive resolutions that promote psychological health (Solomon & Shapiro, 2008). Bilateral eye movements, similar to those experienced during rapid eye movement (REM) sleep, facilitate information transfer between brain hemispheres and aid in the processing of memories and emotions at an adaptive level, leading to reduced distress and integration into memory networks (Shapiro, 2012). Stickgold suggests that EMDR also induces a neurobiological state similar to REM sleep, facilitating the cortical integration of traumatic memories into general semantic networks and reducing the strength of episodic memories and associated negative emotions.

Studies inclusive of brain imaging have shown that bilateral brain stimulation, such as eye movements, tapping, or auditory stimulation, activates brain functions that support focused attention, reorientation, and memory processing (Shapiro, 2012). EMDR therapy produces positive functional changes in the brain and can result in reduced emotional distress, vividness of disturbing images, and improved memory accuracy. As I word it more simply to my clients, bilateral stimulation keeps part of your brain busy while it naturally works through processing that is otherwise stopped or was earlier maladaptive while also causing a dearousal that allows your mind to do what it naturally does.

Why and How I Got Into EMDR

EMDR therapy and training did not come about through my deliberate pursuit; rather, they serendipitously found their way into my life. During the final residency of my master's program, just before seeking licensure, I encountered unexpected challenges that triggered a psychological unraveling I neither desired nor anticipated. As a devoted mother and wife, I willingly chose to undergo a physical separation from my family during a time when they were dealing with chronic health issues and lacked sufficient support.

The decision to attend this residency therefore weighed heavily on me, causing feelings of guilt and leaving me emotionally vulnerable. Adding to the strain, my residency instructor displayed narcissistic traits and subjected me to intense criticism, reawakening within me a trauma response to such abuse that I believed had long been resolved. These attacks, directed not only at me but also at other students, caused many of us to inappropriately question our chosen career paths while I found myself unraveling further.

Returning from this trying residency experience, I was a shattered and fragmented version of myself. Surprised by the significant impact of criticism on my well-being, I recognized the need for therapy and actively sought it out. The therapist I found attentively listened to my struggles with criticism and proposed that I engage in EMDR therapy with her. Initially skeptical, I also remained open to the possibilities this modality offered. Through our sessions, we explored past childhood hardships and workplace mistreatment, unearthing realizations I didn't even know I needed. Gradually, I discovered that I no longer had to merely cope with criticism and its associated challenges; instead, I processed those experiences in a way that they ceased to affect me. Even the weight of my childhood diminished as I underwent this transformative process. I experienced a newfound lightness that exceeded my wildest expectations.

After engaging in my own EMDR therapy at the start of my professional career as a therapist, I sought out EMDR training under the wing of the late Dr. Shapiro and her approved organizations. It changed my life, the way I viewed it, and the way I conceptualized therapy and my clients. To this day, I am still amazed as clients process through horrendous trauma, only to report that they are no longer triggered by that which they pursued therapy for. I still use it on myself, also.

So What Does EMDR Have to Do With Giftedness?

EMDR and giftedness, strangely, go hand-in-hand. This is not to say that EMDR is the only or best modality to use for all gifted people, though it can be the right modality for many. In my EMDR training, I was informed about research suggesting that those with higher IQs did well with EMDR processing. Unfortunately, this supposition is not well-founded yet in peer-reviewed journals and research. However, I have also anecdotally found it to be true. My complex, highly intelligent, gifted clients, that is, seem to work through trauma processing more rapidly and more completely.

If we consider again how gifted persons engage in pattern-finding and meaning-making, it is not so difficult to imagine why and how processing anything, including trauma, can be done rapidly for them. As also attended to in previous chapters, the enhanced cognitive abilities of gifted persons tend to include exceptional memory skills and a heightened capacity to absorb and retain information, leading to advanced learning and knowledge acquisition. We typically think of a gifted individual's ability to process and integrate new information into existing memory networks as advantageous in academic settings. When it comes to trauma and memory processing, gifted individuals may exhibit heightened sensitivity and emotional intensity, resulting in more profound and vivid memories of traumatic events. Due to their advanced cognitive abilities, they may also have a more compound understanding and analysis of traumatic experiences, which can contribute to emotional and psychological responses.

In the context of trauma treatment, the unique cognitive and emotional characteristics of gifted individuals may influence the effectiveness of therapeutic approaches such as EMDR. The advanced cognitive abilities of gifted individuals may facilitate their engagement and understanding of the therapeutic process, allowing them to benefit from techniques like bilateral stimulation and memory reprocessing. However, it is obviously important for therapists to consider the individual needs and sensitivities of gifted clients and tailor the therapy accordingly. Other therapy modalities and skills for both coping with and processing trauma will be discussed in subsequent chapters. An understanding of EMDR will be used as a lens through which this next chapter and its content is understood.

Chapter 7 Conclusion

Chapter 7 explored the significance of Eye Movement and Desensitization (EMDR) therapy in the context of giftedness. EMDR is a therapy modality initially associated with trauma processing but also beneficial for anxiety and depression. Bilateral stimulation, rather than eye movement specifically, is a key component of EMDR, occupying parts of the brain that impede trauma processing and promote a sense of calm. Discovered serendipitously by Dr. Francine Shapiro, this modality has gained international recognition as an evidence-based treatment for trauma.

The neurobiology of memory was identified as closely tied to the effectiveness of EMDR with memories stored in different regions of the brain and assimilated into preexisting memory networks that influence behavior, attitudes, beliefs, and perceptions. It was addressed how traumatic memories can remain unprocessed and trapped, leading to distressing symptoms. EMDR aims to transmute these memories into adaptive resolutions through bilateral stimulation and the facilitation of information transfer between brain hemispheres. Studies have shown positive functional changes in the brain through EMDR therapy, resulting in reduced distress and vividness of disturbing images, and improved memory accuracy.

Anecdotal evidence was offered suggesting how gifted individuals with enhanced cognitive abilities and sensitivity may benefit from EMDR therapy. Particularly, it was identified how a propensity for pattern-finding and meaning-making coupled with heightened emotional intensity may contribute to storing vivid traumatic memories. This intensity, however, also allows thorough processing to occur. The advanced cognitive abilities of gifted individuals enable them to understand and analyze their traumatic experiences, influencing their emotional and psychological responses. In trauma treatment, the distinctive cognitive and emotional characteristics of gifted individuals shape the effectiveness of therapeutic approaches like EMDR, facilitating their engagement and allowing them to benefit from bilateral stimulation, memory reprocessing, and other aspects of the modality.

It was also identified as crucial, however, for therapists to consider the individual needs and sensitivities of gifted clients, adapting the therapy to their specific requirements. That is, while EMDR provides a valuable lens through which we might understand and approach trauma processing for a gifted person, it is not the only or best modality for all gifted individuals. The upcoming chapters will take a brief look into other therapy modalities and coping mechanisms for trauma, further enhancing our understanding of the intersection between giftedness and trauma processing.

Chapter 7 Check-In

Exploration: This chapter explored Eye Movement Desensitization and Reprocessing (EMDR), what it is, why it is used, the neurobiology of memory, and this author's personal experience with it in relation to giftedness.

Conclusion: EMDR is a unique therapy modality used to heal trauma and may be well-suited for gifted individuals, due to their unique abilities to seek patterns and meaning.

Questions to consider include:

1. Did you know about EMDR before this chapter?
2. Can you conceptualize how traumatic memories are stored?
3. Did any of your own trauma or struggles come to the surface for you while reading this chapter?

Nervous system and mental/emotional health:

1. Check in with your body, your breathing, and your experiencing of this chapter.
2. Are there any difficult memories that arose for you while considering this material?
3. What bilateral stimulation can you do to help calm your nervous system (walking, knitting, listening to EMDR music)?
4. If needed, take a break and maybe engage in self-care aimed at calming your body and mind.

Chapter 7 References

Buchanan, T.W. (2007). Retrieval of emotional memories. *Psychological Bulletin, 5*, 761–779.

Byrne, J.H. (2017). *Learning and memory: a comprehensive reference*. Academic Press.

EMDRIA. (2023). *EMDR therapy & Depression*. Retrieved from https://www.emdria.org/about-emdr-therapy/emdr-depression/

EMDRIA. (2021). *EMDR therapy Beginnings: Francine Shapiro*. Retrieved from https://www.emdria.org/blog/emdr-therapy-beginnings-francine-shapiro/

EMDR Institute, Inc.. (2020). *Welcome to EMDR.com*. Retrieved from https://www.emdr.com

Landin-Romero, R., Moreno-Alcazar, A., Pagani, M., & Amann, B.L. (2018). How does eye movement desensitization and reprocessing therapy work? A systematic review on suggested mechanisms of action. *Frontiers in psychology, 9*, 1395.

McClelland, J.L., McNaughton, B.L, & O'Reilly, R.C. (1995). Why there are complementary learning systems in the hippocampus and neocortex: Insights from the successes and failures of connectionist models of learning and memory. *Psychological Review, 102*, 419–457

Nadel, L., & Moscovitch, L. (1998). Hippocampal contribution to cortical plasticity. *Neuropharmacology, 37*, 431–440.

Nadel, L., Ryan, T.L., Hayes, S.M., Gilboa, A., & Moscovitch, M. (2003). The role of the hippocampal complex in long-term episodic memory. *International Congress Series, 1250*(C), 215–234.

Shapiro, F. (2017). *Eye movement desensitization and reprocessing: Basic principles, protocols, and procedures* (3nd ed.). Guilford.

Shapiro, F. (2007). EMDR and case conceptualization from an adaptive information processing perspective. In F. Shapiro, F.W. Kaslow, & L. Maxfield (Eds.), *Handbook of EMDR and family therapy processes* (pp. 3–34). John Wiley & Sons, Inc.

Shapiro, F. (2012). *Getting past your past: Take control of your life with self-help techniques from EMDR therapy*. Rodale.

Solomon, R.M., & Shapiro, F. (2008). EMDR and the adaptive information processing model. *Journal of EMDR Practice and Research, 2*(4), 315–325.

Squire, L.R. (1992). Memory and the hippocampus: A synthesis from findings with rats, monkeys, and humans. *Psychological Review, 99*, 195–231

Squire, L.R., Genzel, L., Wixted, J.T., & Morris, R.G. (2015). Memory consolidation. *Cold Spring Harbor perspectives in biology, 7*(8), a021766.

Chapter 8: Giftedness and the T.I.C.E.S. of Trauma

The comprehensive cognizance of giftedness is characterized by exceptional cognitive abilities, pattern-finding, and meaning-making that lends to a gifted person's depth and complexity. This conceptualization offers a lens through which we can examine the intricate relationship between memory, trauma, and the often intense experiences of gifted persons. Gifted individuals possess advanced intellectual capacities and unique memory processing that shapes their learning and experiences. The impact of trauma on memory becomes particularly significant for gifted individuals, given their heightened sensitivity and intense emotional responses. In the previous chapter, EMDR was considered as a tool to conceptualize trauma processing. This chapter further investigates the relationship between giftedness and memory, examining the role of memory in learning and the impact of trauma on gifted individuals. Subsequent sections then analyze the implications of tailored therapeutic interventions aimed at addressing the specific needs of gifted individuals.

The Body, Trauma, and Classical Conditioning

At the turn of this century, researchers and mental health practitioners started approaching trauma work with an understanding of how traumatic memories are not only held in the mind but in the body as well. In the highly influential book, *The Body Keeps the Score*, psychiatrist and trauma expert Dr. Bessel van der Kolk (2014) explores the effects of trauma on the whole person. This world-renowned publication presents research and personal stories, revealing how trauma reshapes our being, impairs pleasure and self-control, and can erode trust. Dr. van der Kolk also offers suggestions for innovative healing methods like neurofeedback, meditation, yoga, and EMDR, to fully leverage the brain and body's ability to change. With global acclaim, it has topped the New York Times Bestseller List for nonfiction and has been translated into 36 languages.

Other renowned practitioners and researchers have worked to identify how trauma is stored in the body. For example, Dr. Peter A. Levine, a psychotherapist and trauma expert, developed Somatic Experiencing (SE) as a therapeutic approach used to address the effects of trauma and stress-related disorders (Ergos Institute, Inc., 2022). SE recognizes that traumatic experiences can manifest as unresolved sensations in the body, leading to physical and psychological symptoms. Similarly, in her book *The Body Never Lies*, Swiss psychologist and psychoanalyst Alice Miller (2006) dives into the lasting impact of harmful parenting while emphasizing the profound connection between childhood trauma and its enduring effects on both the body and mind. In this book, Miller highlights how these effects can manifest in diverse ways, ranging from physical ailments to emotional turmoil and difficulties in relationships. By emphasizing the resolute truth expressed by the body, Miller underscores the importance of attuning to its messages as a pathway to healing from past traumas.

These practitioners and their publications along with Dr. Shapiro and many others maintain that trauma is not only stored mentally. Rather, there are experts who will insist that it is held at a musculoskeletal level and even in our cells and DNA. Now, whether we can prove trauma coding and historical trauma at a molecular level, we have ample anecdotal and empirical evidence supporting how it impacts people physically. When we consider Dąbrowski's five overexcitabilities and how they manifest in relation to this somatic storage of trauma, we can start to make connections between EMDR, somatic experiences, trauma, and giftedness.

To further explain how the body stores trauma and somatic memories, I would like to remind or introduce you to Russian physiologist Ivan Pavlov's most notable experiment. Pavlov (1925) famously studied the process of **classical conditioning**, which involves pairing a neutral stimulus with an unconditioned stimulus to elicit a conditioned response. In his experiment, Pavlov used dogs and observed their salivary response to food. He noticed that the dogs would salivate in anticipation of the food when they saw or heard the laboratory assistant who regularly fed them, leading Pavlov to investigate further. To understand classical conditioning, as illustrated in Figure 5 below, Pavlov introduced a neutral stimulus, such as a bell or a tone, and paired it with the presentation of food. Initially, the bell had no association with salivation, but after repeated pairings with food, the dogs started to associate the bell with the food and began to salivate in response to the bell alone. In this way, the neutral stimulus (bell) became a conditioned stimulus that triggered a conditioned response (salivation) without the presence of the original unconditioned stimulus (food).

Figure 5. Pavlov's Dog Experiment (Representation)

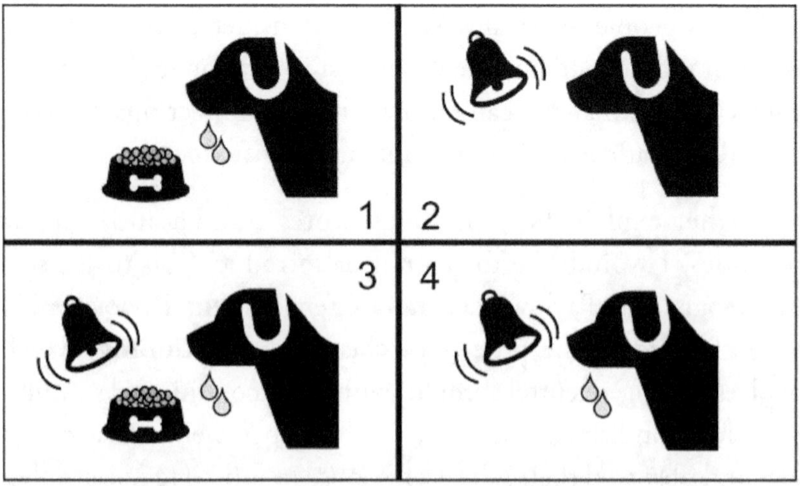

In this illustration of classical conditioning, there is a stimulus (the food) that causes a somatic response (the drooling) and then another stimulus (the bell) that is connected to this entire experience. Now, let us think of this in relation to how the body holds trauma. Consider, for example, a child who is yelled at, and that the yelling causes them to have a stress headache such as is shown in Figure 6.

Figure 6. The Classical Conditioning of Somatic Responses to Trauma

Just like how the food causes a somatic response for the dog (drooling), the yelling causes a somatic response for the child (headache). Now imagine the child is just reading a book, and this is a neutral or even enjoyable activity for the child like the bell ringing is neutral for the dog. As the child is reading another time, though, they are yelled at again for not finishing their chores and develop a corresponding stress headache. This is similar to when the dog sees the food, drools, and the bell is rung at the same time. Later on, just as the dog drools when the bell rings, the child becomes a teen who gets a stress headache every time they read, and they likely do not know it is because they were yelled at while reading when they were younger. This sort of traumatic and somatic learning takes place in childhood and throughout one's life, often eventually burying the unconditioned stimulus (the food or the yelling, respectively).

Dr. van der Kolk's insistence that the body keeps the score highlights the lasting impact of trauma on the body. It emphasizes that even if the initial cause of a somatic response is forgotten, the response itself persists and can be linked back to the traumatic event. By attentively listening to the body's messages, we can uncover the earlier trauma and work towards unlearning maladaptive responses while learning more appropriate ones. Crucially, this process involves examining the imagery, cognitions (thoughts), emotions, and physical sensations associated with the neutral triggers and conditioned responses.

The Body, Trauma, and Operant Conditioning

Now, as many may be aware, classical conditioning is not the only kind of learning taught readily in psychology books. Indeed, **operant conditioning** is also frequently paired with this concept as another option. Operant conditioning, unlike classical conditioning, might seem more direct. B. F. Skinner coined the term *operant conditioning* in 1937 within the realm of reflex physiology.

Although the term was fresh, its concept was not entirely groundbreaking. Skinner's definition of operant behavior as behavior controlled by its consequences closely resembled what was previously known as *instrumental learning* or simply habit. Per Skinner (1938, 2019), operant conditioning is a method of learning that uses rewards and punishment to modify behavior. It is based on the idea that the consequences of a behavior determine the possibility of it being repeated. Behavior that is followed by a pleasant consequence is likely to be repeated while behavior followed by an unpleasant consequence is less likely to continue. There is also the removal of reward or punishment that is considered, as seen in Figure 7 below.

Figure 7. Types of Operant Conditioning

Four types of operant conditioning methods include using:

- Positive reinforcement: the addition of a reward
- Negative reinforcement: the removal of a punishment
- Positive punishment: the addition of a punishment
- Negative punishment: the removal of a reward

When we relate operant conditioning to the concept of trauma coding, it is not so difficult to see how they might interact. For example, if a child gets yelled at for talking too loud (positive punishment), they may grow up talking quietly to avoid punishment. That is, because of the negative consequences and the addition of a punishment attached to talking loudly, this behavior is extinguished or avoided. Let us take this example further and suppose this person has a psychomotor overexcitability and an intrinsic drive to talk loudly and rapidly. If this behavior is met with harsh judgment and difficult treatment, the child may blunt this behavior and associated overexcitability causing additional trauma and impact on their nervous system. Later, when a gifted adult who experienced such blunting quietly orders their meal in a noisy restaurant, friends may wonder why they struggle to speak up. It is possible that they were simply conditioned in childhood to do so, though they have a drive to do otherwise. It is a trauma response.

Sometimes, concepts of positive punishment, like in the example above, and negative punishment can be difficult to comprehend. Negative punishment is when a reward is removed. For example, imagine a child was given a stuffed bear as a reward for getting an A in spelling. Now, imagine this same child forgets to turn in a homework assignment and has this bear taken away as a punishment. They may choose to keep doing their homework after this event to avoid further punishment, or they may give up on trying altogether to avoid such disappointment in the future. Unfortunately, if this is an intense or common form of punishment for a child, they may grow up afraid of losing important things if they are less than perfect. Such fear may manifest in adulthood when a person avoids good things such as a promotion or trip because they do not want it later taken away. Some people also expect resulting difficulty when something good happens, particularly if they make a mistake.

For gifted persons, pattern-finding and meaning-making may feed into the negative outcomes associated with negative punishment such that individuals hypervigilantly look for the bad that may happen next. These individuals may also blunt emotional overexcitability, for example, to avoid having their feelings hurt. When gifted persons are labeled as "not living up to their potential," negative punishment could be responsible. In adulthood, this supposed "underachieving" may present when a gifted individual avoids college because they are afraid to fail or think they are not "good enough" to go. Or a gifted adult such as this may have attended college, feeling that they would be punished harshly for not, though they did not truly want to go. In either case, the reasoning for their actions are based on trauma rather than authentic wants and needs.

When operant conditioning is coupled with classical conditioning, it can intensify the encoding of trauma within the mind and body. For instance, if a child receives food as a reward for positive actions (positive reinforcement), they might associate food with being good. As a result, they may develop a tendency to overeat in order to seek momentary emotional relief or a sense of value (engagement with classical conditioning). However, they may lack conscious comprehension as to why feeling full or engaging in excessive eating is considered positive, as they inherently dislike such behavior. To delve deeper into this phenomenon, it is crucial to examine their bodily reactions, triggers, mental images, thoughts, emotions, and associated sensations, as they hold the key to a more complete understanding of this phenomenon.

The Body and T.I.C.E.S., Trauma, and Giftedness

So what does an understanding of the body and trauma have to do with giftedness? Well, let us loop back to an understanding of asynchronicity, compensation, and overexcitability or OE. As a reminder, asynchronous, gifted individuals tend to compensate for difficulties, adjust to them, and sometimes maladjust. Additionally, gifted individuals tend to have one to several OEs in psychomotor, emotional, sensual, imaginational, and/or intellectual domains that can intensify trauma experiencing and coding in the mind as adjustments are made. Consider, therefore, how classical and operant conditioning layered with intensity can complicate how trauma is remembered, coded, and felt.

Now that we have conceptualized the gestalt of the situation, I would like to introduce another aspect of EMDR that can help us further understand giftedness and trauma more entirely. As a reminder, EMDR utilizes back-and-forth eye movements or other types of bilateral stimulation to activate the information processing system and facilitate the resolution of traumatic memories. When I use EMDR with clients, we start out a processing session by identifying the **T.I.C.E.S.** of the situation. T.I.C.E.S., discovered by EMDR developer Dr. Francine Shapiro (2017), stands for triggering stimuli or target (T), associated imagery (I), an associated negative belief or cognition (C), activated emotions (E), and bodily or **somatic sensations** (S).

As an example of how T.I.C.E.S. are applied, imagine the classical conditioning example where a teenager now gets stress headaches when he reads. Having ruled out attention and eye problems, an EMDR therapist could have him consider the T.I.C.E.S of the situation. For this example, the trigger is reading, the image is sitting with a book they need to complete for an English class, and the negative cognition might be "there is something wrong with me." The emotion may be frustration and shame, and the body sensation may be tension in the head and neck with a tightness in the throat and thoughts of a stress headache. After considering the T.I.C.E.S., the therapist would have the teenager connect with all the elements and especially the body sensations, and float back in their mind to an earlier time when they felt this way. The idea is that many experiences might come up. However, it is probable that the client will float back to a time they were yelled at by their parent, and it caused them similar body sensations. This is where the mystery of the conditioning of body sensations starts to be understood and reworked.

As we explore the T.I.C.E.S. in this scenario, you might notice how the five components also correlate gently with the five OEs. More specifically, a physical trigger may relate to psychomotor OE, the image may relate to imaginational OE, the cognition may relate to intellectual OE, the emotion may relate to emotional OE, and the sensation may relate to sensual OE. And obviously, while there may be a crossover between and within these categories, we can again begin to conceptualize further how trauma and giftedness combine to form a more intense situation. If you consider how trauma results in T.I.C.E.S. that combine with the OE loop considered in an earlier chapter, you can picture this more clearly such as in Figure 8 below. Here, traumatic experiences impact the body and mind while the body and mind are also being influenced by OEs that then trigger back to the body.

Figure 8. Gifted Trauma Response Cycle

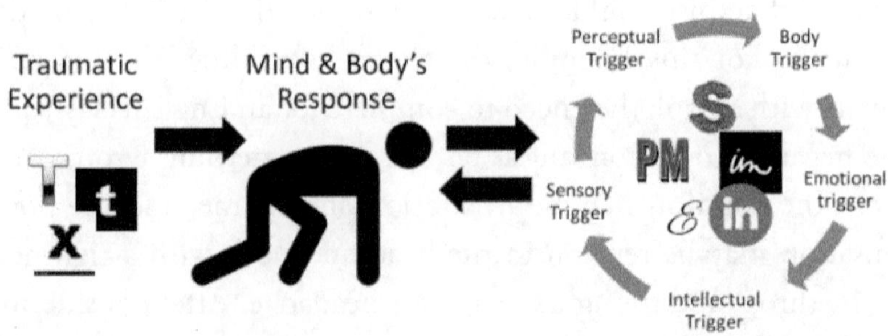

Note: Traumatic experiences may include big T traumas (T), little t traumas (t), and/or complex trauma (x). The body and mind respond to trauma after and while also being impacted by psychomotor (Pm), sensual (S), imaginational (Im), intellectual (In), and emotional (E) overexcitabilities. This process can result in triggers that feed back into a somatic cycle.

A Note About Neurodivergence and T.I.C.E.S.

When contemplating T.I.C.E.S. along with giftedness and neurodivergence, I need to mention some unique particularities that relate to different parts of the T.I.C.E.S. model since the model was developed while considering more **neuronormative** experiences. That is, while neurotypical individuals can generally identify or produce images, cognitions, emotions, and sensations, neurodivergent individuals may struggle with some of these domains due to some neuro-differences that will be discussed here, briefly.

Aphantasia and Synesthesia

Aphantasia is the inability or difficulty creating mental imagery while **synesthesia** is when stimulation in one perceptual pathway leads to experiences in another perceptual pathway. People with aphantasia may not readily visualize images in their mind's eye and instead rely on other forms of memory, such as verbal or conceptual memory (Larner, 2016; Zeman et al., 2015). Those who are aphantasic may also struggle with autobiographical memory for this reason (Dawes et al., 2020; Monzel et al., 2022). Aphantasia is commonly noticed in autistic individuals and those with higher-than-average IQs (Dance et al., 2021; Milton et al., 2021). Therefore, several twice-exceptional (2e) persons, particularly if they are gifted and autistic, may be impacted by aphantasia. 2e persons may also experience synesthesia, reporting that they perceive music as colors or experience tastes as textures (Dance, 2021).

Because of these phenomena, some individuals may not be able to produce a clear image when moving through the T.I.C.E.S. or they may combine imagery and other experiencing of stimuli. This should not discourage the needed work, however, as an aphantasic individual can focus on other aspects of the T.I.C.E.S. or use photographs that represent their target or trigger while synesthetes can allow these perceptions to combine into unique cognitions or senses. It is simply important to make sure guidance and understanding is based in the client's **lived experience** rather than the clinician's often neuronormative expectations.

Alexithymia and Alexisomia

Alexithymia is a psychological condition characterized by difficulties in identifying, describing, and expressing emotions (Preece et al., 2017). Individuals with alexithymia may have a limited emotional vocabulary and struggle to articulate their feelings or understand the emotions of others. This can lead to a sense of emotional detachment. Introspective alexithymia, also referred to as **alexisomia**, may present as a difficulty in identifying body sensations and somatic experiences (Oca, 2020). These **neurodivergences** can be experienced by 2e individuals, especially.

Similar to aphantasia, a person working through the T.I.C.E.S. could skip or modify elements that do not work for them. For example, if cognitions, emotions, or sensations cannot be identified, a therapist might instead ask their client what the experience reminds them of to help them label these. It is important to note, though, that if a 2e client cannot specify part of the T.I.C.E.S. perfectly, other parts of the T.I.C.E.S. can be focused on instead. Difficulty identifying or using any part of the T.I.C.E.S. is not a failing and should not be considered as such. However a person's unique brain works, the T.I.C.E.S. can be used as a tool to address trauma for that individual.

Chapter 8 Conclusion

Chapter 8 explored the relationship between giftedness and trauma through the lens of memory processing and coding in the body. It considered the significance of how trauma and somatic memories are stored in the body, drawing on the works of experts such as Dr. Bessel van der Kolk, Dr. Peter A. Levine, and Alice Miller. This chapter also brought light to how traumatic experiences can impact the body and manifest as physical and psychological symptoms, emphasizing the importance of attuning to the body's messages for healing.

Classical conditioning and operant conditioning were discussed as learning mechanisms that can interact with trauma coding, influencing the behaviors and responses of gifted individuals. Chapter 8 also underscored the role of pattern-finding and meaning-making in gifted individuals, shedding light on how their cognitive abilities and sensitivity shape their experiences of trauma and its effects on memory.

After discussing conditioning, the T.I.C.E.S. model was introduced, providing valuable insights into trauma processing. Developed by Dr. Francine Shapiro, the T.I.C.E.S. model encompasses the triggering stimuli (T), associated imagery (I), negative beliefs or cognitions (C), activated emotions (E), and bodily or somatic sensations (S) related to a traumatic experience. These elements form the foundation for exploring and resolving trauma through EMDR therapy. When applying the T.I.C.E.S. model to gifted individuals, its correlation with the five overexcitabilities (psychomotor, imaginational, intellectual, emotional, and sensual) becomes apparent.

It was also discussed how adaptations may be needed for different neurodivergences and experiences. Regardless, this connection and related contingencies emphasize how trauma impacts both the mind and body of gifted individuals, often amplifying their experiences and responses.

By understanding the body's role in trauma coding, the different conditioning processes, and the T.I.C.E.S. of trauma, tailored therapeutic interventions can be developed to address the specific needs of gifted individuals. Overall, this chapter deepened our understanding of giftedness, trauma, and memory, paving the way for effective trauma treatment strategies, which will be discussed further in subsequent chapters.

Chapter 8 Check-In

Exploration: This chapter explored how the body holds trauma and how overexcitability relates to classical conditioning and the T.I.C.E.S. of trauma processing or triggers/target, images, cognitions, emotions, and body sensations.

Conclusion: All people can learn how to hold trauma through conditioning without remembering why or how. This can later be uncovered and understood using the T.I.C.E.S. and conceptualizing how they combine with overexcitabilities to form intense experiences for gifted individuals.

Questions to consider include:

1. Did an understanding of conditioning cause you to consider how you learned and adapted to or compensated for prior experiences in your life?
2. Did you move through the T.I.C.E.S. of some of your own triggers or experiences?
3. Did you struggle to identify any part of T.I.C.E.S. for yourself?
4. Did any of your own trauma or struggles come to the surface for you while reading this chapter?

Nervous system and mental/emotional health:

1. Check in with your body, your breathing, and your experiencing of this chapter.
2. Are there any triggers, images, cognitions, emotions, or sensations that you need to attend to?
3. What kind of self-care do you need to engage in, given this experiencing?
4. If needed, take a break and maybe engage in this self-care as it relates to your body and mind.

Chapter 8 References

Ergos Institute, Inc.. (2022). *Ergos Institute of Somatic Education Peter A Levine, PhD.* Retrieved from https://www.somaticexperiencing.com

Dance, C.J., Jaquiery, M., Eagleman, D.M., Porteous, D., Zeman, A., & Simner, J. (2021). What is the relationship between aphantasia, synaesthesia and autism?. *Consciousness and Cognition, 89*, 103087.

Dawes, A.J., Keogh, R., Andrillon, T., & Pearson, J. (2020). A cognitive profile of multi-sensory imagery, memory and dreaming in aphantasia. *Scientific reports, 10*(1), 10022.

Larner, A.J. (2016). *A dictionary of neurological signs.* Springer Science & Business Media.

Miller, A. (2006). *The body never lies: The lingering effects of hurtful parenting.* WW Norton & Company.

Milton, F., Fulford, J., Dance, C., Gaddum, J., Heuerman-Williamson, B., Jones, K.,…& Zeman, A. (2021). Behavioral and neural signatures of visual imagery vividness extremes: Aphantasia versus hyperphantasia. *Cerebral cortex communications, 2*(2), tgab035.

Monzel, M., Vetterlein, A., & Reuter, M. (2022). Memory deficits in aphantasics are not restricted to autobiographical memory–Perspectives from the Dual Coding Approach. *Journal of Neuropsychology, 16*(2), 444-461.

Oka, T. (2020). Shitsu-taikan-sho (alexisomia): a historical review and its clinical importance. *BioPsychoSocial Medicine, 14*, 1-9.

Pavlov, P.I. (1925). *Conditioned reflexes: An investigation of the physiological activity of the cerebral cortex.* Oxford University Press

Preece, D., Becerra, R., Allan, A., Robinson, K., & Dandy, J. (2017). Establishing the theoretical components of alexithymia via factor analysis: Introduction and validation of the attention-appraisal model of alexithymia. *Personality and individual differences, 119*, 341-352.

Shapiro, F. (2017). *Eye movement desensitization and reprocessing: Basic principles, protocols, and procedures* (3nd ed.). Guilford.

Skinner, B.F. (1938, 2019). *The behavior of organisms: An experimental analysis.* BF Skinner Foundation.

Van der Kolk, B. (2014). *The body keeps the score: Brain, mind, and body in the healing of trauma.* New York.

Zeman, A., Dewar, M., & Della Sala, S. (2015). Lives without imagery–Congenital aphantasia. *Cortex, 73*, 378-380.

Part Four:
Skill Building and Trauma Treatment

CHAPTER 9: What is Needed (When Dealing with Trauma and Giftedness)

Upon retrospectively examining a well-worn PowerPoint presentation pertaining to the topic of **skill building** and treatment for trauma in relation to giftedness, I observed that I neglected several slides and vital aspects involving building awareness of needs, identifying goals, and acquiring necessary resources. I was not aware enough of the importance of awareness, even more necessitating this chapter. Recognizing the intrinsic importance of identifying needs in relation to trauma, I meticulously explore each of them in dedicated sections about building awareness, identifying treatment goals, **resourcing**, and attending to biology.

Building Awareness

When working with trauma, clients (and ourselves) often do not know where to start. We may not even know we have trauma to process. It is good therefore to clarify what we are seeking out of a therapeutic or processing experience. As such, skill building and trauma treatment really starts with awareness. To build awareness we might first ask questions such as, "Why am I seeking support?" or "What do I want to do?" We might also ask, "How do I want to go about finding and receiving this support or working through my struggles?" The answer to why we seek support may be more clear to some. It often involves wanting to feel better or experience less distress. The other questions may have more initially elusive answers.

When looking into building awareness about what a person wants to do with their trauma-fed distress, they might consider seeking the support of a therapist. As an EMDR practitioner, I generally guide my clients to consider their strengths and needs, identify starting points, and then identify the triggers/targets, images, negative cognitions, emotions, and sensations (T.I.C.E.S.) as discussed in previous chapters. Clarifying needs, such as knowing a client does not want to panic anymore, helps bring the goals of therapy into focus. Identifying a client's strengths helps them know what they already do well, which can be used to support treatment. Being strength-oriented also helps us remember what we can do rather than what we struggle with, in a way that encourages growth and supports a sense of self-efficacy.

Identifying starting points often involves understanding what is the most distressing or pressing (urgent) to a client, after which the T.I.C.E.S. can be identified. As an example of building awareness around the *what* of processing, if a client reports they are feeling overwhelmed and are most distressed by their panic attacks, this can be used as the target for the T.I.C.E.S. and associated work. Of course, before doing any deep trauma work, an attuned therapist will make sure the client is relatively stable and prepared with sound grounding and affect-management skills, as will be discussed in the following chapter.

When contemplating the methods and processes involved in trauma work, individuals seeking healing have multiple avenues to explore. They can reflect upon their existing skills, seek information from various sources such as online resources or books, and seek social support by exchanging ideas with peers who have faced similar challenges. It is important to acknowledge that all of these options are valid when addressing trauma. However, I would naturally encourage individuals, if they have the means, to consider professional support. I present this suggestion not as a sales pitch, but rather because professional assistance is particularly crucial in trauma work, due to the potential for decompensation and negative disintegration.

When it comes to the *how* of seeking awareness, I have a few suggestions. I generally encourage any person to engage in **mindfulness**, which is an intentional, non-judgmental type of noticing without attachment. Through mindfulness, we simply observe sensations and needs without analyzing them. I also (again) encourage people to pay attention to triggers, images, cognitions, emotions, and sensations (T.I.C.E.S.) while simply observing them, describing them, and participating with their wise minds. **Wise-mind** integration will be discussed further in the next chapter. For now, know that it involves watching and considering with your emotional mind, watching and considering with your rational mind, and then considering where these two minds agree. When decisions are made with our wise minds, we often feel positive about them and reduce the experiencing of cognitive dissonance, or the psychological discomfort that arises when there are conflicting beliefs, attitudes, or values. And yes, this discomfort can also be somatic.

Identifying SMART Treatment Goals

It may seem obvious that when a person has trauma, they simply want it to stop hurting or affecting their life. When setting goals for trauma, however, it is important to remember that goals should be SMART and safe. Safety involves sometimes working with a trained professional who understands the risks associated with trauma processing. Also, the communication and feelings of safety need to be explored on a personal level. Knowing when you do or do not feel safe matters and is so important for any mental health work.

SMART goals are something I present and teach to my first-year college students as a way to conceptualize effective goal setting. An acronym and concept first proposed by consultant and corporate planning director George T. Doran (1981), SMART goals are now generally understood as goals that are specific, measurable, achievable, relevant, and timely. There are sometimes other words that are associated with each letter, though the concepts stay more-or-less the same. Given the example of a person who does not want to panic, we need to consider if this is a SMART goal. Well, not panicking is specific enough because we can clarify whether there is the presence of panic or the absence of it. It is also therefore measurable. When considering if not panicking is achievable, however, this may be difficult to predict. Certainly, a lack of panic attacks is relevant to the person who is suffering. This goal may not be achievable in a realistic amount of time, though, and may not therefore be a SMART goal to set.

So what would be a SMART goal to set for a person with panic attacks or other symptoms related to trauma? To figure this out, I will share a general goal I have for all trauma work. For me and my clients, the general goal is:

> *Reduce the intensity, duration, and frequency of negative symptoms or experiences while increasing something positive.*

For a person with panic attacks, a specific and relevant goal may therefore be:

> *In the next month, I intend to decrease my panic attacks from daily at about an hour per attack, to five times a week or less with a shorter duration, and I will go from not functioning during attacks to doing something during them, no matter how small.*

Notice that this goal gives a time, a specific and measurable desire, and it is relevant. I would also negotiate with the client given what I know and what they believe about whether this goal is achievable. Generally, when we seek to reduce negative symptoms in increments, it can seem more realistic. Additionally, notice how from a strength-based perspective, there is the addition of not only what will be reduced, but what can be added. In this example, there is the addition of doing *something* rather than *nothing* during attacks, which can again build a sense of self-efficacy and engage with a person's nervous system differently. Doing something different also changes the script from feeling powerless or out of control to feeling some control, no matter how little. Sometimes, we may discuss or elect a specific something, such as saying a client will do ten sit-ups or engage in deep breathing or a mammalian ice dive (which will be explained later, I promise).

Resourcing

Building awareness and goal setting may seem like obvious aspects of any journey into trauma management and treatment. This section, however, may find people puzzled. What is **resourcing**? In the context of mental health practice, resourcing refers to the process of seeking or providing individuals with tools, strategies, and support to enhance their emotional well-being, coping skills, and overall resilience (Sisto et al., 2019). It involves helping individuals access and utilize internal and external resources to effectively manage their mental health challenges and promote their overall psychological well-being. Resourcing techniques may include relaxation techniques, self-care practices, social support networks, therapy, and other interventions aimed at building emotional strength and resilience.

At the beginning of a processing journey, resourcing is crucial for setting individuals up for success. Once external sources of support are identified, such as friends, family, therapists, groups, community centers, and information in libraries and on the Internet, individuals may sometimes feel unsure of how to proceed. Drawing from solution-focused and EMDR techniques (Shapiro, 2017), I provide a list of ways to engage in internal resourcing specifically tailored to the gifted population.

- Firstly, I recommend identifying natural or developed strengths, abilities, or talents that individuals already possess. These can serve as valuable resources. With gifted individuals, these strengths may manifest in functional domains, intellectual capacity, pattern-finding, meaning-making, compensatory skills, and more.
- Next, I encourage individuals to recall a time when they were successful, allowing them to focus on what they can do right and the actions they took to achieve that success. This taps into the gifted person's propensity for creative and adaptive problem-solving, offering a helpful resource.
- Additionally, individuals can identify role models or individuals (even fictional characters) they admire and explore how they can embody or incorporate their qualities. This can provide inspiration and guidance.
- It is also important to identify exceptions to difficulties or negative cognitions, acknowledging that alternative options exist beyond their hardships. For example, if a person always feels like they shut down with difficulty, they can consider a time when they did not shut down and contemplate how they did this. This exercise also helps individuals identify their strengths.
- Lastly, it is important to highlight the recognition of overexcitabilities (OEs) as strengths, particularly with gifted individuals. Despite the fact that OEs may not always be seen in a positive light, each of the five intensities holds inherent value and associated abilities, making them valuable resources. A person can explore for themselves or with a professional about how they may benefit from, and therefore use, their OEs to help with their healing process.

By engaging in these internal resourcing techniques, individuals can enhance their self-awareness, tap into their strengths, and navigate their mental health journey more effectively. Considering aspects of resourcing that are specific to gifted individuals helps us further conceptualize the intersection of giftedness and trauma where treatment is concerned.

Don't Forget About Biology

It is probably clear at this point in the book that I take a therapeutic and developmental approach to trauma treatment and processing. However, it is absolutely necessary that I address physiological, medical, and biological concerns as a part of whole-person processing. For example, if a client comes into session suggesting they are tired and they have experienced unexpected weight gain, I might look at depression as a cause of these symptoms. It is wise, though, to start with biology by asking if the client has a history of diabetes or thyroid issues, for example. I would also encourage them to see their primary care doctor or favorite naturopath to rule out medical causes for their physiological symptoms. Additionally, there are many health conditions that cause or mimic anxiety and depression. It would be a shame to not attend to these.

Additionally, there are fields like functional neurology and functional medicine that might be helpful in navigating these spaces with minimal trauma and less invasive intervention while considering the body and mind specifically. According to Meyer et al. (2017) in their article about functional neurology and clinical applications of chiropractic manual therapy, it was maintained that "disturbances of the physiology in the nervous system, especially those in the brain, can have many detrimental effects on the body. These disturbances are proposed to be often reversible or at least to have the potential for improvement" (para. 9). By addressing the body integratively, we also enhance **bottom-up processing**.

According to The Institute of Functional Medicine (2023), functional medicine, an umbrella term under which functional neurology resides, is a medical approach that seeks to identify and treat the underlying cause of disease. When considering issues from a functional medicine perspective, a single symptom or diagnosis may have multiple contributing factors. For instance, depression can be caused by various factors including inflammation. Similarly, a cause like inflammation can result in different diagnoses such as depression. The specific manifestation of each cause varies based on an individual's genes, environment, and lifestyle. When considering the whole-person perspective, which is encouraged with gifted individuals and others, functional medicine can achieve lasting benefits beyond symptom relief since treatments target the correct underlying cause. Again, however, this is only one modality that helps us consider the value of approaching trauma treatment from different perspectives.

Chapter 9 Conclusion

Chapter 9 sought to highlight the significance of building awareness of needs, identifying goals, and acquiring necessary resources in the context of trauma management and treatment. It emphasized the importance of starting with awareness and asking important questions about seeking support, understanding personal goals, and determining the desired approach for working through struggles.

This chapter also explored the concept of SMART goals, emphasizing how they need to be specific, measurable, achievable, relevant, and timely. An example of this tool was given in relation to therapy goals. Furthermore, this chapter introduced the concept of resourcing, which involves providing individuals with tools, strategies, and support to enhance emotional well-being, coping skills, and overall resilience. The chapter provided techniques for internal resourcing, such as identifying strengths, recalling past successes, finding inspiration in role models, recognizing exceptions to difficulties, and embracing overexcitabilities as strengths.

And finally, we briefly discussed the importance of ruling out or integrating an awareness of physiological or medical concerns when considering symptoms. It is always important to take a whole-person approach to assessing giftedness and trauma while identifying other possible root causes of suffering. As such, involving a person's primary care team, naturopath, or functional medicine practitioner is wise.

By engaging in these practices, individuals can enhance self-awareness, tap into their strengths, and effectively begin to manage their trauma-related challenges. Further exploration of trauma treatment from the top-down and bottom-up will be presented in the chapters to follow.

Chapter 9 Check-In

Exploration: This chapter explored how a person might prepare for a trauma-processing journey while remaining safe and SMART (SMART goals).

Conclusion: Trauma work should not be taken lightly, and preparation involves building awareness, identifying goals, and resourcing. For gifted individuals especially, this all needs to be considered in relation to their strengths and needs.

Questions to consider include:

1. What is the purpose of awareness when considering trauma work and where might you need to increase awareness in your own life?
2. Did you come up with any of your own SMART goals or goals for others in your life?
3. What are your natural resources and strengths?
4. Did any of your own trauma or struggles come to the surface for you while reading this chapter?

Nervous system and mental/emotional health:

1. Check in with yourself about your own level of awareness in relation to needs and trauma?
2. Are there any triggers, images, cognitions, emotions, or sensations that need attending to?
3. Can you use your strengths now?
4. If needed, take a break and maybe engage in self-care as it relates to your strengths and overexcitabilities.

Chapter 9 References

Doran, G.T. (1981). There's a S.M.A.R.T. way to write management's goals and objectives. *Management Review. 70* (11). 35–36.

The Institute for Functional Medicine. (2023). *What is functional medicine?* Retrieved from https://www.ifm.org/functional-medicine/what-is-functional-medicine/

Meyer, A.L., Meyer, A., Etherington, S., & Leboeuf-Yde, C. (2017). Unraveling functional neurology: a scoping review of theories and clinical applications in a context of chiropractic manual therapy. *Chiropractic & manual therapies, 25*, 19. https://doi.org/10.1186/s12998-017-0151-1

Shapiro, F. (2017). *Eye movement desensitization and reprocessing: Basic principles, protocols, and procedures* (3nd ed.). Guilford.

Sisto, A., Vicinanza, F., Campanozzi, L.L., Ricci, G., Tartaglini, D., & Tambone, V. (2019). Towards a transversal definition of psychological resilience: A literature review. *Medicina, 55*(11), 745.

Chapter 10: Skill Building & Treatment Options Top-Down

Now that we understand some of how trauma and giftedness intersect and how to prepare for processing, you might be asking: *Now what?* The answer to this is to *do something*, which often amounts to skill building and/or treatment. Trauma therapies and treatment can be categorized into two distinct approaches: **top-down** and bottom-up. Top-down approaches focus on the cognitive and logical aspects of the brain along with stabilization and affect management. Bottom-up approaches focus on the body, its sensory receptors, and psychodynamic elements such as childhood experiences and personality development. In this chapter, we will explore top-down approaches to treating trauma and how skill building can be used to help individuals manage their symptoms, the importance of social support, and how giftedness impacts these factors.

The top-down approach to treating trauma is the most prevalent therapy today and relies on our ability to perceive with our conscious mind and focuses on the cognitive, frontal lobes of the brain. This approach is helpful when stabilization is needed or when we are unable to address the cascade of events that leave us feeling anxious, depressed, or unsafe. However, it is important to remember that trauma responses are generally automatic and unconscious, and when a person is experiencing trauma or triggers, their prefrontal cortex actually goes offline. This means that a logic-first approach can be difficult to access since trauma responses deactivate thinking areas and activate the lower (primitive) areas of the brain. As such, having some coping skills practiced and in place is helpful because their use is more automatic.

It is important to note that while some options for skill building and treatment are offered in this chapter, it is not an exhaustive list nor meant to be a how-to guide for treating trauma. Rather, this chapter will expose readers to options for top-down approaches to trauma treatment so it can be understood and sought as needed. Certainly, this book does not replace the guidance of a trained professional that is aware of a client's specific circumstances and exceptionalities. It is always wise, particularly with trauma processing, to seek support.

Skill Building

Traumatic experiences can have a profound impact on individuals, often leaving them feeling helpless, overwhelmed, and disconnected. Skill building is a key component in trauma treatment that takes a top-down approach to helping individuals manage their trauma-related symptoms. It involves identifying existing skills and strengths or learning new skills to help a person cope with their symptoms and improve their quality of life. Skill building and identification is important for mental health treatment because it also builds a person's sense of self-efficacy or the belief that a person can influence change in their own life. In this section, therefore, we will delve into various strategies and techniques that empower individuals to regain some control over their lives, develop top-down resilience, and foster healing and recovery.

Mindfulness and Grounding

Mindfulness is a technique that involves paying attention to the present moment without judgment. It can help individuals become more aware of their thoughts and feelings, so they might learn to manage them more effectively. By staying in the moment, also, individuals can reduce dissociative episodes or become grounded in the here-and-now, rather than thinking about past difficulties or future concerns. Like mindfulness, grounding techniques involve anchoring into the present and often engaging the senses in what is current. My favorite grounding technique involves literally planting my feet firmly on the ground and feeling where the souls of my feet place pressure on my shoes or on the floor covering. Sensing that pressure and connection has a grounding effect that is experienced while remaining aware of *only* the sensation is possible. Variations of this exercise can be done with one's hands on their chair or on the steering wheel of a car, or by feeling and even experiencing a fabric, plush toy, or rock.

Developing Coping Skills

Coping skills are strategies and techniques that individuals use to manage and navigate challenging situations, emotions, and stressors in their lives. These skills are valuable tools that promote adaptive and healthy responses to various difficulties. Coping skills can be learned and developed over time, empowering individuals to effectively cope with adversity and maintain their well-being. Some common types of coping skills include the following:

- Relaxation techniques, such as deep breathing exercises, progressive muscle relaxation, guided imagery, and meditation.
- Engaging in active problem-solving by identifying the problem, brainstorming solutions, and developing action plans to take a proactive approach to address challenges effectively.

- Positive self-talk can be used by practicing self-encouragement, affirmations, and replacing negative thoughts with positive and *realistic* ones to improve self-esteem and resilience.
- Engaging in hobbies and activities, such as exercise, art, music, or sports, which serve as healthy outlets for stress and promote relaxation. They can also act as a distraction from distress.
- Using time management techniques by organizing tasks, prioritizing responsibilities, and setting realistic goals to reduce feelings of overwhelm and increase productivity.
- Engaging all five of your senses in the world around you and labeling what you see, feel, smell, hear, and/or taste. This is also a mindfulness and grounding activity.
- Making healthy lifestyle choices, such as maintaining a balanced diet, getting regular exercise, ensuring sufficient sleep, and minimizing substance use to contribute to overall well-being and resilience. This can help a person feel generally better, so they can do more bottom-up work and deal with other life stressors effectively.
- Using humor and laughter by finding moments and engaging in activities that elicit laughter to distract from difficulties, release tension, improve mood, and promote a positive outlook.
- Enacting a mammalian ice dive reflex (A WHAT!?). Engaging with one of my absolute favorite skills, a person who feels panicked can dunk their head in a bowl of water, holding it there as able to activate a biological response that slows breathing, heart rate, and blood pressure. I have since amended this skill by simply strapping an ice pack to my forehead at the third eye area. Do not take my word for it, though. Look it up!

- Knowing when to seek support. An important coping skill involves knowing when you have exceeded the reach of your skillset. In such situations, it is wise to seek social support, professional help, and even crisis intervention. It is OK and wise to know your limits and what resources are available if you do.

Treatment from the Top Down

Emotional dysregulation and an inability to manage distress are common symptoms of trauma. Skill building in areas of emotional regulation and distress tolerance equips individuals with tools to identify, understand, and manage their emotions in healthy ways. Some therapeutic approaches that help with these tasks include cognitive behavioral therapy (CBT), dialectical behavior therapy (DBT), acceptance and commitment therapy (ACT), and expressive arts therapies.

Cognitive Behavioral Therapy (CBT)

Cognitive behavioral therapy (CBT) is a type of therapy that focuses on changing negative thought patterns and behaviors. It can help individuals learn to identify and challenge negative or destructive thoughts and replace them with more positive or constructive ones. CBT is one of the most structured and well-researched therapies with sound empirical evidence supporting its use (The Beck Institute for Cognitive Behavior Therapy, 2023). Many individuals enjoy the use of worksheets and homework that are built into this modality. It is important to note, however, that CBT may not work well with gifted adults and some gifted children if they see it as inappropriately discounting beliefs and experiences. Many in the neurodivergent and gifted community identify it as unhelpful or even infantilizing, though this is not identifiably true of all gifted and neurodivergent persons. Awareness of this finding, though, is wise.

Dialectical Behavior Therapy (DBT)

Dialectical behavior therapy (DBT) is a type of evidence-based psychotherapy that was initially developed by psychologist Dr. Marsha M. Linehan (2014) to help individuals struggling with emotional dysregulation, self-destructive behaviors, and difficulty managing intense emotions. DBT combines elements of CBT with mindfulness. It operates on the philosophy of dialectics, which emphasizes finding a balance between what might seem like opposing forces or perspectives. The therapy aims to help individuals create a life worth living by enhancing their emotional regulation skills, interpersonal effectiveness, distress tolerance, and mindfulness abilities.

As a neurodiversity-affirmative DBT practitioner, I particularly appreciate taking a dialectic approach to validating a person's experiences while working on opposite action, wise-mind practices, and **radical acceptance** skills especially. The first part of this practice involves using the word *and* instead of *but*. For example, a client may come to me and say that they want to feel better *but* they are just so overwhelmed. In saying this, they say that their overwhelm prevents them from feeling better. I encourage them, instead, to say that they want to feel better *and* they are just so overwhelmed. This allows both the wanting to feel better and the overwhelm to exist together without one preventing the other. It is a minor semantic change, and it is powerful.

Opposite action, then, involves simply and deliberately doing the opposite mentally and behaviorally of what is done when distressed. Opposite action aims to help individuals regulate their emotions by challenging problematic patterns of behavior. It also helps begin the process of somatic reset. As an example of opposite action, I noticed one day in high school that when I was upset or headachey, I would furrow my brows. So, I decided to experiment with this by raising my eyebrows when I found myself in this state.

To my appreciation, I found doing this guaranteed one or two things. First, willfully raising my eyebrows would automatically improve my mood, which was lovely (it is seriously difficult to be in a bad mood with your eyebrows raised). Also, I noticed that if you walk around with your eyebrows unnaturally raised, people might think you are a little odd or mischievous, which is fun as well. What I stumbled upon as a teenager was opposite action. This concept seems to work with posture, expression, word choices, and emotional states.

A **wise-mind** practice, as depicted in Figure 9 below and adapted from Lineham's DBT training manual, is an exercise that helps individuals cultivate a balanced state of mind, integrating emotions and rational thinking. It aims to promote clarity, mindfulness, and effective decision-making by accessing a wise mental state. The idea behind it is to identify where different ideas and inclinations come from, mindfully making decisions from where the rational and emotional minds agree or overlap. That is, a person considers decision making that is balanced and agreeable to both rational and emotional selves.

Figure 9. Wise Mind Depiction

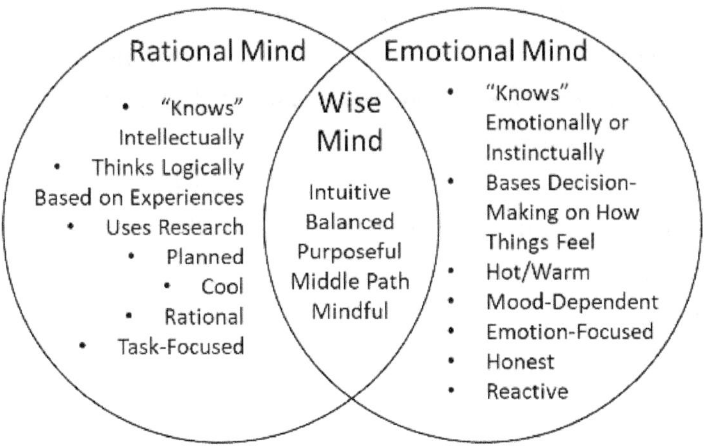

Accompanying a wise-mind practice, radical acceptance is the practice of fully and completely accepting reality as it is, without judgment, resistance, or attempts to change it. It involves acknowledging and embracing the present moment, including painful or difficult experiences, without attempting to deny or avoid them. Radical acceptance also involves letting go of the struggle against what cannot be changed and finding peace within oneself. It does not mean approving of or condoning the situation, but rather choosing to accept it as an undeniable reality. Radical acceptance can be exceptionally difficult with trauma, though it is also difficult to work through trauma if it is not identified as a reality of one's lived experience.

Acceptance and Commitment Therapy (ACT)

Acceptance and commitment therapy (ACT) is a form of psychotherapy that focuses on helping individuals develop psychological flexibility and achieve a meaningful life by accepting their experiences and committing to actions aligned with their values (Hayes, 2006). This concept and modality is similar to the DBT concept of radical acceptance. The main premise of ACT is that suffering is a natural part of the human experience, and that attempts to control or avoid unwanted thoughts, emotions, and sensations can often lead to more distress and limitations. Instead, ACT emphasizes accepting these inner experiences while taking committed action toward creating a rich and meaningful life. By developing psychological flexibility and engaging in values-driven actions, individuals can potentially enhance their well-being and increase resilience, also. This approach is often well-accepted, though expecting a traumatized person to just accept their past needs to be done with great care.

Expressive Arts Therapies

Expressive arts therapies encompass a range of therapeutic approaches that utilize various forms of artistic expression as a means of promoting healing, personal growth, and psychological well-being (Dunphy, 2014). These therapies recognize the inherent power of the arts in facilitating self-expression, exploration, and transformation. Expressive arts therapies integrate different art modalities, such as visual arts, music, movement, drama, and writing into the therapeutic process. The focus is on the creative and expressive aspects of art rather than the final product. By engaging in the artistic process, individuals can tap into their inner experiences, emotions, and narratives in a non-verbal and non-threatening manner. Sometimes also used for bottom-up processing, the key principle underlying expressive arts therapies is that the creative process itself can be therapeutic and serve as a form of communication and self-discovery.

The Value of Safety and Social Support

Traumatic experiences can disrupt one's sense of safety, trust, and self-worth. There is therefore a need for a holistic and multi-dimensional approach to treatment. Part of this approach involves building a foundation of safety and stabilization through validation and skill building. This can certainly be done with a licensed professional or peer group. Safety and validation can also be experienced through sound social support.

Social support plays a crucial role in coping with trauma and its aftermath. It refers to the assistance, comfort, and emotional sustenance individuals receive from their social networks, such as family, friends, peers, and community. As a therapist, I often assess the level of social support a person has. This can be done by exploring their thoughts about and access to family and friends, a peer group, religious or spiritual groups, or other social structures, such as those found in the workplace or in schools.

There are several ways in which social support can help with trauma coping. First, it can offer opportunities for psychological support and emotional validation. Since traumatic experiences can evoke intense emotions and distress, social support can provide a safe space for individuals to express their feelings without judgment or shame. It can help sufferers feel understood, accepted, and less alone in their struggles. Social support can also act as a protective factor by buffering the impact of stress and trauma. Having supportive relationships can mitigate the negative effects of trauma on mental and physical health. It helps individuals build resilience and cope more effectively with adversity. And, social support can help those feeling alienated by trauma find a sense of belonging.

Aside from psychological support, social support also brings with it practical assistance in times of need. Since trauma can disrupt various aspects of an individual's life, such as daily routines, work, or securing safe housing, practical assistance with tasks, resources, or shelter, may be particularly meaningful for trauma sufferers who are in crisis. Practical support can alleviate stress and help individuals regain a sense of stability. The information and guidance gained through social networks can also provide valuable information about available resources, treatment options, and coping strategies. Additionally, trusted individuals can offer guidance and help individuals navigate the complex process of seeking help and healing.

And finally, social support can produce coping role models for those affected by trauma. Observing others who have successfully coped with trauma can inspire hope and resilience. Social support can connect individuals with role models who have overcome similar challenges, providing encouragement and guidance on the path to recovery. Understanding and sharing experiences with others who have gone through similar traumatic events can provide a unique form of support. Peer support groups or communities allow individuals to connect with others who can empathize with their experiences, share insights, and provide a sense of shared understanding and validation.

It is important to note that the quality and availability of social support can vary among individuals. Some may have strong existing networks while others may need to actively seek out and build supportive relationships. Professional support from therapists, counselors, or support groups can also play a significant role in augmenting social support. Overall, social support can provide emotional, practical, and informational resources that can aid individuals in navigating the challenges of trauma and facilitate their healing and recovery process. This stated, it is important to know that some people have very little social support and therefore need additional support in other areas.

Considerations Made for Top-Down Skill Building and Treatment Approaches as It Relates to Giftedness and Trauma

Skill building is a fundamental aspect of trauma treatment, empowering individuals to overcome the challenges posed by traumatic experiences. By providing a range of skills and techniques, trauma survivors can regain control, foster resilience, and promote healing and recovery. Through the integration of skill building into treatment approaches, individuals can proceed towards reclaiming their lives and moving forward with renewed strength and hope. However, considerations still need to be made for how this is done specifically with the gifted community.

It is understood that giftedness involves qualities including advanced cognitive abilities, rapid pattern-finding, and meaning-making that lend to depth and complexity, asynchronous development and compensation or masking, and overexcitability (OE)/heightened intensity in psychomotor, sensual, imaginational, intellectual, and emotional domains. What needs to be further understood is how these qualities impact not only trauma but also skill building and treatment of it. We will therefore consider these qualities in clusters of cognitive components, asynchronicity and compensations, and in relation to the OEs, as they relate to top-down approaches.

Cognitive Components

In relation to advanced cognitive abilities, rapid pattern-finding, and meaning-making, we need to remember that what may seem like new or complex information to a neurotypical client may not be new or complex to a gifted client. That is, they do not need to be instructed on a concept several times, and it should not be assumed that they do not already know what is being shared. To this point, I cannot tell you how many times a gifted client or peer told me they ended up teaching their counselor rather than being taught new skills. Because of this, gifted clients often get bored with therapy just as they become bored in school. Therapy, therefore, for gifted clients requires some level of depth and complexity, making top-down approaches sometimes meaningless to the meaning-maker. If a coping skill or treatment has meaning or sound reasoning for its use, it is more likely to be utilized by a gifted individual.

Asynchronicity and Compensation

In relation to asynchronous development and compensation and/or masking, we need to recall how not all skills are obvious, which may seem like a contradiction in relation to the previous section. However, needs may not be apparent either due to compensatory efforts or to masking. As such, gifted individuals may need extra attention and digging when it comes to finding out what is really needed in therapy. I have seen several severely depressed, anxious, or traumatized clients who were seen before me and were identified as "**just fine**" and even praised for doing "so well." Again, just like in school where struggles were not apparent or the gifted student did not rock the boat, gifted individuals often present as "just fine" when they may be internally unraveling. As gifted persons, we need to be aware of how we may mask difficulties, and as professionals and parents, we need to dig a little deeper past what may seem obvious.

Overexcitabilities (OEs)

When considering giftedness, overexcitability (OE), and top-down trauma treatment and skill building, this is where we must really pay attention. Just like there is no one-size-fits-all trauma treatment, there is also not a one-size-fits-all conceptualization of giftedness and trauma, particularly when it comes to the expression of OEs. The good news is, however, if we can understand an individual's OEs, we may better understand what top-down skills and treatments work best for them.

Let us start with psychomotor OE (*Pm*OE). *Pm*OE involves a notable surplus of energy and the psychomotor expression of emotional tension in a person's body or speech. We may consider this person when thinking about that kid in class who really needs his recess so he can run in order to later focus, or the coworker that can talk for five minutes straight without seemingly taking a breath. When it comes to skill building with *Pm*OE, the effort is two-fold. First, they may need to use this excitability and cope by doing physical activity or talking through difficulties. They also may need help managing this OE, however, if it seems to interfere with feelings of safety. So, in some cases, a *Pm*OE may need to take a walk, and at other times, they may need to engage in some calm grounding.

Now let us consider the sensually OE or *S*OE. *S*OE individuals have a heightened experiencing of sensory and aesthetic pleasure that involves a deep appreciation for various senses along with the sensual expression of emotional tension. For a person with the

*S*OE, therefore, skills and treatment options that involve engagement with the senses and somatic work can be super helpful. For example, grounding with a sensory toy or looking for what an individual with *S*OE can touch, taste, hear, see, and smell in their environment can be helpful and appealing. On the other hand, a person's *S*OE may become easily overstimulated by sensory input and may benefit from relaxation techniques or avoiding sensual stimuli. This can be done by sitting in a dark room with their eyes closed or taking a bath. So in other words, if an individual with *S*OE is under-stimulated or needs a distraction, they can engage with their senses while if they are overstimulated, they may need to retreat from them.

To the imaginational OE or *Im*OE, the world may be more expansive. Persons with *Im*OE tend to engage in vivid imagery, fantasy, and sometimes magical thinking. *Im*OE individuals may also create immersive fantasy worlds, engage in dramatic narratives, and use spontaneous imagery to express emotions. They are known to have a low tolerance for boredom, often seeking novelty and stimulating experiences to fuel their imagination. In relation to finding skills and treatments that work well with *Im*OE, therefore, it is important to consider how they may live in a world of possibilities. As such, grounding an *Im*OE individual with problem-solving and time-management skills can be super important because it allows them to engage with these possibilities while honing in on the best options for them. Additionally though, it helps to remember that their fantasy world may be a safe space that they can actively escape or dissociate into. Along with understanding, they may need help coming back from this dissociative departure. Aside from this though, support with boredom and frustration tolerance may be valuable for individuals with *Im*OE while acknowledging their need for novelty at times as a means of distraction.

An *Im*OE counterpart in ways, intellectual OE or *In*OE is marked by heightened mental activity and intense intellectual engagement. It often includes curiosity, concentration, sustained effort, reading passion, keen observation, and precise planning. *In*OE individuals tend to excel in questioning, problem-solving, and metacognition. They often thirst for truth, possess tenacity, and exhibit critical thinking and independence. Persons with *In*OE might also be judged as too in their heads though, sometimes neglecting their emotions or the emotions of others. Because of this intellectual intensity, *In*OE individuals benefit from both engagement with their intellect and mindful departures from it. When exploring treatment options or skills, an individual with *In*OE might appreciate psychoeducation, understanding the scientific underpinnings of therapeutic decisions or modalities, or engaging intellectually with their own problem-solving. However, if someone with *In*OE is intellectually overstimulated and mentally shut down, it can be helpful to engage with other senses that are unrelated to their intellect. *In*OE may also benefit from a wise-mind practice to find a balance between emotional and rational thinking.

Finally, the emotionally OE or *E*OE may have heightened feelings and empathy, diverse emotions, deep attachments, and emotional sensitivity. Persons with *E*OE may be labeled as highly sensitive or emotionally intelligent, or be misunderstood as lacking emotional intelligence at times. Individuals with *E*OE often connect deeply with others, animals, and places, displaying compassion and responsiveness. And while self-reflection and inner dialogue can shape their well-differentiated self-awareness, loneliness can also be a common experience for them. Because of the tendency to be empathetic while experiencing loneliness, a person with *E*OE may benefit from strong social support and attachment work. They may benefit, too, from expanding their emotional vocabularies to gain greater emotional insight. Acceptance of their emotional intensity can be super helpful while improving upon emotional regulation and distress tolerance skills. Additionally, because of their tendency towards emotional thinking, a gifted mind with *E*OE may benefit from a wise-mind practice where they consider their rational mind and negotiate between these parts when making decisions.

Chapter 10 Conclusion

This chapter explored how trauma therapies can be categorized into top-down and bottom-up approaches with top-down approaches focusing on the cognitive and logical aspects of the brain while bottom-up approaches focus on the body and sensory receptors. This chapter especially emphasized the importance of skill building in trauma treatment and identified various strategies for coping and managing trauma-related symptoms from the top-down.

Within this chapter, we discussed mindfulness and grounding techniques as effective ways to stay present and manage dissociation. We also explored coping skills such as relaxation techniques, problem-solving, positive self-talk, engaging in hobbies and activities, time management, and using humor and laughter. This chapter mentioned the importance of seeking support when needed and highlights the value of professional support in coping with trauma.

Furthermore, some top-down treatment approaches for trauma were then discussed, including cognitive behavioral therapy (CBT), dialectical behavior therapy (DBT), acceptance and commitment therapy (ACT), and expressive arts therapies. Principles and techniques involved in each of these therapies were explored while emphasizing the importance of emotional regulation, distress tolerance, and mindfulness. We then emphasized the role of safety, validation, and social support in trauma treatment while highlighting the significance of social networks in providing psychological support, practical assistance, and coping role models.

Chapter 10 concluded by acknowledging the need for considerations specific to the gifted community in skill building and trauma treatment approaches, taking into account the unique characteristics and experiences of gifted individuals. This is particularly true in relation to cognitive differences, asynchronicity and compensation, and the five overexcitabilities.

Chapter 10 Check-In

Exploration: This chapter explored how trauma can be coped with and treated from the top down with special considerations made for gifted individuals.

Conclusion: Skill building and top-down approaches empower people with coping mechanisms and effective therapies while encouraging social support. The influence of giftedness needs to be considered, however, for tailored and sensitive treatment.

Questions to consider include:

1. Have you used top-down approaches and skills in your own life? What are your favorites?
2. Did you learn about any new skills or treatment options in this chapter?
3. Did any of your own trauma or struggles come to the surface for you while reading this chapter?

Nervous system and mental/emotional health:

1. Check in with your body, your particular overexcitabilities, and your thoughts.
2. Are there any triggers, images, cognitions, emotions, or sensations that need attending to?
3. What kind of skills can you incorporate into your self-care practice?
4. If needed, take a break and maybe engage in some of your favorite grounding or coping skills.

Chapter 10 References

The Beck Institute for Cognitive Behavior Therapy. (2023). *Understanding CBT*. Retrieved from https://beckinstitute.org/about/understanding-cbt/

Dunphy, K. (2014). The effectiveness of expressive arts therapies: A review of the literature. *Psychotherapy and counselling journal of Australia, 2*(1).

Hayes, S.C., Luoma, J.B., Bond, F.W., Masuda, A., & Lillis, J. (2006). Acceptance and commitment therapy: Model, processes and outcomes. *Behaviour research and therapy, 44*(1), 1-25.

Linehan, M. (2014). DBT skills training manual. Guilford Publications.

Chapter 11:
Skill Building & Treatment Options Bottom-Up

Trauma can have a profound impact on individuals, regardless of their backgrounds or abilities. For gifted individuals who tend to possess exceptional intellectual abilities along with great depth and complexity, the effects of trauma can be particularly complex and challenging. This chapter, therefore, delves into the intersection of trauma and giftedness while exploring treatment options that adopt a bottom-up approach.

As a reminder from the previous chapter, top-down approaches to trauma treatment focus on the cognitive and logical aspects of the brain along with stabilization and affect management. We discussed some top-down approaches and skill building that might be used at the start of and throughout one's treatment and in everyday life. Bottom-up approaches focus on the body, its sensory receptors, and psychodynamic elements, such as childhood experiences and personality development. These aspects of treatment and experience are often disguised as pain or tension, making them less obvious to ourselves or others.

If we consider symptoms and struggles like an iceberg with one-tenth of its icy mass above the surface, top-down processing would address the manifestations of stress and trauma that reside above or on the surface while bottom-up symptoms, processing, and experiences are below as seen in Figure 10.

Figure 10. Top-Down and Bottom-Up Factors

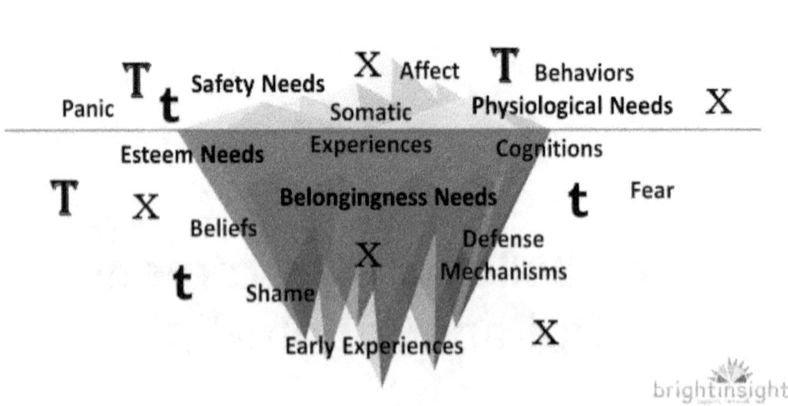

Note: Traumatic experiences may include big T traumas (T), little t traumas (t), and/or complex trauma (x). Some behaviors, experiences, and symptoms manifest above the water line where they can be seen and easily noticed while others may sit below the surface, requiring more bottom-up processing.

Though there are many types of treatment options for trauma processing to help decrease negative symptoms and improve one's quality of life, some are more highly revered and supported in the literature. A simple Google search for bottom-up approaches yields several articles, including one from *Psychology Today* where trauma therapist, national speaker, and author Amanda Ann Gregory, LCPC (2021) reports that common approaches to bottom-up therapy include eye movement desensitization and reprocessing (EMDR), somatic experiencing, internal family systems (IFS) work, and expressive arts therapy. Expanding on this list, integrative trauma therapist, host of Therapy Chat and Trauma Chat podcasts, and the founder of the Trauma Therapist Network, Laura Reagan, LCSW-C (2021) identifies the following list of bottom-up approaches:

- Yoga therapy
- Somatic Experiencing
- Eye Movement Desensitization and Reprocessing (EMDR)
- Sensorimotor Psychotherapy
- Brainspotting

- Focusing
- Accelerated Experiential Dynamic Psychotherapy (AEDP)
- Hakomi Method
- Art Therapy
- Drama Therapy
- Dance/Movement Therapy
- Play Therapy
- Sand Tray Therapy
- Equine-Assisted Psychotherapy

An obvious EMDR enthusiast myself, it is likely clear that I encourage this approach. In my own practice, however, I also integrate gestalt therapy tools and IFS or parts work to help clients identify parts of themselves, such as their inner children, inner critics, rebellious teens, parental forms, protectors, shadow parts, and so on. Additionally, we do a lot of body or somatic work to find where the body is storing traumatic messages and what they are saying. Once these messages, sensations, and parts are identified, they can be dealt with.

Bottom-Up Approaches for Gifted Individuals

Often, individuals ask me what the best trauma treatment for a gifted client is. My response to this question is similar to when I am asked what the best careers or livelihoods are for gifted folx. Simply stated, it depends on the person. Indeed, while gifted people have shared qualities and characteristics, they are also each unique. As each person is unique, and each traumatic event or upbringing is different, so too are the approaches to treating trauma. There is no one-size-fits-all treatment, just like there is not just one kind of gifted person. As such, practitioners who work with gifted and neurodivergent persons need to be flexible and creative. This is particularly true since they are not the populations used to test therapy modalities and interventions. They also benefit therefore from understanding more about each person's identity and unique-to-them qualities.

Understanding Gifted Identity

When selecting where to start with treatment for a gifted person, their uniqueness and identity should be considered. In his article about gifted identity, therapist and director of the Center for Identity Potential Andrew S. Mahoney (2001; 2011) considers the importance of validation, affirmation, affiliation, and affinity in the development of a secure sense of self among gifted individuals. These four constructs form the basis of the Gifted Identity Formation Model (GIFM), which Mahoney has formulated to aid counselors and educators in comprehending the unique needs of gifted individuals. The GIFM outlines the following definitions for each construct:

- **Validation**: The inherent need for acknowledgment and acceptance of one's giftedness by others.
- **Affirmation**: The requirement for positive feedback and encouragement from others to foster a positive self-concept.
- **Affiliation**: The desire for social connections with individuals who share similar interests and abilities.
- **Affinity**: The yearning for a sense of belonging and connection to a broader community or group.

Within his work, Mahoney highlights the interesting nature and interconnectivity of these constructs. For instance, a lack of validation or affirmation may result in feelings of isolation and disconnection, subsequently influencing one's sense of affinity and affiliation with others. By gaining a comprehensive understanding of these needs, counselors and educators are better equipped to provide effective support to gifted individuals as they develop.

In my own research, which also manifested an identity development theory, it was observed that understanding innate qualities and a person's experiences, including strengths and struggles, enabled individuals to take actions that allowed them to objectively identify and meet needs, thus fostering growth and eventually a strong sense of identity (Williams, 2023). This tendency is illustrated in Figure 11.

Figure 11. Awareness as Growth

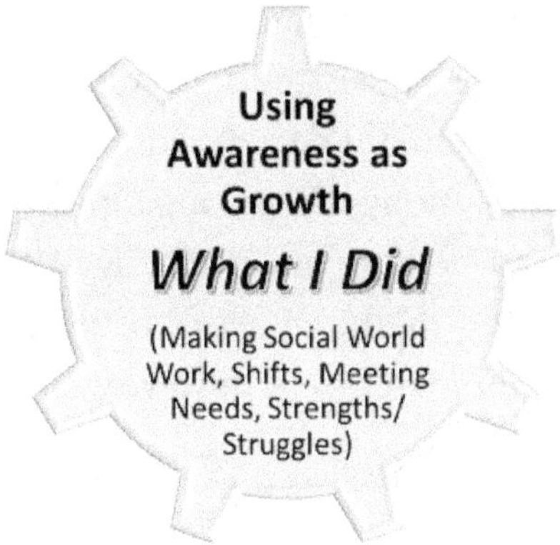

USING AWARENESS AS GROWTH

HAVING AN AWARENESS OF STRENGTHS & STRUGGLES

- NOTICING ASYNCHRONICITY
- NOTICING COMPENSATION

TRYING TO MAKE SOCIAL WORLD WORK:

- SOCIAL LEARNING
- ASSESSING SOCIAL DYNAMIC/ CUES

EXPERIENCING SHIFTS IN AWARENESS/ BEHAVIOR

- DIVERGENCE FROM SOCIAL-CULTURAL STRUCTURES
- DEVELOPING DEEPER SELF-UNDERSTANDING

MEETING NEEDS

- IDENTIFYING NEEDS
- OBJECTIVELY FINDING WHAT WORKS

GROWING FROM EXPERIENCE/CURIOSITY

As you might imagine, these strengths and struggles may have to do with pattern-finding and meaning-making, overexcitabilities, and other gifted characteristics. Mahoney might also conclude that this awareness and strength to grow involves validation, affirmation, affiliation, and affinity in different contexts as different aspects of identity are formed.

In relation to identity formation, a therapist or layperson doing trauma work with a gifted person will want them to experience growth. Therefore, they might consider if aspects of a secure identity are in place by asking the following:

- ❍ Does this gifted person have a sense of validation, affirmation, affiliation, and affinity?
- ❍ Is this gifted individual aware of their strengths, struggles, and overexcitabilities? (If so, what are they?)

- Has this gifted person learned to adjust or make shifts in themselves or their environments, thus impacting their social world?
- Does this gifted individual know what they need to be fulfilled or at least OK?

These questions can help frame a pathway for trauma work by first seeing where the foundation or sense of self resides. Without a secure-enough sense of self, a processor might decompensate while working through traumatic memories. Along with strong top-down skills, a secure sense of identity can help a person manage their affect between sessions, despite doing the heavy work of trauma processing in session. Identity development itself, however, can be more of a bottom-up process.

Understanding Needs

As part of the identity development process for gifted persons, and central to developing sound therapy goals, a person needs to know what they need. This needs identification can also help a person understand what modality is best for them or their client. As an example, imagine a person who comes in for therapy or trauma work and reports that they feel a lot of tension in their back. They also report a history of ear infections as a child and that they think they struggle with auditory processing. For this person, who is already aware of some struggles, it may be clear that they need to do bodywork and not receive only auditory instructions or stimulation. This person, that is, might benefit from EMDR with tactile or visual bilateral stimulation. Having them do only auditory bilateral stimulation would not align with their identity or needs. For a client who has a lot of negative self-talk, they might benefit from starting with internal family systems work while preparing to do EMDR to desensitize whatever traumatic memories fuel these internal criticisms and judgment. Ultimately, a starting place for bottom-up processing depends on what the client needs in therapy and in daily life.

Goodness of Fit for Giftedness and Trauma

Considering the goodness-of-fit model (Thomas & Chess, 1977), it is presumed that all people have unique temperaments that need to be accepted and adapted to, rather than fighting them or imposing outside objectives. That is, it is up to caregivers, therapists, educators, and other professionals to adjust an environment to build on a child's or client's strengths and offer support, rather than exaggerate someone's struggles. I look at this as *not limiting* someone because of my needs and rather meeting them where they are in relation to their needs. So, if a person has aphantasia and has had a negative experience with EMDR, I might suggest a different modality or a workaround while allowing them the autonomy to choose their path. Autonomy and acknowledging self as expert is central to good therapy for anyone, especially for gifted persons who sometimes seek autonomy voraciously.

Openness and Experimentation with Gifted

Because of the sometimes perfectionistic, skeptical, and critical mindset of gifted persons (and this is not seen as a bad thing), it is important to framework carefully. That is, the work being done should not be a promise of perfect peace, nor should it be identified as all-or-nothing or a demand. Rather, it is helpful to gifted persons to be open to trying whatever approach is used, even if there is skepticism. I also find it helpful to explain the science or *why* behind any approach I use. Additionally, it is good to understand that there is no wrong way of doing therapy or a particular modality while exploring different approaches as needed. It is helpful to avoid all-or-nothing or extreme language though, reminding clients that they are working on decreasing the intensity, duration, and frequency of negative symptoms while increasing positive experiences.

One thing I like to do with gifted clients especially, is try out tasks and modalities as *experiments*. Sometimes, we experiment in session, and sometimes, clients experiment with different skills or tasks at home. Calling them experiments also removes the demand of perfection or compliance or a perceived demand, which might be met with avoidant responses. Rather, those engaging in an experiment can see if something works for them or not. So, for example, I might encourage a person to pay attention to their body sensations over the coming week while floating back (EMDR float-back, Chapter 8) to see if these sensations connect to experiences. If clients are able and willing to do this, they report back on the experience. If they do not try this, well, it was just an experiment, and it can be conducted in session. The pressure to be perfect is therefore removed.

The idea of openness and **experimentation** can be extended beyond the therapist's office. In fact, I encourage gifted individuals to experiment with different tasks and skills they may have avoided before, just to see what they are like. I also encourage people to be willing to be surprised. By allowing surprise and mystery, gifted clients can work around the perfection and demand avoidance that may otherwise limit them.

A Note About Treatment Resistance

Before concluding this chapter, it is important to address the issue of treatment resistance. Many gifted clients I work with have been mistakenly labeled as "resistant to treatment." In reality, this resistance often arises because the treatment modality or the practitioner's skill set does not align with the client's unique identity and needs. It is not the fault of the client but rather a lack of knowledge, creativity, or insight on the part of the practitioner. It is crucial to acknowledge that therapists who lack training or insight are not necessarily bad therapists, but they may not be the right fit for the client. Therefore, the responsibility falls on us as practitioners to continuously improve while clients advocate for themselves when faced with this damaging label, such as is seen in Figure 12.

Figure 12. What is Treatment Resistance?

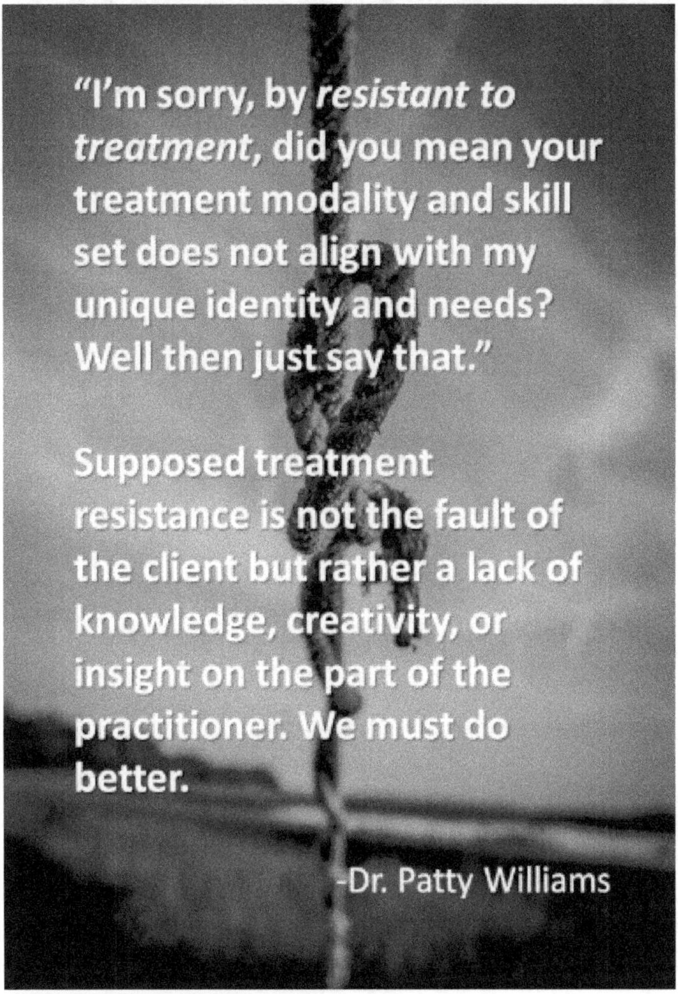

Now, this is not to say that resistance in a therapy setting should not be addressed. Resistance is an element we all feel at points in our lives where we struggle and do not wish to move forward, for subconscious reasons sometimes. Bringing awareness to these energies makes sense and is part of sound practice. Treatment resistance or labeling a client as resistant, however, is a different issue. Esteemed American author and psychotherapist Virginia Satir (1916-1988) had more to say about this topic. Satir, who made significant contributions to the field of family therapy and was renowned for creating the *Virginia Satir Change Process Model*, believed resistance should be reframed as dignity. That is, by reframing resistance as dignity, we can understand that individuals often exhibit resistance in certain situations when the presented context fails to provide an environment that respects and upholds their personal sense of dignity (Satir, 1991). Again, this is a whole other issue and one worth addressing in session. Labeling the client as otherwise difficult should be avoided.

Chapter 11 Conclusion

This chapter explored the intersection of trauma and giftedness, focusing on treatment options that adopt a bottom-up approach. Unlike top-down approaches that address the cognitive aspects of trauma, bottom-up approaches emphasize the body, sensory receptors, and psychodynamic elements. Various bottom-up interventions such as EMDR, somatic experiencing, art therapy, and others were listed.

It was also explored in this chapter how when working with gifted individuals who possess exceptional intellectual abilities and complex inner worlds, it is crucial to consider their unique identities and needs. Validation, affirmation, affiliation, and affinity play vital roles in developing a secure sense of self for gifted individuals. Therapists and caregivers must understand the strengths, struggles, and social dynamics that shape their clients' identities. This understanding can guide the selection of appropriate treatment modalities and interventions.

It was also noted how identifying and meeting the individual needs of gifted clients is essential for effective trauma treatment. Flexibility and creativity were recognized as key since there is no one-size-fits-all approach. The therapist-client relationship should foster autonomy though, acknowledging the client as the expert in their own experiences. The goodness-of-fit model was used to highlight the importance of adapting the environment to support and build on the strengths of gifted individuals, rather than focusing solely on their struggles.

Openness and experimentation were also explored in relation to giftedness, and it was explained how these can help clients overcome perfectionism and skepticism. This is done by allowing people to try different modalities and tasks as experiments, without the pressure of achieving perfection. By embracing openness, curiosity, and a willingness to be surprised, gifted individuals can explore different approaches and tasks, expanding their growth and healing opportunities.

In summary, trauma treatment for gifted individuals requires a comprehensive understanding of their unique identities, strengths, and needs. By adopting bottom-up approaches, therapists can address the complex interplay between trauma and giftedness, helping individuals find healing, resilience, and a sense of self that allows them to thrive and even experience post-traumatic growth, which will be explored subsequently in Chapter 12.

Chapter 11 Check-In

Exploration: This chapter explored how trauma can be coped with and treated from the bottom-up with special considerations made for gifted individuals.

Conclusion: Bottom-up approaches help people process trauma through the body where it is often disguised as pain or tension. There are several recommended modalities for this process such as EMDR, somatic work, and IFS. It is important to make sure the modality matches the client's needs, not just the therapist's or society's neuronormative expectations.

Questions to consider include:

1. Have you used bottom-up approaches and skills in your own life? What are your favorites?
2. Did you learn about any new treatment options or ideas in this chapter?
3. Did any of your own trauma or struggles come to the surface for you while reading this chapter?

Nervous system and mental/emotional health:

1. Check in with your body, your particular over-excitabilities, and your thoughts.
2. Are there any triggers, images, cognitions, emotions, or sensations that need attending to?
3. What kind of experiment or openness can you incorporate into your self-care practice?
4. If needed, take a break and maybe experiment with new grounding or coping skills.

Chapter 11 References

Gregory A. A. (2021). *How bottom-up treatment can address trauma strategies to help the adult brain engage with past trauma.* Retrieved from https://www.psychologytoday.com/us/blog/simplifying-complex-trauma/202112/how-bottom-treatment-can-address-trauma.

Mahoney, A.S. (2001). *The gifted identity formation model. Roeper Review, 20*(3), 222-226.

Mahoney, A.S. (2011). *The gifted identity formation model.* Retrieved from https://www.sengifted.org/post/the-gifted-identity-formation-model

Reagan, L. (2021). *Trauma treatment modality series: "Top-down" and "bottom-up" approach to therapy.* Retrieved from https://traumatherapistnetwork.com/trauma-treatment-modality-series-top-down-and-bottom-up-approach-to-therapy/

Satir, V. (1991). *The Satir model: Family therapy and beyond.* Science and Behavior Books

Thomas, A., & Chess, S. (1977). *Temperament and development.* Brunner/Mazel.

Williams, P. (2023). *Understanding how twice-exceptional (2e) individuals navigate adolescence: A grounded theory study.*

CHAPTER 12: Processing Trauma and Giftedness Altogether

So let's pull it all together. In Part One of this book, we considered what giftedness is, identifying how gifted persons tend to possess unique depth and characteristics including advanced cognitive abilities, rapid pattern-finding and meaning-making, compensation, asynchronous development, and overexcitability. Then, we built an understanding of the challenges, protective factors, identification difficulties, and non-cognitive characteristics associated with giftedness and twice-exceptionality. We learned how this understanding is crucial to comprehending the needs of gifted individuals. Next, trauma was defined as the lasting adverse effects of emotionally disturbing or life-threatening events, and we further explored the differences between big T, little t, and complex trauma types.

In Part Two and Chapters 4, 5, and 6, we learned how any type of trauma can interact with giftedness in various ways. For example, gifted individuals with advanced cognitive abilities may intellectualize and deeply analyze trauma while their pattern-finding and meaning-making tendencies can affect how trauma is coded within the brain. Asynchronicity and compensation for developmental differences or difficulties can also influence how gifted individuals experience and respond to trauma. Sometimes, they mask their struggles. Additionally, it was explored how psychomotor, intellectual, sensual, imaginational, and emotional overexcitabilities can impact the experience and processing of trauma separately, or together.

In the third part of the book, I introduced EMDR therapy, which focuses on seeking patterns and meaning. While EMDR may be well-suited for gifted individuals in healing trauma, it was introduced more to help the reader conceptualize how healing happens. More specifically, since trauma can be held in the body and affect individuals unconsciously, EMDR's T.I.C.E.S. framework (trigger/target, image, negative cognition, emotion, and body sensations) and an understanding of overexcitabilities were attended to since they can help us uncover and understand intense experiences in gifted individuals.

In this fourth part of the book, we considered how effective trauma work involves building awareness, setting goals, and resourcing. We explored tailored approaches to considering the strengths and needs of gifted individuals and skills that could help with top-down processing that is more cognitive and behavioral in nature. Next, we addressed the need for bottom-up approaches, which involve processing trauma through the body, and modalities such as EMDR, somatic work, and IFS to name a small few. However, it was also impressed upon us how the chosen modality needs to match the gifted client's needs rather than conforming to societal expectations.

Altogether, a comprehensive understanding of giftedness, its interaction with trauma, and appropriate therapeutic approaches are essential to providing effective support and treatment for gifted individuals who have experienced trauma. So what now? Well, I'm glad you asked.

What do we do with all this (possibly) new information? This depends on who it is for. Is this information being used so you might better understand a peer, friend, colleague, or partner? Did you pick up this book to help you understand your family members, children, or students? Are you seeking to better help your clients or patients? Are you wanting to better understand yourself and your needs? All of this is fine. However, the position you come from shapes what you might *do* next. We will explore each of these areas, though, to help us conceptualize how we use this information. And keep in mind, these are simple conceptualizations. It is my hope that your use of this information goes beyond what we discuss.

Understanding Gifted Peers and Trauma

Our friends, colleagues, and partners are important to us. They are our peers and the people we mirror with the most. As such, if you are seeking information about giftedness and trauma so you might help or understand your peers, you are pretty amazing to me. When we take the time to learn about our peers, we solidify their importance to us.

However, it needs to be maintained that, though we now understand more about giftedness and trauma, this does not mean we know what an individual gifted person who has trauma is experiencing. Rather, we can instead ask mindful questions or offer information that might be helpful to them. And be careful about giving advice. Unsolicited advice can be annoying at best and harmful at worst.

If you have an idea or insight that might help someone, ask to offer it. For example, if a spouse does not understand why they keep talking when they want to stop, ask them if you might offer some insight. If they agree, tell them about overexcitabilities and how some people with psychomotor overexcitability may have a drive to talk, particularly when excited or under stress. You might also offer that their need to feel understood could stem from complex childhood experiences. If this person is not a close acquaintance, however, maybe share more superficial information or resources, such as the *Living With Intensity* book (Daniels & Piechowski, 2009).

Even if you do not offer information or resources for gifted peers experiencing trauma, you can certainly use this information to remain insightful and understanding of certain behaviors or processes. Any time we learn about others or seek to understand them more deeply, we are leading with compassion, something I value greatly and encourage.

Understanding Gifted Family Members, Children, or Students with Trauma

Family members, children, and students are generally important-to-us individuals who are not necessarily peers. For children, students, and family members from different generations than our own, being trauma-informed can look different. When working with people with different chronological realities, we can reduce the bias associated with assumptions or lack of knowledge related to age. It is also helpful to realize the possibility of an age- or status-related power differential and associated possibility of harm. With family, children, or students, a person might be taking the role of teacher, mentor, or parent, and therefore, a message might need to be delivered differently. Sometimes, this involves gaining permission while other times it involves a shift in how we speak or interact.

A good example of this is when we kneel down to talk quietly to a frightened child. We are aware they may need to feel safe so we adjust to this need. As another example, if a teacher notices that their gifted student is struggling to finish a book where a character is abused or neglected for example, rather than reprimanding this student, they might inquire as to the emotional or somatic impact this story has on them. Taking this approach involves being trauma-informed and proactively considering if there is a reason for the student's behavior beyond simple disobedience.

As suggested by Dr. Ross Greene (n.d.) in his many publications, on his *Lives in the Balance* website, and in literature about

Collaborative & Proactive Solutions used to work with children, "Kids do well if they can," (Greene, 2021, para. 2). What this means, and more explicitly per Greene, is that if a child were able to do well, they would, and if they had the skills necessary to use adaptive behavior, challenging behavior would not present. In the example of the student who is not reading their assigned book, they may not have the skills, awareness, or support to navigate how the book triggers traumatic material. And while a parent, family member, or educator may not know what to do about this, it is good to be aware so as not to perpetuate or accentuate harm. Also, referrals can be made or encouraged, so such individuals can work with a trained professional.

Understanding Gifted Clients and Patients with Trauma

It may seem obvious that therapists and psychologists should be minimally trained on this significant neurodivergence. In fact, understanding this experience may explain why you maybe picked up this book. However, you might also be shocked to know how many trained professionals are not trained in giftedness. When I was in my master's program for clinical mental health counseling, I think I saw one short paragraph in one textbook about giftedness. I am not over- or under-exaggerating. The topic of giftedness was an afterthought at best.

There is so much about giftedness that is misunderstood. Particularly, in the general population and even within the gifted population, there is a belief that everyone is gifted in their own way or that people are only gifted in certain areas. While all people have strengths and differences and anyone can potentially realize their fullest potential with appropriate awareness and support, being gifted is not something everyone experiences. Giftedness is not something we set out to achieve. No, as was addressed earlier, giftedness is a neurological, whole-person difference. It does not mean a person is better or worse, either. It *just is*.

So, as a mental health professional such as a coach, case manager, therapist, psychologist, or psychiatrist, it is important for you to know and understand this difference. Giftedness is not a diagnosis. It is a different way of existing when compared to neuronormative society. Along with this difference comes different approaches to conceptualizing trauma and trauma treatment. And when you notice a client or patient is possibly gifted, a great place to start is with Dąbrowski's (1966) overexcitabilities (OEs).

As an example of how I might explore giftedness and trauma with a gifted client, I start by asking about the OEs. For clients who happen to be aware of this concept, we explore what OEs they have. For my many clients who do not know about OEs, this can be an amazingly impactful conversation and moment of growth and awareness as clients realize their intensities have a name and that they are not broken or "too much."

Along with and beyond awareness of OEs, it is also helpful to identify other characteristics of giftedness and how it impacts and interacts with trauma. This process often validates and normalizes the gifted client's experience. This process, too, can be amazingly impactful as clients see and internalize a new and deep understanding that they are not alone nor misunderstood. Being understood is important since many gifted individuals feel chronically misunderstood or like there is something wrong with them or the way they think and feel, particularly if they have not found peer groups or literature about giftedness. Their developmental trauma can also feed this negative cognition. Once a gifted person learns that there are others like them, there can be a major shift in the conceptualization of self.

As presented in my identity development theory seen in Figure 13 below, the process of securing a sense of identity for gifted persons can involve having like peers and family members, having supportive professionals, and then using awareness as growth, as attended to in the previous chapter (Williams, 2023). As a reminder and as also depicted in this graphic, awareness as growth involves an understanding of innate qualities and a person's experiences, including strengths and struggles, that then enable individuals to take actions that allow them to objectively identify and meet needs. This process fosters growth and eventually a strong sense of identity. When normalized and nurtured in professional settings and other environments, a gifted client may grow through and from trauma more effectively.

As also attended to in Chapter 11, gifted individuals have unique needs when it comes to developing a strong sense of self. These needs can be summarized by four key elements: validation, affirmation, affiliation, and affinity (Mahoney, 2011). *Validation* refers to the fundamental need for recognition and acceptance of one's giftedness by others. *Affirmation* is the requirement for positive feedback and encouragement to foster a positive self-perception. *Affiliation* represents the desire for social connections with individuals who share similar interests and abilities. And finally, *affinity* captures the deep longing for a sense of belonging and connection to a larger community or group. By understanding and addressing these needs in a therapeutic or otherwise professional setting, we can support the healthy development and well-being of gifted individuals as they process their trauma.

Figure 13. Gifted (2e) Identity Development Theory

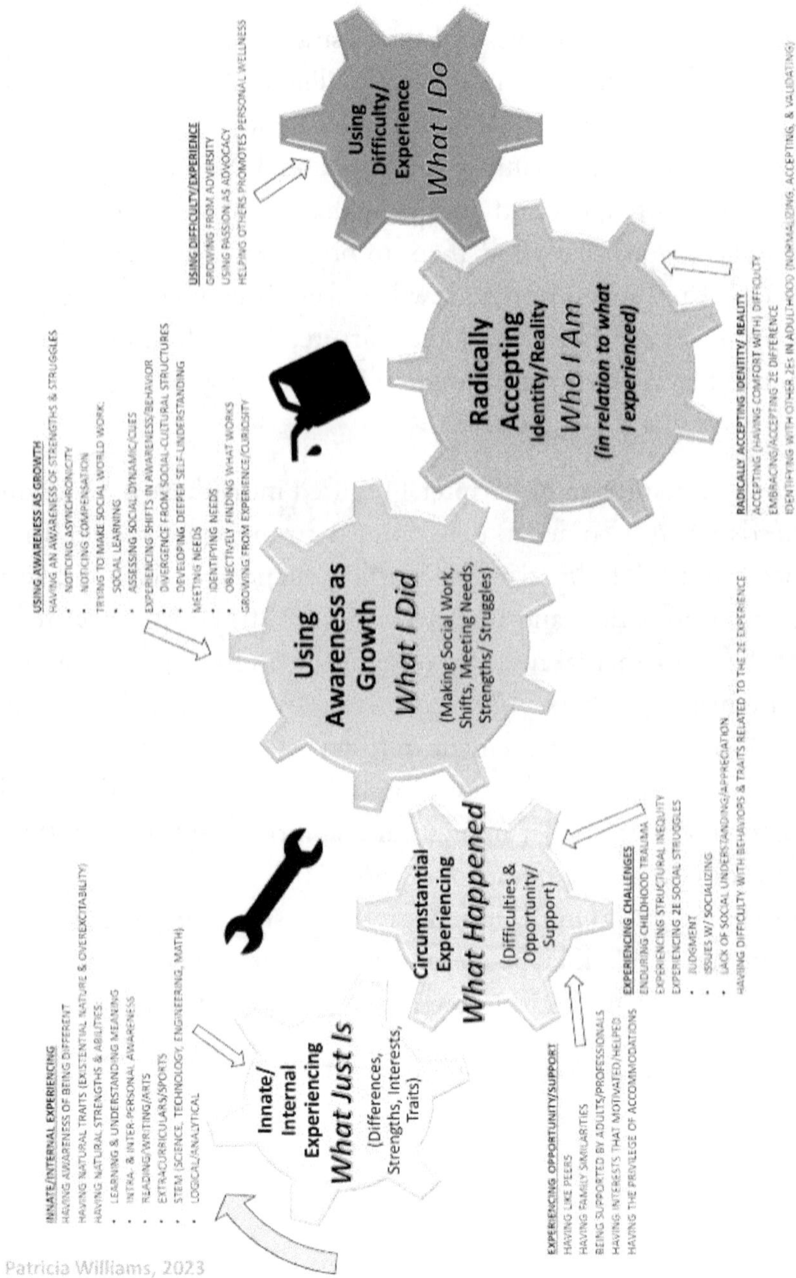

Understanding Your Own Giftedness and Trauma

Now, whether you intended to or not, it is quite possible that you picked up this book because you needed to understand your own giftedness and trauma. Even if you do not identify as gifted (though individuals drawn to these topics often are), reading this book because you want to help or understand gifted people you know, this is wonderful and compassionate. I call such folx *gifted adjacent*. If you know you are gifted or if this information is resonating with you on a personal level, though, well, there may be more to explore.

Whether you are realized gifted or not, the information within this text can be used on a personal level. On one hand, and if you feel you are able, this information can be used to inform your own **autopsychotherapy** process. Often frowned upon by the therapeutic and behavioral health community, I must insist that autopsychotherapy is valid and useful for gifted individuals especially. What is autopsychotherapy, though?

Autopsychotherapy, as also explained by Dąbrowski (1966), is a self-guided and introspective journey of personal growth and development. It involves individuals exploring their own thoughts, emotions, behaviors, and experiences to enhance self-awareness and achieve personal transformation. Rather than being avoided and reserved for professionals, this process encourages individuals to dive deeply into their inner world, confront internal conflicts, and strive for self-improvement and self-realization. Using autopsychotherapy, individuals can gain a profound understanding of themselves, their values, and their potential, leading to personal growth and the fulfillment of their unique abilities and talents. Autopsychotherapy is highly valued within Dąbrowski's theory of positive disintegration as a means to foster self-directed growth and cultivate a more advanced personality structure.

Granted, just because a person is able to do autopsychotherapy, that does not mean they should discount traditional therapy support for trauma processing. This is particularly true since several helpful modalities require specialized training and an understanding of how to titrate in and out of trauma work appropriately. So use the information within this book wisely to inform your own process and seek support from an informed position as needed.

Chapter 12 Conclusion

This chapter focused on considering how to use the newfound information about giftedness and trauma for different populations and purposes. Whether we read this book to help and understand our peers, friends, colleagues, partners, family members, children, students, clients, or selves, understanding a person's unique experience is crucial in offering support and empathy. It is important to recognize that, while we may have gained knowledge about giftedness and trauma, we cannot fully comprehend the unique experiences of an individual who is both gifted and traumatized. Instead, we can approach these individuals with mindful questions, provide relevant information, and avoid giving unsolicited advice. When sharing insights, it is essential to seek permission and gauge the level of closeness in the relationship.

For family members, children, and students who may be in a different power dynamic, a trauma-informed approach is necessary. This involves being sensitive to emotional and somatic responses and understanding that challenging behavior may stem from underlying trauma rather than defiance. Adopting the perspective that *kids (or people in general) do well if they can* emphasizes the importance of recognizing and addressing the skills, awareness, and support needed to navigate challenging situations. Ultimately, the use of this information should lead to greater compassion, insight, and the promotion of professional intervention when necessary.

We also explored in this chapter how understanding gifted clients and patients with trauma is essential for mental health professionals as the intersection of giftedness and trauma requires specialized knowledge and approaches. Unfortunately, the training of many professionals often overlooks the unique needs and experiences of gifted individuals. Giftedness should not be seen as a universal attribute nor a goal to achieve but rather as a neurological and whole-person difference that impacts how individuals perceive and process trauma. Recognizing and exploring the concept of overexcitabilities (OEs) can be a valuable starting point when working with gifted clients, fostering awareness, validation, and a deeper understanding of their intensities. Additionally, addressing other characteristics of giftedness and their interaction with trauma can help normalize the experiences of clients and promote a sense of belonging. It is crucial for mental health professionals to support the healthy development and well-being of gifted individuals by addressing their unique needs for validation, affirmation, affiliation, and affinity.

Lastly in this chapter, it was considered how for individuals who resonate with the information on giftedness and trauma on a personal level, it can be used to inform their own process of self-exploration and growth. Autopsychotherapy, a self-guided journey of introspection and personal development, can be a valuable tool in gaining self-awareness, achieving personal transformation, and nurturing one's unique abilities and talents. However, it is important to recognize the limitations of self-guided therapy and seek professional support when needed, especially in the context of trauma processing. By utilizing this knowledge wisely and seeking support from informed professionals, individuals can navigate their own giftedness and trauma with greater understanding and insight.

While this chapter provided valuable insights into how to use information about the intersection of giftedness and trauma, it should serve as a stepping stone rather than a stopping point for our exploration. Our venture continues as we delve deeper into another significant aspect: post-traumatic growth within the context of giftedness. In the upcoming chapter, we will expand on the material offered about trauma and giftedness, exploring the transformative potential and resilience that gifted individuals can experience in the aftermath of trauma. This exploration of post-traumatic growth adds a new dimension to our understanding, enriching our knowledge of how giftedness and trauma intertwine, and offering valuable guidance for individuals, professionals, and their loved ones who choose to embark on this journey.

Chapter 12 Check-In

Exploration: This chapter offered a recap of the information offered in the previous eleven chapters and explored ways a person might use it to support and understand different gifted individuals.

Conclusion: The importance of context while validating and showing compassion for gifted individuals facing trauma was explained. The importance of recognizing the unique needs of gifted persons and addressing overexcitability was also explored while considering the value of autopsychotherapy and specialized support.

Questions to consider include:

1. Did you consider how you might apply the information offered in this book?
2. Do you have ideas about how this information applies to you personally?
3. Did any of your own trauma or struggles come to the surface for you while reading this chapter?

N**ervous system and mental/emotional health**:

1. Check in with yourself and your T.I.C.E.S.
2. Are there any triggers, images, cognitions, emotions, or sensations that need attending to?
3. Can you do any autopsychotherapy or do you need extra support for yourself or others?
4. If needed, take a break and consider what you need to do moving forward to be well.

Chapter 12 References

Dąbrowski, K. (1966). The theory of positive disintegration. *International Journal of Psychiatry, 2*(2), 229-249.

Daniels, S., & Piechowski, M.M. (2009). *Living with intensity: Understanding the sensitivity, excitability, and emotional development of gifted children, adolescents, and adults.* Great Potential Press, Inc..

Greene, R. (n.d.). *Lives in the balance.* Retrieved from https://livesinthebalance.org

Greene, R. (2021). *Collaborative & proactive solutions: F.A.Q.*. retrieved from https://livesinthebalance.org/wp-content/uploads/2021/06/FAQ-21.pdf

Mahoney, A.S. (2011). *The gifted identity formation model.* Retrieved from https://www.sengifted.org/post/the-gifted-identity-formation-model

Williams, P. (2023). *Understanding how twice-exceptional (2e) individuals navigate adolescence: A grounded theory study.*

Part Five: **Conclusions**

(13) Giftedness and Post-Traumatic Growth

(14) Hanging Threads and Antarctic Flamingos

(15) Concluding Thoughts and Reflections

Chapter 13: Giftedness and Post-Traumatic Growth

While Chapter 12 provides valuable insights into the intersection of trauma and giftedness, our exploration does not end there. In fact, it serves as a stepping stone on a path towards the topic of giftedness and post-traumatic growth. **Post-traumatic growth (PTG)** refers to the positive psychological changes that individuals can experience following a traumatic event or upbringing. It encompasses personal transformation, increased resilience, and the development of new perspectives and values. Understanding how gifted individuals navigate and harness their unique traits and abilities in the face of trauma opens up a new dimension of exploration.

Gifted individuals possess advanced cognitive abilities, rapid pattern-finding skills, and heightened intensity in various domains, which can greatly influence their responses to trauma. Their cognitive capabilities enable them to intellectualize and process trauma with depth and complexity. Moreover, their pattern-finding abilities allow them to make meaning out of traumatic experiences, shaping their journey toward PTG.

Asynchronous development and compensation often observed in gifted individuals also play a role in PTG. While asynchronous development refers to the gaps between different areas of development, the compensatory skills that accompany it can manifest as a coping mechanism in the context of trauma. Gifted individuals may compensate for their struggles, that is, by leveraging their strengths and adapting in unique ways. This adaptive compensation process can contribute to their PTG as they navigate through, and in response to, their trauma.

Furthermore, the presence of overexcitabilities (OEs) in gifted individuals adds another layer to the exploration of PTG. Psychomotor, intellectual, sensual, imaginational, and emotional overexcitabilities intensify the experience and impact of trauma. These heightened sensitivities can shape the individual's PTG journey, influencing their emotional processing, creativity, and overall resilience. By recognizing and understanding how gifted individuals engage with post-traumatic growth, we gain a comprehensive view of their potential for personal transformation and resilience.

This exploration expands our knowledge of how giftedness interacts with trauma and provides insights into the unique pathways that gifted individuals may follow in their healing and growth. In the upcoming sections, we will dive more deeply into the specific dynamics of PTG within the context of giftedness. Through research findings and theoretical frameworks, we will explore how gifted individuals cannot only overcome trauma but also thrive and experience personal growth as a result. By shining a light on the transformative potential within the intersection of giftedness and trauma, we aim to provide valuable guidance and support for professionals, individuals, and their loved ones who are navigating this complex journey.

Defining Post-Traumatic Growth

According to trauma researchers and professors Lawrence Calhoun and Richard Tedeschi (2014), post-traumatic growth or PTG is the positive psychological change experienced as a result of the struggle with highly challenging life circumstances. Per these authors, such positive change might include:

- Greater appreciation of life
- Strengthening of close relationships
- Increased compassion and/or altruism
- Identification of possibilities and/or purpose
- Greater awareness and utilization of strengths
- Enhanced spiritual development
- Creative growth

Per my own research about positive developmental trajectories for twice-exceptional individuals (Williams, 2023) outcomes also often include:

- Developing deeper self-understanding
- Identifying needs
- Meeting needs
- Objectively finding what works
- Growing from experience/curiosity
- Growing from adversity
- Using experience to fuel passion as advocacy
- Helping others promotes personal wellness

So, the common themes involve personal growth, fulfillment, and overall well-being, per what is explained by Tedeschi and Calhoun and according to my own experience and research, collectively. In other words, *post-traumatic growth is the presence of personal growth, fulfillment, and overall well-being that is created or fortified as a result of or in conjunction with a traumatic experience or upbringing.*

Post-Traumatic Growth and Positive Disintegration

So, we established that PTG is a phenomenon that can arise from experiencing and navigating through traumatic events. It is a process through which individuals undergo positive changes and personal development following their encounters with adversity.

PTG can be fostered by positive disintegration, as proposed by Dąbrowski (1966).

PTG as a specific construct was not directly addressed by Kazimierz Dąbrowski in his work. Dąbrowski's theory of positive disintegration primarily focuses on the concept of personality development and the disintegration process that individuals may undergo to achieve higher levels of personal growth. However, the ideas and concepts within Dąbrowski's theory can be related to the notion of PTG.

Per Dąbrowski, healthy personality development often necessitates the disintegration of the existing personality structure. This disintegration can be accompanied by psychological tension, self-doubt, and feelings of anxiety and/or depression. These challenging experiences create an opportunity for individuals to engage in a deeper examination of themselves and their potential. As individuals explore the depths of their being, they begin to question their current state and envision possibilities for personal growth and development. This process of self-reflection and introspection can lead to higher levels of personality development.

It is often through the positive disintegration process that individuals can experience PTG, emerging stronger, more resilient, and with a greater sense of purpose and meaning in their lives. While trauma may initially disrupt and challenge individuals, it can also serve as a catalyst for personal transformation and positive change. By embracing the disintegration process and engaging in self-examination, individuals can navigate the aftermath of trauma and experience personal growth that transcends their pre-trauma state. This growth may encompass various aspects of their lives, including their beliefs, values, relationships, and overall well-being.

It is important to note, however, that PTG is a complex and individualized process. Not everyone will experience it in the same way or to the same extent. Additionally, we do not want to confuse concepts of PTG and positive disintegration, erroneously suggesting that trauma is necessary for the positive disintegration process. Rather, positive disintegration offers a framework for understanding the potential for growth and development that can arise from traumatic experiences. By acknowledging the potential for PTG and recognizing the transformative power of disintegration, individuals can approach their journey of healing and recovery with a sense of hope and possibility. This understanding can inform therapeutic interventions and support systems aimed at facilitating personal growth and helping individuals navigate the challenges and opportunities that arise in the aftermath of trauma.

Giftedness and Post-Traumatic Growth

I very purposely considered Dąbrowski's theory of positive disintegration in relation to PTG before looking more specifically at PTG and giftedness for a couple of reasons. First, though Dąbrowski's work is often cited and related to giftedness, he did not specifically study gifted individuals when developing his theory. As such, it seems more appropriate to first relate it to PTG alone without involving this topic. Additionally, it is with an understanding of PTG and positive disintegration that I further consider the interaction of PTG and giftedness. In other words, these theoretical frameworks shape the way I discuss the remainder of this chapter.

PTG and the Gifted Brain

Chapter 4 explored the interesting interaction between trauma and the gifted brain, focusing on advanced cognitive abilities, pattern-finding, and meaning-making. It focused on unique cognitive dimensions within gifted individuals and how trauma can intersect with these characteristics, posing challenges and vulnerabilities. Upon examining the complexities of this interplay, however, we gained valuable insights into the experiences of gifted individuals and how these cognitive strengths offer pathways towards not only healing but also tremendous growth.

Recognized for these advanced cognitive abilities and rapid pattern-finding skills, gifted persons tend to also demonstrate creativity and ingenuity. While cognitive strengths and creativity can lead to difficulties with feeling connected or understood, they can also help gifted individuals seek growth. According to educational psychology researcher, author, and professor James Kaufman (2018), an aptitude for creativity seen in those with advanced cognitive abilities can have a notable impact on traditional positive outcomes such as academic or professional success. Creativity, per Kaufman, can transformatively foster personal happiness while cultivating a sense of purpose and meaning in life. For the gifted and existential meaning-maker, this is imperative.

In Chapter 4, we explored how the gifted brain exhibits neurological differences in brain volume, gray matter, white matter, neuroplasticity, and the association with the cognitive abilities of gifted individuals. This unique neurology contributes to rapid learning, cognitive processing, and the formation of new neural pathways. While these differences increase susceptibility to trauma, they also allow the realization of healing and growth. Since gifted individuals may be more attuned to noticing and making connections to traumatic experiences, that is, they are also more capable of making connections to strengths, meaning, and opportunities, particularly when there is a growth mindset encouraged. Additionally, their tendency to intellectualize situations can help a gifted person move past emotion to find practical relief. The resourcefulness of gifted individuals, in this instance, is an absolute benefit.

Gifted individuals, with their clear propensity for meaning-making, ascribe significance and purpose to events and experiences. It is also not a far stretch to imagine how positive messaging and meaning can be derived from traumatic lives or experiences. While we never wish trauma or difficulty on anyone, it is through difficulty that we often grow most. Finding meaning in their efforts and having a sense of life purpose can empower gifted individuals and promote well-being.

By considering the intersection of PTG and the gifted brain, we also consider how the vulnerabilities and challenges faced by gifted individuals can be strengths and opportunities for growth. Granted, it undoubtedly helps to emphasize the importance of recognizing and supporting the unique cognitive characteristics of gifted individuals in trauma-informed manners while identifying pathways for growth, healing, and self-realization for gifted individuals when trauma is involved.

Gifted Asynchrony, Compensation, and PTG

In Chapter 5, we explored the complex interactions between developmental asynchronicity, compensation, and trauma within the context of giftedness, twice-exceptionality, and neurodivergence. By exploring the intricate dynamics and connections among these phenomena, we gained deeper insights into the challenges faced by gifted individuals and the potential pathways for growth and resilience that can emerge at their intersection.

The discussion in Chapter 5 began by highlighting the concept of asynchronous development where various skills and abilities develop at different rates, often leading to a mismatch between cognitive and emotional development. It is true that asynchronicity can contribute to social difficulties and struggles with belonging. It is also true that the presence of asynchronicity helps gifted persons develop compensatory skills. The concept of gifted compensation, as a reminder, involves the utilization of strengths to compensate for difficulties or disabilities. While compensation can lead to masking behaviors and concealing one's authentic self, it is also a valuable adaptive skill. When we recognize and validate the experiences of gifted individuals, including their struggles and vulnerabilities, it is likely we will create a supportive environment that promotes authenticity and well-being. In the process of supporting strengths and struggles while acknowledging constructive adaptation, we also create an environment where PTG can be more fully realized.

It is important to note again how Chapter 5 explores the notion of underachievement and its impact on gifted individuals. It is crucial to recognize that the label of underachievement is often based on a narrow definition of success that prioritizes productivity and tangible outcomes, disregarding the multidimensional aspects of giftedness. The pressure to conform to external expectations and the internalization of being an underachiever can perpetuate self-judgment and contribute to trauma. To foster PTG, it is essential to shift the focus from mere achievement to a holistic approach that prioritizes the individual's overall well-being. By acknowledging and supporting the unique strengths and interests of gifted persons, we can create an environment where PTG is more likely to be realized.

The interconnectedness of asynchronicity, compensation, and trauma in the lives of gifted individuals were highlighted throughout Chapter 5. It is crucial to grasp and effectively address these dynamics in order to promote the mental well-being, resilience, and self-actualization of gifted individuals. By adopting a comprehensive and developmental outlook, we can cultivate an inclusive and trauma-informed approach to support the distinct needs and experiences of gifted individuals. This approach most significantly fosters their growth and overall well-being, enabling individuals to develop PTG and other positive, developmental outcomes.

Heightened Intensity and PTG

Central to the gifted experience lies the potential for remarkable growth even in the face of adversity. In Chapter 6, we explored how Dąbrowski's concept of overexcitability (OE) intersects with the intensive influence of trauma. That intersection, in turn, offers valuable insights into the journey of PTG. By exploring the dynamics that emerge when heightened sensitivities and traumatic experiences collide, we can gain understanding about the transformative implications for personal development and well-being.

We began Chapter 6 by revisiting the inherent nature of overexcitability, recognizing its innate qualities and the five distinct types that encompass psychomotor, sensual, intellectual, imaginational, and emotional domains. It was important to emphasize that overexcitability should be embraced as a biological difference rather than perceived as negative or excessive. This understanding, when embraced, can empower gifted individuals to adapt and devise strategies that celebrate the affirmation of neurodivergence.

Let's explore each OE in relation to trauma, briefly. Psychomotor overexcitability (*Pm*OE) can manifest as excess energy and emotional tension. Next, sensual overexcitability (*S*OE), as a reminder, involves heightened sensory pleasure and aesthetics, but it can also be misunderstood and judged by society, leading to unique trauma experiences. Intellectual overexcitability (*In*OE) brings heightened mental activity and critical thinking, influencing how traumatic events are processed and analyzed. Imaginational overexcitability (*Im*OE) fosters unrestricted imagination and vivid visualization, which can intensify emotional responses and anxieties when catastrophizing occurs. And finally, emotional overexcitability (*E*OE) involves heightened emotional intensity and sensitivity, influencing the deep encoding of traumatic memories.

Gifted and intense (overexcitable) individuals may face negative judgments, impacting their self-esteem and contributing to complex trauma. However, when OEs are accepted and even celebrated, they can contribute to the realization of PTG. Additionally, if individuals harness their OEs and use them meaningfully, they can be accessed more mindfully, contributing to an individual's sense of self-efficacy.

Examples of accepting and harnessing each of the OEs to promote PTG are as follows:

- A gifted individual with psychomotor overexcitability (*Pm*OE) can use their excess energy and emotional tension to work through struggles physically. They may need to expel excess energy or use it to encourage wanted behaviors.
- A gifted and sensually overexcitable person (*S*OE) could use their heightened senses to seek out positive sensual experiences to promote growth while radically accepting this aspect of their being.
- An individual with intellectual overexcitability (*In*OE) can use their heightened mental activity and critical thinking to work through difficulties and identify positive or constructive outcomes.
- Someone with imaginational overexcitability (*Im*OE), a strong imagination, and vivid visualization abilities might imagine possibilities for growth and recovery where others are not able to do so.
- An emotionally overexcitable (*E*OE) or highly sensitive person (HSP) who feels deeply might use this ability to foster compassion for themselves and others while being radically accepting of this difference in a way that fosters a sense of identity.

Throughout Chapter 6, and this book as a whole, are insights that illustrate the profound interplay between OEs and trauma, which form a complex psychological profile for gifted individuals. It is clear that each OE adds unique layers to the experience and perception of trauma. OEs can also intensify the healing experience for gifted individuals, resulting in PTG. It is important to acknowledge that the interaction between OEs and trauma is unique to each gifted individual with diverse combinations and interactions that contribute differently to the realization of PTG and other forms of positive developmental outcomes.

Giftedness, Trauma, and PTG...Oh My!

It would seem after reading this chapter, and indeed after reading the entire book, that being gifted is neither a gift nor a curse, or maybe it is both. This is a common theme among and within gifted communities, where the value of this gift is debated. In her often-cited article about what she called the *asset-burden paradox of giftedness*, author, professor, and former school counselor Jean Sunde Peterson (2012) shares how a comprehensive 15-year case study of a gifted individual resulted in this key revelation: Giftedness is both an asset and a vulnerability throughout formative years especially. This seemed particularly true as the research participant grappled with the aftermath of trauma and developed coping mechanisms for survival and healing from ages 15 to 30.

In my own research and work, I have found that social, cognitive, and non-cognitive elements impact gifted and twice-exceptional (2e) individuals intensely, though there might also be an increased opportunity for successful development related to these struggles and strengths. In later works, Peterson again (2018) seemed to echo these findings and the reality that development is qualitatively different for gifted and 2e persons, specifically:

> *Rapid information processing, sensitivities, intensities, asynchronous development, and overexcitabilities may all have impact on developmental task accomplishment during adolescence. Those aspects likely also affect how development is experienced, regardless of school achievement level, home context, sociocultural heritage, context, and interpersonal skills. (Peterson, 2018, para. 52)*

Though this difference does not speak to PTG exactly, it does support the assertion that *gifted is different*. That difference, again, can translate to growth or developmental potential, a concept well-discussed by Dąbrowski.

Relating this all back to identity development, I remind you of the part of a positive developmental trajectory where gifted and 2e persons use awareness as growth, as depicted in Figure 14 below and previously in Figure 13. That is, after experiencing and realizing their innate qualities, their difficulties, and their opportunities in life, gifted individuals used that awareness as growth before radically accepting strengths, struggles, and who they were (Williams, 2023). And, if what happened included trauma, you had better believe that their growth could be identified as PTG.

Figure 14. Awareness as Growth Gear

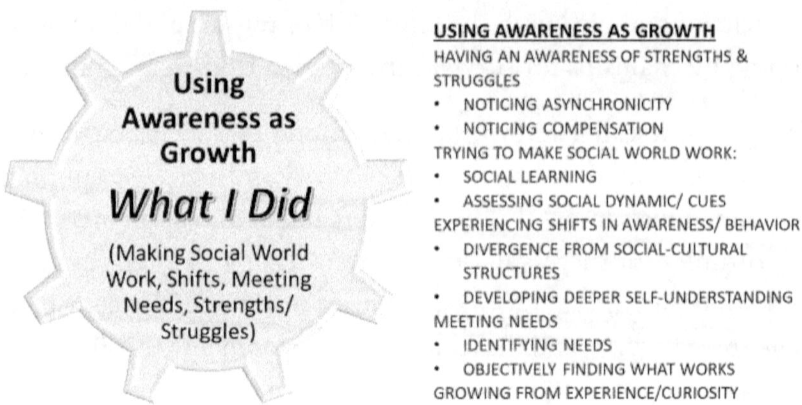

Note: At this stage of identity development, gifted individuals used an awareness of strengths and struggles along with nature and nurture to inform growth, as also depicted in Figure 10 in Chapter 11.

So while it is true that giftedness is a double-edged sword of sorts, sometimes allowing a deep experiencing of pain and struggle, it also brings with it a great possibility, maybe a probability, of joy and growth; that is, a great developmental potential.

How Can PTG Be Encouraged in Gifted Individuals?

If it is true that giftedness involves a propensity for potential, as research and anecdotal evidence suggests it does, then how do we foster PTG in the lives of gifted persons? For this, I have a suggestion. To explain it simply, most growth happens when there is great potential and great opportunity. And, the more the opportunity, the exponentially more the growth. I illustrate his idea in Figure 15.

Figure 15. Growth Equals Potential by Opportunity

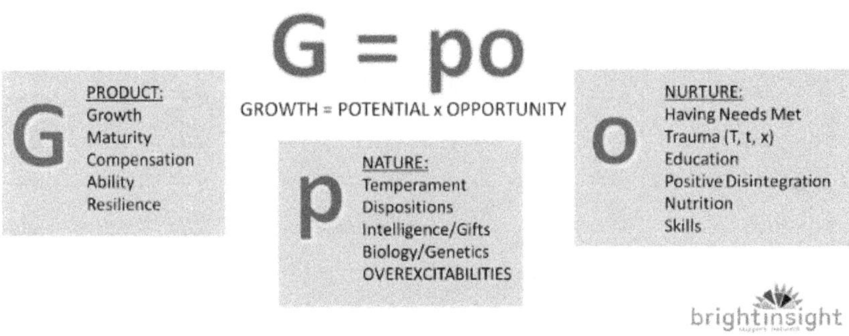

So, where the product is growth (G), seen as also maturity, compensation, ability, and resilience for example, components that produce this product are potential (p) and opportunity (o). Here, opportunity is looked at as nurture or impacts such as trauma, having needs met, education, positive disintegration, nutrition, support, and skills. Opportunities can be created, though it should be noted that they also can involve a level of privilege. Potential, on the other hand, is more innate and can be considered as nature. Potential can involve a person's temperament or dispositions, intelligence or giftedness, biology, genetics, and certainly overexcitabilities. And

I should also mention here that this depiction is open to debate as a quality such as compensation may find itself in other areas. So keep in mind that this is a rough idea and conceptualization to enhance your understanding.

Regardless of the details of this depiction, it can be concluded that growth or positive developmental outcomes are based on opportunity and potential or nature and nurture. Indeed, the greater a person's potential or the greater their opportunity, the potentially greater the growth outcome. Keep in mind that growth, therefore, is not exclusive to the gifted individual. However, we can see how gifted qualities may impact nature and nurture or potential and opportunity such that greater growth or PTG is realized. We can also conclude that if you want to increase the chances of PTG or growth otherwise for any person, gifted or not, you must increase opportunity for such, purposefully through therapy, skill building, social support, education, adopting healthy habits, or otherwise.

Chapter 13 Conclusion

We began this chapter by exploring post-traumatic growth (PTG), defining it as the positive psychological change experienced after facing challenging circumstances. We learned how PTG can bring about a greater appreciation of life, strengthened relationships, increased compassion, identification of possibilities and purpose, enhanced awareness and utilization of strengths, spiritual development, and creative growth. Additional outcomes include deeper self-understanding, identifying and meeting needs, finding effective strategies, growing from experience and adversity, using experience for advocacy, and promoting personal wellness. PTG signifies personal growth, fulfillment, and overall well-being resulting from traumatic experiences.

Next, we explored how PTG can be fostered by positive disintegration, a concept proposed by Dąbrowski. Although Dąbrowski's theory did not address PTG specifically, his theory can be related to PTG. Positive disintegration involves the disintegration of one's existing personality structure, leading to self-reflection, questioning, and the exploration of personal growth and development. Through this process, individuals can experience PTG, emerging stronger, more resilient, and with a greater sense of purpose and meaning. It's important to understand that PTG is a complex and individualized process, and trauma is not necessary for positive disintegration. However, recognizing the potential for growth and the transformative power of disintegration can inform therapeutic interventions and support systems that facilitate personal growth and recovery after trauma.

After addressing more theoretical underpinnings of PTG, we considered how different characteristics of giftedness might result in PTG. It was therefore explored how gifted individuals possess advanced cognitive abilities, rapid pattern-finding skills, and a propensity for meaning-making. While we were reminded that gifted individuals may struggle with connection and understanding, they can also utilize their creativity and intellectualization to seek growth and find relief. Their unique neurological profile allows for rapid learning and the formation of new neural pathways, increasing the facilitation of healing and growth. By recognizing and supporting the cognitive strengths of gifted individuals in trauma-informed ways, pathways for growth, healing, and self-realization can be identified. These pathways of processing empower gifted individuals and promote well-being.

Another grouping of gifted characteristics, we next explored asynchronicity, compensation, and PTG in the context of giftedness. We were reminded that asynchronicity, or the seemingly uneven development of skills and abilities, can lead to social challenges and a sense of not fitting in. However, this asynchrony also fosters the development of compensatory skills, meaning that gifted individuals utilize their strengths to overcome difficulties. While compensation can sometimes lead to unwanted masking behaviors, it is also a useful and adaptive strategy.

In our final consideration of gifted qualities, we explored the intersection of Dąbrowski's overexcitabilities (OEs) and PTG in gifted individuals. The five OEs (psychomotor, sensual, intellectual, imaginational, and emotional) were highlighted as inherent qualities to be embraced. Each OE has distinct effects on trauma experiences. Harnessing and embracing OEs can contribute to PTG and enhance self-efficacy. By understanding the complex interplay between OEs and trauma, we recognize their roles in intensifying the healing process for gifted individuals, leading to PTG.

Nearing the end of the chapter, we considered trauma, giftedness, and PTG altogether while exploring the complex nature of giftedness, acknowledging that it can be both a gift and a vulnerability. We learned how even research suggests that being gifted entails unique social, cognitive, and non-cognitive elements that impact individuals intensely with the potential for successful development. The rapid information processing, sensitivities, intensities, asynchronous development, and overexcitabilities associated with giftedness contribute to a qualitatively different developmental experience. This difference supports the notion that giftedness offers growth and developmental potential.

Identity development in gifted individuals, which involves becoming aware of innate qualities, navigating difficulties and opportunities, and accepting strengths and struggles, was also considered. It was concluded that if trauma is part of this journey, the resulting growth can be identified as PTG. Recognizing and validating the experiences of gifted individuals, including their struggles, promotes authenticity and well-being, creating an environment where PTG can be realized alongside identity development. Knowing this, we can better promote the mental well-being, resilience, and self-actualization, and ultimately facilitate PTG and positive developmental outcomes by acknowledging and supporting the unique strengths and interests of gifted individuals.

One final and significant point, we considered an equation for growth, understanding that it takes both potential and opportunity (or nature and nurture) for growth to happen. While we may not be able to influence potential much since it is an innate quality, it is through the mindful and purposeful seeking of opportunity that we create better conditions for PTG and other positive developmental outcomes while understanding that privilege can impact this element. Ultimately, we identified how giftedness, while presenting challenges, also carries the potential for joy, growth, and significant developmental opportunities. I have never known this not to be true.

Chapter 13 Check-In

Exploration: This chapter offered a recap of the information offered while considering, differently, how giftedness and trauma can also result in post-traumatic growth (PTG).

Conclusion: While there are several risks and difficulties involved with being gifted, there are also strengths and characteristics that can contribute to PTG. Positive growth can also be promoted by experiencing supportive opportunities.

Questions to consider include:

1. Did you consider how you or someone you know experienced PTG?
2. Do you think you can encourage PTG by understanding this information?
3. Did any of your own trauma or PTG come to the surface for you while reading this chapter?

Nervous system and mental/emotional health:

1. Check in with yourself and your T.I.C.E.S.
2. Are there any triggers, images, cognitions, emotions, or sensations that need attending to?
3. Can you identify any growth opportunities in the midst or as a result of your struggles?
4. If needed, take a break and consider how to encourage positive growth in your own life.

Chapter 13 References

Calhoun, L.G., & Tedeschi, R.G. (2014). *Handbook of posttraumatic growth: Research and practice.* Routledge.

Dąbrowski, K. (1966). The theory of positive disintegration. *International Journal of Psychiatry, 2*(2), 229-249.

Kaufman, J. (2018). Creativity as a stepping stone toward a brighter future. *Journal of Intelligence, 6*(2), 21. https://doi.org/10.3390/jintelligence6020021

Peterson, J.S. (2012). The asset-burden paradox of giftedness: A 15-year phenomenological, longitudinal case study. *Roeper Review, 34*(4), 244-260. https://doi.org/10.1080/02783193.2012.715336

Peterson, J.S. (2018). Giftedness: Asset and vulnerability. *Encyclopedia of adolescence* (pp. 1593-1608). Springer International Publishing. https://doi.org/10.1007/978-3-319-33228-4_97

Williams, P. (2023). *Understanding how twice-exceptional (2e) individuals navigate adolescence: A grounded theory study.*

Chapter 14: Hanging Threads and Antarctic Flamingos

Sometimes after mentally devouring a new book with lots of new or interesting information, we are left with more questions than answers. This is OK! Anticipating this, I did what any middle-aged American writer might do: I took to Facebook. After offering a list of chapter titles for folx to consider, I made this request:

As I complete my book about giftedness and trauma, I am looking for hanging threads and questions! Within this book, I address the following topics as chapters:

(1) What is Giftedness?

(2) So Why the Focus on Giftedness?

(3) What is Trauma?

(4) Trauma and the Gifted Brain

(5) Asynchronicity, Compensation, and Trauma

(6) Heightened Intensity and Trauma

(7) What is EMDR and How Does It Relate to Giftedness?

(8) Giftedness and the T.I.C.E.S. of Trauma

(9) What is Needed (When Dealing with Trauma and Giftedness)

(10) Skill Building and Treatment Options Top-Down

(11) Skill Building and Treatment Options Bottom-Up

(12) Processing Trauma and Giftedness Altogether

(13) Giftedness and Post-Traumatic Growth

Given these topics or others you can think of, what questions do you have? I would love to address them ALL as appropriate and able!

And let me tell you, my gifted Facebook community did not let me down! I received so many questions that I had to apply a qualitative coding process to organize requests. What resulted was this non-exhaustive list of questions and answers related to trauma and giftedness that may not have been more fully addressed in the book. These questions or topics are divided into sections that consider the following:

- Levels of giftedness and trauma
- Demand avoidance, trauma, and pajamas
- Rejection sensitivity and trauma
- **Imposter syndrome** and trauma
- Giftedness and aging
- Giftedness and marginalized populations
- Belonging, relationships, and trauma
- Giftedness, parenting, and trauma
- Giftedness, **dysautonomia**, EDS, the HPA axis, and vasovagal involvement
- Giftedness, autism, and ADHD
- Stigma, labels, and acceptance
- **Misdiagnosis**, **missed diagnosis**, and misunderstanding
- Compensation, masking, and therapy woes

- When school lets you down
- Is it trauma and what can I do?
- Why EMDR?
- The impact and importance of healing

I hope this list and associated question and answers help you more deeply understand the intersection of giftedness and trauma.

Levels of Giftedness and Trauma

To start the question and answer portion of this text, I will first consider special psychological profiles and populations that were not specifically addressed in earlier chapters. The first question I received about this asked if high or profound giftedness versus mild giftedness correlates differently with trauma. To begin my reply to this question, I need to initially explain how the identification of leveled giftedness is akin to functioning labels (labels that judge a person's ability to function in day-to-day life), which I avoid in an effort to be more neurodiversity-affirming. That said, there are an identified five levels of giftedness in existing literature and research that each needs special consideration. These five levels are coined in some spaces as: mildly, moderately, highly, exceptionally, and profoundly gifted (Gross, 2000). In the *5 Levels of Gifted* books by Deborah L. Ruf (2022), however, she prefers to number these one through five or label them as moderately gifted to gifted, highly gifted, exceptionally gifted, exceptionally to profoundly gifted (4), and exceptionally to profoundly gifted (5). And while levels four and five appear to be the same, Ruf insists that because of limitations of IQ tests, the distinct differences between these two levels reside in individuals' behaviors.

Since each of these five levels relates to an IQ level with some exceptions per Ruf's measures, they are not perfectly assessed. That said, it can be suggested that with each increasing variation, there is an increase in minority status. That is, while one in six to one in forty-four individuals in the general population might be considered mildly gifted, fewer than one in every one million people are imagined to be profoundly gifted (Gross, 2000). With the variation seen in the first category, one can also see the potential for difficulty with these measurements. What can be concluded, however, is that the higher a person's IQ and intelligence or level of giftedness, the more rare they may be in relation to the general population.

Because of the rarity of more highly gifted individuals, it is readily understood how finding like peers can be a challenge. Additionally, with more highly to profoundly gifted individuals, research suggests an increased risk of socio-affective concerns, social isolation, and pressures to conform (Gross, 2000). Because of their rarity, there is an increased risk of misunderstanding. Add to this the more intensely rapid processing that takes place for these individuals, and you have an increased opportunity for trauma encoding that can go haywire. However, the more highly gifted an individual, the greater possibility for novel problem-solving and ingenuity, though this is not a rule. It should be noted that while we might expect more highly gifted individuals to have a greater measure of overexcitability, this has not been well-substantiated in research and can therefore be debated.

Demand Avoidance, Trauma, and Pajamas

Many participants in this Q and A request asked about demand avoidance, often seen as **pathological demand avoidance (PDA)** or, as more constructively presented, a persistent or pervasive drive for autonomy. A psychological profile initially seen as a subtype of autism before the rise of the **neurodiversity movement**, PDA has since been more broadly applied and is often addressed in gifted circles. PDA is a tendency for some individuals to perceive a demand placed on them as a neurological threat that launches a fight, flight, freeze, or fawn response. For children, we might notice this when they admittedly refuse to go to school, do their homework, or clean their rooms. As you can imagine, this often results in harsh discipline and judgment, rather than understanding and calm. For adults, PDA may manifest as difficulty with task completion and particularly when the perceived demand is great. For example, many adult **PDAer**s have difficulty completing and submitting tax documentation, even if they are receiving refunds. Not completing such tasks and being judged or punished for this as children or adults can have a lasting and difficult impact on people's sense of self-worth, self-efficacy, and identity. It is not a stretch to imagine how this might also impact complex trauma.

According to my favorite gender nonconforming autism and neurodiversity support specialist podcaster, Kristy Forbes (2021), PDA is a neurobiological response to demand interpreted as a threat that they handle by making peace with and being radically accepting about. Per Forbes, traditional approaches to managing PDA, such as cognitive behavioral therapy and reward/punishment methods, do not work. However, radical acceptance and creativity often do. For example, Forbes shares that they communicate safety to their brain by sometimes staying in their pajamas, even for presentations. In other words, by being in their pajamas, their brain receives the signal that it is time to relax and there is no demand on them that may be interpreted as a threat.

The concept of removing demand and threat can be extended to ourselves and our children. And though we probably cannot do everything in our pajamas, we can think of how to remove the threat of demands in creative and accepting ways. A simple example of this I use with parents is to cut up an apple and place it in front of their child who is likely to eat it. If we instead ask them if they want the apple, they may see the demand for a response as, believe it or not, a threat. Another strategy is to offer options to ourselves or our children or view tasks as experiments, as discussed in Chapter 11.

Rejection Sensitivity and Trauma

Often paired with PDA is RSD or rejection-sensitive dysphoria. And though there seems to be a PDA-RSD connection, PDA is generally associated with autism while RSD is paired with ADHD. According to William W. Dodson (2022), M.D., LF-APA, a clinician who spent his career working in adult ADHD medicine, RSD is a common and disruptive manifestation of emotional dysregulation often observed in adults with ADHD. Although RSD is not an official diagnosis, it is a brain-based symptom inherent to ADHD rather than reportedly being caused by trauma. The term "dysphoria" signifies the severe emotional and physical pain experienced by individuals with RSD when faced with real or perceived rejection, criticism, or teasing.

Because the intensity of an RSDer's emotional response is judged as disproportionate to the triggering event, it can be met with harsh judgment while further encoding the trauma of the rejection and judgment. According to Dodson, around a third of adult ADHD patients report RSD as the most impairing aspect of their condition, particularly since managing the associated emotional pain or RSD can be challenging. As such, being aware of RSD can help us be more radically accepting of it and sensitive to its presence.

Imposter Syndrome and Trauma

Impostor syndrome, a phenomenon reported by many gifted folx, refers to the experience of high-achieving individuals who, despite their evident accomplishments, struggle to internalize their success. They might constantly doubt themselves and fear being exposed as frauds while finding it challenging to accurately attribute their achievements to their genuine competence (Bravata et al., 2020). This may be particularly true with fast learners who do not have to study like their peers to receive high marks. It may also be true for us when we may easily conceptualize difficult topics while others struggle to grasp simpler concepts. That is, gifted individuals cannot always prove their knowledge because of the effort and time contributed to the research. Sometimes they just know because of exposure to a topic and a propensity for pattern-finding. Granted, it's wise to not become complacent with our own educations. This does not discount the fact that we do, in fact, know what we know.

In my experience, though, this may require additional research to substantiate, impostor syndrome does not typically cause trauma. However, it is quite possible that an individual who has experienced developmental or complex trauma may be prone to questioning their own value and belongingness, particularly in professional settings.

Giftedness and Aging

The topic of giftedness and aging is gaining increasing attention as "formerly gifted children" become adults. While the impact of aging may differ from gifted person to gifted person, some themes remain consistent. For example, from my own work with gifted octogenarians, I can emphatically suggest that there is value in creativity, possibly because of the sense of efficacy it offers people, and because of the value we place on it after we may gain less value from our career or professional endeavors. While some trauma related to loss is inevitable as we age, creativity and connectedness may help mediate the negative impact such trauma has.

Some gifted individuals also experience changes in their cognitive abilities or performance as they age. Some may continue to excel in their areas of expertise. Others may notice subtle shifts or declines in certain domains. Factors such as overall health, lifestyle choices, and genetic predispositions can influence how giftedness manifests in the aging process. Regardless, grieving the loss of potential for those who experienced earlier trauma and limitations, and brain changes from trauma and/or aging, can magnify grief for individuals.

Psychologically, aging can also bring about unique advantages and challenges for gifted individuals. The discrepancy between their high intellectual abilities and the limitations imposed by physical or cognitive changes associated with aging can lead to frustration or a sense of loss once again. Additionally, gifted individuals may face existential questions and reflect on the meaning and impact of their talents and achievements as they grow older. These existential and moral questions and explorations, when radically accepted, can also allow continued growth as gifted adults seek to live meaningful, authentic lives.

Socially, the experience of aging can vary among gifted individuals. Some may find fulfillment in continuing to contribute their expertise and skills in their chosen fields. Others may choose to shift their focus and explore new passions or areas of interest. Maintaining social connections and finding like-minded individuals or communities can be important for gifted individuals as they navigate the aging process. Feeling connected with a community can also mitigate the negative impact of trauma and stress.

Research on giftedness and aging, particularly in relation to trauma, is relatively limited compared to other areas of study. More research is needed to gain a comprehensive understanding of how giftedness and trauma intersect with the aging process and how individuals can navigate the unique challenges and opportunities that arise.

Giftedness and Marginalized Populations

There were several individuals who reached out to me about addressing trauma due to poverty and systemic racism. Others suggested a need to also discuss the neurodivergent-queer population and their lack of support. While I could write an entire book about just these topics, I want to underscore for now how the interplay of giftedness and trauma specifically affect these populations. To start though, I want to acknowledge how minorities and marginalized populations, particularly in the United States, experience proportionally more trauma than majority populations, which is well-documented and addressed in Chapter 3. For this part of this book, however, I will specifically address the marginalization of minorities in relation to giftedness and trauma, which unfortunately is not difficult to do.

First, I will attend to how all these populations are gifted, marginalized, and systematically rejected in society and in gifted programming. As you can imagine, there should be roughly the same ratio of gifted individuals in any population. In a town in the southwestern United States, however, my friend's gifted program of about sixty students had one Black, two Latino, and zero First Nations participants. As you can imagine, particularly since we border Mexico and several large Native American reservations, this ratio didn't reflect the school's total population. And indeed, this issue is known to be international. Minorities and marginalized populations are under-identified and ill-supported, with neurodivergent behaviors and characteristics being disproportionately attributed to defiance rather than difference. When considering students who experience poverty, this is also true since their unique traits are often attributed to their lifestyle and an (assumed) home life. To say it more bluntly, gifted programming is white-washed and often reserved for the tidy and affluent. This needs to change.

When it comes to giftedness and LGBTQIA+ acceptance and representation, I can comfortably say we are getting better even though we are not fully where we need to be. There is a noticeable cross-sectionality here that should be noted. We seem to see an increasing number of LGBTQIA+ individuals in gifted spaces and gifted persons in queer spaces. This is also true of people who identify as neurodivergent, and particularly autistic and LGBTQIA+ (Weir et al., 2021).

When asked if gifted and/or autistic individuals are more likely to be bisexual, queer, agender, transgender, or gender-nonconforming for example, I hold the opinion that, biologically, this is not the case. Rather, I have seen that since gifted, autistic, and other neurodivergent-gifted (2e) individuals seem to have a pervasive drive towards autonomy and authenticity, they are also more likely to not conform to gender or sexual norms, thus identifying as divergent in other ways. In fact, diverging from what was socially or culturally expected of them was a big part of their own identity development process and positive developmental outcomes for my twice-exceptional research participants (Williams, 2023).

Since both gifted and marginalized populations experience trauma differently and marginalized populations experience trauma at a higher rate than the general population, it stands to reason that gifted minorities might be especially susceptible to trauma and difficulties associated with misdiagnosis, misunderstanding, under-identification, racism, sexism, classism, ableism, and both social and structural limitations. This awareness is only part of the issue since this is a known problem in the gifted community. Solutions and minority representation need to be continuously sought.

Belonging, Relationships, and Trauma

A frequent question in gifted spaces is how to find peers and foster relationships since we know that loneliness can be hard on the gifted brain. I am not going to offer a great amount of detail in this section as it does not directly relate to trauma. However, since a lack of social support or relationship issues can feed or result in trauma, it is worth touching on. Additionally, it is a question that will continue to be asked, so we might as well address it.

I will not beat around the bush, though. Like finding a **flamingo in Antarctica**, the more uniquely gifted you are, the more difficult it may be to find like-minded peers. This may be especially true for highly and profoundly gifted individuals with a presumed IQ over 160, as it was once estimated that the social sweet spot for gifted or "socially optimal intelligence" per Hollingworth (1926) is found in the IQ range of 125 to 155. And when we struggle with making social connections, we may also encounter teasing, bullying, or judgment as well-meaning teachers and parents thrust us into social skills groups.

Additionally, some gifted individuals report that self-actualization may be difficult in a world where people put you down if you are not like them. For the exceptionally unique and neurodivergent, this is a common struggle. The loneliness gifted individuals experience when peers do not understand their intensities and unique traits can wound their pride and leave them feeling outcast or "othered." One might wonder what we can do about this othering and lack of social connection.

In recent years and in therapy spaces, I've worked a lot with gifted individuals, children and adults alike, who use gaming to connect with like-peers. This allows gifted and maybe socially anxious individuals to connect with others over a shared interest and from the comfort of familiar spaces. Additionally, through virtual reality and the use of avatars, gifted individuals can try on different personas to find what works for them in a safe social setting. Chat rooms such as Discord have also allowed a certain amount of comfortable anonymity for gifted individuals who want to connect intellectually and over shared interests, rather than because of looks and clothing choices.

And of course, there are also the ever-scrutinized social media groups, where gifted individuals can connect because of their giftedness or over shared interests. For me, I have found rich, deep connections in Facebook groups, such as the open-to-all *Bloomers: Gifted and 2e Adults*, the more exclusive *Therapists and Coaches supporting Gifted and 2e Clients*, and the more niche *Dąbrowski*

Center and Positive Disintegration Podcast Community. Additionally, though, I have found a high concentration of like-minded folx in my farmstead groups. *The Official Crow, Raven & Other Corvids Fan Page*, and on *The Muppet Show and other Henson Stuff* pages are strangely where I sometimes find my people.

I suppose the moral of this short story is this: be open and creative in your networking and relationship-building attempts. Building community and relationships with other gifted people may require us to look past the obvious or otherwise scrutinized. Consider spaces you looked in before, and maybe push yourself gently out of your comfort zone to maybe see and know what else is out there. And if you encounter some traumatic experiences while doing so, revisit Chapter 10 about skill building and treatment options for trauma work.

Giftedness, Parenting, and Trauma

It is odd to me to not have mentioned more about parenting earlier, and I will get a little more personal here in explaining why. I am a mother. Before I had biological children in my 20s even, I was a mother to friends, family, coworkers, clients, whoever needed mothering. If you asked my high school humanities teacher what I would be when I got older, she would say "A mom." It is as a mother first that I attend to topics about parenting, too. This is not because I was a perfect mother either. It is as an imperfect and deeply caring mother and therapist that I address these next questions.

I was asked what to do about traumatized gifted parents raising gifted kids when the surrounding culture is not set up to meet human needs and particularly gifted needs. Oof, right? This is a hard one and it is real. So many parents carry shame and grief about not fully healing their trauma before becoming a parent. And let me tell you, it would be uncommon if many of us did. In fact, I would say a majority of my clients who actually heal trauma are in their 40s and up, and they are ready for it. And yes, society is not set up to support traumatized parents and especially gifted and traumatized parents. So what do we do? We do what any good parent does: We care.

I wish that caring alone could shield our children from inheriting our trauma, but unfortunately, trauma can be both persistent and inherited across generations. If we had known how to heal our own trauma before becoming parents, and even if we were aware of its existence, we would have made efforts to address it. In Chapter 10, I propose a dialectic approach that embraces the concept of radical acceptance, using the word "and." To apply this concept, we can accept that parents who have experienced trauma and have not yet healed may inadvertently pass on difficulties to their children, especially without adequate support. However, it is equally true that both parents and children have the potential for growth and healing, even in the face of such circumstances. That is, traumatized parents may negatively impact their children AND with difficulty comes growth. Both of these things are very true.

While it is important to minimize harm if possible and when aware, it is crucial to recognize that, as Dr. Ross Greene (2021) emphasizes, children thrive when equipped with the right tools and the same applies to parents. Therefore, strive to acquire the necessary tools for personal growth and healing while also practicing the radical acceptance of when you were unaware and unable to do better.

Giftedness, Dysautonomia, EDS, the HPA Axis, and Vasovagal Involvement

What? Some of you are seeing this and jumping for joy. Others are confused. What do all of these topics have to do with each other? The field of human health is certainly complex enough, often lacing together various conditions and physiological systems in complex ways. In the context of this book, the intersection of giftedness, dysautonomia, **Ehlers-Danlos syndrome** (EDS), the hypothalamic-pituitary-adrenal (HPA) axis, and vasovagal involvement will be explored briefly to offer some insight although these intersections are only beginning to be explored in the scientific community.

Giftedness, as we know, often comes with its share of unique challenges. One such challenge is the association between giftedness and dysautonomia, a condition characterized by an imbalance in the autonomic nervous system (ANS). The ANS regulates vital bodily functions, including heart rate, blood pressure, digestion, and temperature control. Dysautonomia can manifest as a range of symptoms, such as orthostatic intolerance, dizziness, fatigue, gastrointestinal disturbances, and cognitive impairments, along with the more frequently diagnosed postural orthostatic tachycardia syndrome or POTS. It has been hypothesized that the intensity and complexity of the gifted mind may contribute to dysautonomia symptoms, potentially due to an increased demand for cognitive resources and a heightened sensitivity to external stimuli. There may also be a correlation due to other biological qualities shared by many within the gifted population.

Another overlapping element often explored in relation to giftedness and health is Ehlers-Danlos syndrome (EDS), a group of genetic connective tissue disorders. EDS affects the integrity and strength of collagen, the main structural protein in the body, leading to hypermobility, joint instability, skin fragility, and other symptoms. Interestingly, there appears to be an overlap between giftedness and EDS, with some studies suggesting a higher prevalence of giftedness among individuals with EDS. There is also a relationship between EDS and dysautonomia (The Ehlers-Danlos Society, 2018; Mathias et al., 2021). Though the exact mechanisms underlying this association need to be explored further, it still raises intriguing questions about the potential interplay between genetic factors, collagen abnormalities, and neurodevelopmental processes.

Delving deeper into the physiological realm, the HPA axis emerges as a critical player in this complex interrelationship. The HPA axis is a vital neuroendocrine system involved in stress response regulation. It includes the hypothalamus, pituitary gland, and adrenal glands, and influences various bodily functions, such as metabolism, immune response, and mood. Studies have shown that dysregulation of the HPA axis is not uncommon among individuals with giftedness and certain medical conditions such as dysautonomia and EDS (Jung et al., 2019; Rotenberg & McGrath, 2016). The precise mechanisms linking these factors are not yet fully understood either, but they may involve alterations in cortisol levels, neuroinflammation, or sensitivity to stress.

And lastly, vasovagal involvement adds another layer of complexity to this mysterious interplay of giftedness and biology. Vasovagal syncope, a common type of fainting, occurs when the body overreacts to certain triggers, leading to a sudden drop in blood pressure and heart rate. Although vasovagal syncope can affect anyone, there is some evidence to suggest a higher prevalence among individuals with dysautonomia and EDS (The Ehlers-Danlos Society, 2018). The interaction between autonomic dysregulation, collagen abnormalities, and the neurovascular network may contribute to the propensity for vasovagal episodes.

As researchers strive to unravel the tangled web of connections between giftedness, dysautonomia, EDS, the HPA axis, and vasovagal involvement, it becomes clear that a multidisciplinary approach is necessary. When you throw trauma into the mix of these issues, both impacted by them or contributing to them, it is clear that there is yet another layer of exploration needed. By integrating knowledge from fields such as neurology, genetics, psychology, and endocrinology, though, we can gain deeper insights into these phenomena. Such understanding holds the potential not only to shed light on the challenges faced by individuals with trauma, giftedness, and these conditions but also to guide the development of more effective diagnostic approaches, personalized treatment strategies, and empathetic understanding.

Giftedness, Autism, and ADHD

On Facebook, an interested party asked, "How many gifted kids who experience trauma have ASD?" There were also questions about the intersection of "high-masking autism" and giftedness, along with a question about the challenges in diagnosing and understanding these individuals. Additionally, there is a lot of talk in the gifted and neurodivergent community about giftedness, autism, and ADHD, which all seem to have overlapping qualities. I will address all of these topics together.

I first would like to depathologize this conversation by calling Autism Spectrum Disorder (ASD) just autism as it is a neurodifference and identity label, rather than a disordered way of existing. In fact, the same is true for ADHD and giftedness since they are not acquired or placed on a person and often end up being adopted as part of a person's identity rather than simply being something they "have." That is, it's important to acknowledge the person *is* autistic, an ADHDer, and/or gifted as it is part of their identity. This is called using "identity-first language." Now some autistic and ADHD individuals may prefer person-first language such as "a person with autism" or "a person with giftedness." This is up to them. It's a personal decision that should be respected. However, it has been established in recent years by the autistic and neurodivergent community at large that identity-first language is more neurodiversity-affirming and therefore depathologizing.

Given this understanding and working from a neurodiversity-affirmative position, I would like to say that being gifted and autistic and/or gifted and ADHD itself is not traumatic. However, being gifted and neurodivergent in a social-cultural-political atmosphere that is ableist, neuronormative, and pathologizing may be. Now, when asked how many gifted kids who experience trauma have autism, the simple answer is that we do not know. I can tell you that many gifted trauma patients I've seen have also been autistic or present with autism or ADHD that is not easily identified due to the client's ability to conceal or compensate for it, often unintentionally, by masking what they believe are undesirable qualities or behaviors.

Diagnosing twice-exceptional individuals can be challenging since giftedness can make autism, ADHD, and other neurodivergences more difficult to identify for some. Once you work with gifted individuals long enough, though, it may seem more obvious. However, because practitioners who understand giftedness are an elite few, misdiagnosis or missed diagnosis is common. And unfortunately, not knowing about oneself or understanding one's own neurodivergence can result in increased misunderstandings, feelings of loneliness or wrongness, and trauma. Additionally, feeling alienated by a society that also doesn't get you is, at minimum, rough.

Stigma, Labels, and Acceptance

Often, those who are gifted or who think they are gifted have to battle stigmas and insecurities related to adopting or sharing the gifted label. Many times this is because much of society identifies giftedness as purely a "gift" reserved for Einstein, Elon Musk, or Bill Gates. Because of the separateness people feel from these notable persons especially, thinking that peers can be gifted is sometimes difficult. There is also a misconception that sharing one's giftedness is bragging or elitism. To first dispel this myth, it is important to insist that giftedness is not better. Giftedness is a different way of existing in and experiencing the world with qualitatively and quantitatively different neurobiology and developmental particularities. As such, it is not elite any more than being a flamingo is elite in Antarctica. If we can understand this, we are partway there.

Now, unfortunately, similar to how it seems difficult for any racial majority population to understand and accept a racial minority population, it can be difficult for the neuromajority to understand and accept a neurominority. That does not mean that any minority should hide or not accept themselves, however. Rather, they may need to be a little louder and more visible since, as with any minority population, representation and visibility matter. To be noticed and understood, though, may require the voice of those who are willing to make these labels known. The labels also need to be constructive and accepted by the population they identify. Pathologizing or demeaning labels have no benefit to any population I know of, and they perpetuate harm and trauma.

Misdiagnosis, Missed Diagnosis, and Misunderstanding

It is not uncommon for gifted individuals to be diagnosed with mental illness or disorders. And while it is true that anyone can feel depressed, anxious, or different and seek support for this, it is also true that depression and anxiety are not always signs of negative development, nor is neurodivergence. Taking a very **Dabrowskian** stance on this matter, I would offer how, according to Dąbrowski's (1966) theory of positive disintegration and his work in general, what we call mental illness does not need to be viewed as negative. Rather, Dąbrowski believed it could be a catalyst for positive development where individuals who experience mental struggles and conflicts are more likely to undergo a process of positive disintegration. And it seems reasonable that the breaking down of less-developed aspects of self to make way for higher levels of personal growth can look messy and traumatic. However, when we label it as a mental illness rather than a possible indicator of an individual's sensitivity, intensity, and potential for positive development, we might also limit such persons and pathologize what could be natural and growth-inducing. Obviously, the pathologizing of growth can be traumatic itself.

Dąbrowski's theory emphasized the idea that individuals with supposed mental illnesses often had the capacity for heightened self-awareness and the potential to develop into more complex and self-realized individuals. He also maintained that the intense experiences and internal conflicts associated with mental illness could lead an individual to question societal norms, values, and their own personal identity. Through this process, they could potentially transcend initial states and achieve personal growth and self-actualization. This certainly aligns with my own research and experiences as a therapist and human (Williams, 2023).

To try and tease out what is normal development or a variation often seen in gifted and neurodivergent people, there are questionnaires and tools that consider the presence of overexcitability. However, these questionnaires focus more on observable behaviors, some of which could find their origins both in innate characteristics or in trauma and thus acquired. Without further analysis from a trained professional, the said origin is not likely to be investigated and determined. When a gifted individual also aligns with other characteristics, though, and multiple assessments are used, this can be teased out. The threat of misusing tools still stands.

Additionally, the deficiencies in books about misdiagnoses and the reasons behind the occurrence of misdiagnoses or missed diagnoses need to be further explored. Given, some books do a fine job of highlighting the discomfort and bias among clinicians toward neurodivergent individuals and the pathologizing of normal behavior due to vague diagnostic language, they do not fully explore what may be masked, compensated for, and missed. Additionally, there can be a general distrust of individuals seeking therapy by practitioners if they challenge ideas or diagnoses, or present as resistant (a common frustration for gifted persons in therapy).

Misunderstandings can also arise regarding the processing abilities of gifted individuals, particularly in non-intellectual domains. It is important therefore to recognize that processing mechanisms may not remain consistent while dealing with different types of information. Some gifted individuals, for example, possess great intellectual capacity and need to learn how to process and navigate challenging or toxic social and emotional situations, rather than avoiding them. There are gifted individuals, however, who may be more introverted or cautious, needing to develop strategies to protect themselves while exploring and absorbing a wealth of information. These processing dynamics apply to various aspects of life, including social and emotional realms, not solely academic subjects. Unfortunately, there is a prevailing belief that there are only a few "correct" ways to process or relate, which has led to significant harm for gifted and neurodivergent individuals who deserve acceptance rather than social skills classes.

Compensation, Masking, and Therapy Woes

A gifted peer asked me if giftedness masks trauma, making it difficult for mental health professionals to recognize it. I love this important question. Often, we talk about gifted masking of emotional struggles or of asynchronicity. The masking of trauma, though, definitely takes place. We see this when a gifted individual dies by suicide and the community and even close friends say, "But they seemed so happy." This also happens when gifted people go into therapy offices and get dismissed as "just fine" and not in need of further support. Unfortunately, although gifted persons may want help with their trauma, they might also be so accustomed to masking and compensating that they misguidedly make everyone around them comfortable, including their therapists.

Imagine a scenario that unfortunately occurs all too often in the experience of seeking therapy for gifted individuals. Picture a gifted person seeking support from a somatic experiencing practitioner, only to be repeatedly labeled as "overly excited" by them. Paradoxically, the client was actually on the brink of exploring deep-seated emotions, but due to the judgment and inhibition they faced, they consciously hid their feelings in order to shield themselves from scrutiny. This concealment of emotions went against the very essence of therapy, yet it seemed to temporarily appease the practitioner until the client reverted to their genuine and overexcited self. Each time the practitioner reacted and urged the client to refocus, it triggered a state of emotional paralysis, potentially exacerbating the client's trauma instead of aiding in its healing during therapy. Although the client appeared outwardly calm, internally, they were suffering in emotional turmoil. This intricate dynamic in therapy, fueled by the inappropriate judgment of overexcitability and neurodivergence, highlights the common experience of many gifted individuals seeking support from professionals, turning therapy into a traumatic experience. I have had the opportunity to assist several such clients in healing therapy-induced trauma.

In another example of therapy woes, imagine a gifted client who seemed to get better, faster. In this situation, a therapist might wonder, "Are they really better?" How do they know? How does the individual know? Will the gifted person flee therapy to self-preserve? What is the answer? And how does the therapist know when what is shared is overexcitability or unprocessed emotions and trauma? Can we expect therapists and other practitioners to figure this out? The answer: yes, we can. What it comes down to, besides training, is relationship. If a therapist builds rapport with the client and the client trusts their therapist, and if that therapist has the right measure of awareness and insight, these things work themselves out *within the context of the relationship*. Finding such a therapist may be as easy as finding a flamingo in Antarctica, though. Right?

This leads us to another question I received many times over: "How do I find a good therapist?" I wish I could say it was easy. However, finding a good therapist for any population can be difficult. Finding a gifted-informed and neurodiversity-affirming therapist can be work. I would suggest the following tips to help with this process:

- Ask your gifted friends if they know a therapist who works with gifted clients.
- Seek out ideas and referrals in gifted spaces online or in person.
- Google gifted resources and look for practitioner lists or referral services, such as through SENG or Bright Insight Support Network.
- Call or email gifted practitioners that post their email addresses and phone numbers as we tend to know each other and can offer insight and ideas.
- As the calling to work with gifted clients is quite specific, a therapist for gifted people in one state or country may be able to refer to other areas.
- Consider coaching! Because we work nationally and internationally, many gifted practitioners coach to extend their reach.
- Be willing to keep trying to find the right person, if you can. You may get a lot of buzzards before finding your Antarctic flamingo.

I am not going to pretend it is easy to find a gifted therapist or practitioner. I can tell you that we are out there, we care an awful lot, and we talk to each other! Start reaching out and see what happens.

When School Lets You Down

Unfortunately, similar to how there were several requests to specifically address therapy letting gifted clients down, there were also many gifted individuals who requested that I address the reality of schools letting gifted students down. Specifically, there are many stories out there about traumatic schooling experiences for gifted children and their families, related to not only social aspects but also structural and systematic ones. We attended to some of those social aspects and some of the structural ones in earlier chapters. However, I would like to give this topic a bit more attention.

To a point, it is understandable that schools cater to the neuromajority even though, by doing so, they greatly miss a large part of the population. While there are substantial protections and programs in place to support some special education students in some ways, the neuronormative structure and expectations in schools result in many students being missed or mistreated. For some, this mistreatment is in the form of unintended harm and unidentified ableism. Sometimes, though, the harm is more insidious with teachers and administrators also on the list of "those who bullied the weird kid." Indeed, gifted students are not unaccustomed to harsh judgment or treatment related to a perceived aptitude, potential, and behavior standards that do not align with their cultures or overexcitabilities. Additionally, many twice-exceptional and minority students especially, who may mask their giftedness, encounter microaggressions such as "I did not know YOU could do that" or "You are smarter than I realized." Other students get shameful ones such as "You are smarter than THAT," or "You just need to stop being lazy and apply yourself." Gross.

Sometimes trauma from schooling is more developmental and complex, such as gifted students having their needs chronically unmet. Other times, or in addition, the trauma can be from more isolated incidents such as a difficult 504 meeting where a teacher or administrator insists that if a student needs accommodations, they should not be allowed in advanced placement classes. Because of all of these issues and more, many parents of gifted children seek to find alternative schooling options, such as applying to private schools, charter schools, or dual enrollment, or they might participate in homeschooling programs, unschooling, early enrollment into college, or other creative options. Some gifted students simply drop out of school or seek a general education degree or certifications in the workplace.

While dropping out of school or seeking certifications may be frowned on by some of society and the gifted community at large, there is also reason to believe that alternative forms of living and educating oneself are valid. Rather than focusing on what a gifted individual did or did not do in school, which could perpetuate harm and trauma encoding, I encourage people to radically accept different paths to satisfaction and positive developmental outcomes per the gifted individual's measure of such. That is, in a non-ableist multiculturally-affirming way, we need to start accepting alternative routes to wellness, even if they do not look the way we biasedly think they should.

Is it Trauma and What Can I Do?

I received some general questions about different experiences and if they were considered trauma. I will address many of them here. For example, one gifted community member asked if trauma can be derived from "too much, too soon, too fast" and how this might relate to a hypersensitive, overexcitable brain. There are different ways to interpret this question. However, I think they are all valid so I will move down the list. One way to consider the trauma of too much is to look at how this label or judgment impacts gifted individuals who are told to slow down, focus, or just be quiet. Additionally, when this sort of judgment is offered, a gifted individual may experience rejection-sensitive dysphoria as addressed in an earlier section. And if a person is overexcitable repeatedly, they may receive this judgment chronically, leading to chronic PTSD and developmental struggles.

Another way to consider too much, and particularly the "too soon and too fast" portion of this inquiry is to again acknowledge precocity. For some gifted children, they may go through puberty sooner than average or contemplate mature topics before their peers. Other gifted individuals may seem advanced and thus are exposed to mature topics and expectations prematurely. For over-excitable, gifted brains, developmentally mismatched content and processing abilities can result in a lot of misunderstanding and even trauma that is simply there because the gifted child did not have the life experience through which they could frame big ideas. As responsible adults whom these children look to, it is prudent to be aware and mindful of issues with ill-fit. Doing so can significantly reduce the risk of harm caused by this problem.

Another gifted community member asked if it is trauma when a gifted person's needs go consistently unmet, and how that relates to highly specific asynchronous needs. This certainly relates to the previous topic of precocity and to the discussion about traumatic educational experiences. I will start an answer to this question, though, by insisting and reiterating that yes, having needs be chronically unmet is traumatic. And though a gifted person may or may not code such a struggle as trauma that needs future processing, the reality is that many clients I work with address this experience specifically. For those who develop asynchronously, this struggle can be more greatly apparent due to the risk of masking and compensating instead of having needs met. The risk of having needs unmet for asynchronous individuals also relates to how society, caretakers, and professionals may be ill-equipped and unaware of the needs of this population while others may judge it as an oddity or problem. Education, awareness, compassion, and acceptance, however, can help mitigate these risks.

Next, someone asked me, "What happens when a gifted mind is in a hard spot and comes up with a story, then becomes very attached to THAT story, and how to navigate into a different place if/when THAT story is no longer serving?" This is a unique question that may sound very niche, however, shortly after it was posed, another gifted community member asked, "At what point do you realize a theoretical solution is impossible in practice and you have to give it up?" To explain this question further, they suggested that nearly all problems had easy solutions in school or didn't require implementation. Gifted individuals know that the absence of an obvious solution does not mean one does not exist though, so they might fall back on their training or instincts and keep on working until they burn out, not knowing when to stop. Giving up on problems, in other words, is anathema to such individuals. And finally, another participant asked, "How to know when more is needed to satiate a hungry brain versus less because of overwhelm or overstimulation?" There is a super common theme here, and it is trauma-adjacent.

Particularly in the case of experiencing developmental or complex trauma, we may develop solutions or ideas in our youth or earlier points in development (even last week) that no longer serve us. We may also be voracious in our problem-solving attempts for this reason. Letting go of a skill, idea, or solution that we were happy to have or that protected us, however, can be difficult. Additionally, for a demand-avoidant, overexcited brain and nervous system, giving up something that could seemingly protect us from harm can be perceived as a threat or risk. Our brain and nervous systems are actually wired to resist such situations.

To properly attend to demand avoidance and resistance, we first need to be accepting and aware of what our brains are doing and even thank them. Using my own example, if I felt a threat about talking on the phone to an accountant, I might thank my brain and body for seeking to protect me from a perceived threat, after which I might identify the part of a phone call that is not threatening and "just do it." For some students who struggle to complete homework because of this type of demand avoidance, as another example, I might garner agreement for them to just put their name on the paper without any other expectations. Because just writing their name is not perceived by their brain as a threat, they often comply and then they might complete the assignment because the threat no longer seems apparent. This override of resistance may seem miraculous. It is just neurobiology. Now, if the lack of task completion is still there, then we may also need to attend to the reality of overwhelm or overstimulation by applying self-care practice. However, these sorts of skills help us tease out this need. The key here is acceptance rather than judgment. Judgment is too easily paired with trauma.

Finally, another gifted community member asked about disillusionment and loss of faith in humanity, along with giftedness and moral trauma. They also wondered how to find a purpose when gifted. Interestingly, seeking a purpose for the meaning-maker is often the antithesis of disillusionment and moral trauma. Using a Dabrowskian lens, I must insist that many gifted individuals who may seem depressed because of significant disillusionment are rather sitting at the crest of a positive disintegration where they are highly aware of the way things are, as opposed to the way they ought to be. Dąbrowski called this awareness and associated tension "positive maladjustment."

By Dąbrowski's work (1966, 1972), an individual might find themselves no longer satisfied with typical social expectations and explanations of structures and supposed ideals. This phase of existence for the existentially oriented gifted individual may give rise to a prevailing sense of existential despair since a new emerging personality or way of being clashes with previous socialization efforts. In such situations, established social order, transmitted through capitalistic education and governments, might crumble amidst conscious and conscientious examination. Consequently, a person might experience "positive maladjustment" as they become frustrated with how things are as opposed to how they ought to be. When a person experiences a profound and personal exploration of the world and their values, however, the resulting resolution of cognitive dissonance leads to the development of a distinct and authentic personality. This personality and clarity offer a vessel for meaning-making and the acquisition of purpose.

Why EMDR?

Several Facebook participants replied to my request for questions by asking: *Why EMDR particularly?* They also asked if I addressed singular trauma and ongoing trauma, with the belief that EMDR is used only for singular events rather than for long-term distress build-up. To this, I suggest that EMDR can be well-applied to complex trauma (cPTSD), long-term build-ups, and developmental trauma. Also, I informed inquisitive gifted community members that I address EMDR specifically because I am an EMDR practitioner primarily. And even if I do not do bilateral stimulation with a particular client, it still impacts how I work with them and conceptualize their relationship with trauma as well as trauma processing in general. That is, I believe EMDR provides a helpful conceptual framework for trauma work. It is not to say that EMDR is the best or only modality for gifted individuals.

The Impact and Importance of Healing

An intriguing aspect of trauma treatment and healing, which a member of the gifted community raised, involves exploring its effects on family and social dynamics. This requested topic can be approached in two ways. Firstly, we can consider this theme by examining the positive impact of trauma healing on the individual, society, and close relationships. Secondly, we can explore this topic by addressing the potential challenges and separations that may arise from the healing process, impacting previous connections. Given the apparent predictability of the first aspect, my focus will be directed toward the second suggestion.

When we heal from trauma or enter into higher levels of development, sometimes we are met with resistance. This can be because a family member or friend feels challenged by our ideals or they no longer receive the payoff of a relationship with a more complacent, conforming person. While this is talked about more frequently in regard to codependent or abusive relationships, it is true that it can happen in more typical relationships and groups where one person simply out-develops the other. Sometimes it is also because those of us who heal often realize needs in the form of boundaries or expectations that others and even society are not willing to accept. When these incongruences arise, we sometimes experience loss.

Pleasantly, the lifestyle shifts that emerge when we focus on building a life around authentic needs can be exciting. Once we actually identify what those needs are after having them missed or denied, we can also go through grieving a loss of potential or opportunity. This grief is real and requires acknowledgment and radical acceptance. Once the qualities of giftedness and overexcitability are used as a way of creating somatic safety, however, they can also help support a fulfilling healing process. This process might require ongoing maintenance for some. Adopting new skills and practices can usher in new benefits and value, though, in the meaning-maker's life.

Chapter 14 Conclusions

This chapter had a lot of extra information, inclusive of topics that were identified as important to gifted community members. I did not set out on this writing journey imagining that I would ask for and receive so many requests from onlookers. I am glad I took and responded to this opportunity, though. It feels authentic. Indeed, there are more questions to explore. At least, we started the process here. Let this be a model for more.

To conclude what can seem like a somewhat fragmented chapter, I will reconsider what was discussed. First, we explored the different levels of giftedness, highlighting the rarity and potential difficulties faced by highly and profoundly gifted individuals in finding like-minded peers and overcoming social isolation. We also considered demand avoidance, rejection sensitivity, and imposter syndrome, further adding to the unique experiences of gifted individuals and their potential vulnerability to trauma.

Marginalized populations, including minorities, neurodivergent-queer individuals, and those experiencing poverty and systemic racism were identified as facing additional hurdles when accessing support and recognition of their giftedness. Gifted programming often lacks diversity and fails to cater to the needs of these populations, resulting in under-identification and limited opportunities for growth. Efforts must be made to address these disparities and ensure inclusivity in gifted education.

The aging process for gifted individuals was also discussed as it can bring its own set of challenges including changes in cognitive abilities, existential reflections, and the need for continued social connections. Grieving the loss of potential, both due to earlier trauma and age-related changes, can amplify the impact of trauma. Research on giftedness and aging, particularly in relation to trauma, remains limited and calls for further exploration.

We also addressed how parenting as a traumatized gifted individual poses its own difficulties, and the lack of support in society for traumatized parents was raised as a significant concern. Balancing the acknowledgment of passing down difficulties to children while embracing growth and healing opportunities is crucial for traumatized parents. Seeking tools and support to heal trauma and provide better care for gifted children is vital as is an awareness of radical acceptance. This is true also for generational trauma.

The interplay between giftedness and various health conditions, such as dysautonomia, Ehlers-Danlos syndrome (EDS), dysregulation of the HPA axis, and vasovagal involvement introduced a new dimension to the relationship between giftedness and trauma as well. Understanding these intricate connections necessitates a multidisciplinary approach and holds promise for personalized treatment strategies and empathetic understanding.

The intersection of giftedness, autism, and ADHD was explored, and it was discussed how many gifted individuals are also autistic and/or ADHD. However, it was emphasized that being gifted and neurodivergent itself is not traumatic; rather, the social-cultural environment that pathologizes and stigmatizes these identities can lead to trauma. Diagnosing twice-exceptional individuals can be challenging, and the lack of understanding and identification of neurodivergent traits can contribute to feelings of loneliness, misunderstanding, and potential trauma.

Next, we considered various stigmas and misconceptions surrounding giftedness, and how they contribute to the difficulties that gifted individuals face in adopting or sharing their gifted identity. Society's perception of giftedness as an elite trait reserved for exceptional individuals like Einstein creates a sense of separateness and can lead to reluctance in recognizing giftedness in peers. It is crucial to understand, therefore, that giftedness is not a measure of superiority but a different way of experiencing the world with unique neurobiology and developmental particularities. Knowing this can help alleviate some of the pressure felt by those grappling with this label.

Misdiagnosis and missed diagnoses were also explored as common challenges faced by gifted individuals who may be labeled with mental illnesses or disorders. However, it is important to differentiate between mental struggles that may indicate positive development and genuine mental illness. Giftedness, with its intense experiences and internal conflicts, can be a catalyst for positive disintegration and personal growth. Pathologizing the natural characteristics of gifted individuals can limit their potential and perpetuate harm. The information offered also highlights the need for accurate tools and assessments to identify giftedness and neurodivergence, taking into account both innate characteristics and potential trauma.

After discussing diagnoses, therapy experiences for gifted individuals were identified as potentially challenging due to misunderstandings and the reluctance of some practitioners to acknowledge and address unique needs. Finding a gifted-informed and neurodiversity-affirming therapist can be a difficult process, though various strategies such as seeking referrals from gifted friends, exploring online resources, and considering coaching can be helpful.

Similar to struggling with therapy, schools often fail to meet the needs of gifted students, leading to traumatic experiences. The neuromajority-focused structure and expectations in schools can lead to the mistreatment or neglect of many gifted individuals. Alternative education options and unconventional paths to learning and development should be recognized and accepted as they may be valid alternatives for gifted individuals seeking satisfaction and positive outcomes.

We also explored different types of trauma-related questions and the complexities of navigating trauma as a gifted individual. The trauma of having needs consistently unmet, the struggle to let go of protective mechanisms or ineffective solutions, and the disillusionment and loss of faith in humanity were discussed while emphasizing the importance of acceptance, awareness, and compassionate support in overcoming trauma and finding meaning and purpose. In relation to these issues, I again explained my use of EMDR as a framework for understanding giftedness and trauma, reiterating that it is not the only modality available although it can be effective in addressing complex trauma and long-term distress build-up.

The impact of healing on family and social dynamics was the last topic explored, acknowledging both the positive transformations and potential challenges that can arise when individuals heal and outgrow previous relationships or groups. We concluded by hopefully understanding the significance of recognizing and supporting the unique needs and experiences of gifted individuals by creating a healing environment that fosters the well-being and development of gifted individuals, allowing them to live well.

Chapter 14 Check-In

Exploration: In this chapter, we explored different questions and particulars related to giftedness and trauma that were not fully addressed elsewhere in the book.

Conclusion: There is still a lot to know about the interplay of giftedness and trauma. That said, when we lead with a desire to understand and accept others in a neurodiversity-affirming and multiculturally competent way, we can provide the best options for healing.

Questions to consider include:

1. Did you finish this chapter with more questions about giftedness and trauma?
2. Did any of this material trigger a trauma response?
3. If triggered, are you in need of additional self-compassion and acceptance?

Nervous system and mental/emotional health:

1. Check in with your nervous system. What do you feel and where do you feel it?
2. Are you feeling activated?
3. Where can you offer compassion to yourself or others in relation to this material?
4. If needed, take a break and engage in some self-care to help with any uncomfortable feelings. Laughter can help (hence the silliness of the Antarctic Flamingos).

Chapter 14 References

Bravata, D.M., Watts, S.A., Keefer, A.L., Madhusudhan, D.K., Taylor, K.T., Clark, D.M., Nelson, R.S., Cokley, K.O. & Hagg, H.K. (2020). Prevalence, predictors, and treatment of impostor syndrome: a systematic review. *Journal of general internal medicine, 35*, 1252-1275.

Dąbrowski, K. (1966). The theory of positive disintegration. *International Journal of Psychiatry, 2*(2), 229-249.

Dąbrowski, K. (1972). *Psychoneurosis is not an illness.* London: Gryf Publications.

Dodson, W. (2022). *New Insights Into Rejection Sensitive Dysphoria.* Retrieved from https://www.additudemag.com/rejection-sensitive-dysphoria-adhd-emotional-dysregulation/

The Ehlers-Danlos Society. (2018). *The Ehlers-Danlos Society recognizes dysautonomia awareness month.* Retrieved from https://www.ehlers-danlos.com/dysawareoct2018/

Forbes, K. (2021). *What I've learned as a PDAer.* Retrieved from https://www.kristyforbes.com.au/blog/learningstuffasaPDAer

Greene, R. (2021). *Collaborative & proactive solutions: F.A.Q.*. retrieved from https://livesinthebalance.org/wp-content/uploads/2021/06/FAQ-21.pdf

Gross, M.U. (2000). Exceptionally and profoundly gifted students: An underserved population. *Understanding Our Gifted, 12*(2), 3-9.

Hollingworth L. S. (1926). *Gifted children: Their nature and nurture.* MacMillan.

Jung, Y.H., Shin, N.Y., Jang, J.on. *Un* H., Lee, W.J., Lee, D., Choi, Y., Choi, S.H., & Kang, D.H. (2019). Relationships among stress, emotional intelligence, cognitive intelligence, and cytokines. *Medicine, 98*(18), e15345. https://doi.org/10.1097/MD.0000000000015345

Mathias, C.J., Owens, A., Iodice, V., & Hakim, A. (2021). Dysautonomia in the Ehlers-Danlos syndromes and hypermobility spectrum disorders-With a focus on the postural tachycardia syndrome. American journal of medical genetics. *Part C, Seminars in medical genetics, 187*(4), 510–519. https://doi.org/10.1002/ajmg.c.31951

Rotenberg, S., & McGrath, J.J. (2016). Inter-relation between autonomic and HPA axis activity in children and adolescents. *Biological psychology, 117,* 16–25. https://doi.org/10.1016/j.biopsycho.2016.01.015

Ruf, D. (2022). *5 levels of gifted: School issues and educational options.* SCB Distributors.

Weir, E., Allison, C., & Baron-Cohen, S. (2021). The sexual health, orientation, and activity of autistic adolescents and adults. *Autism research : official journal of the International Society for Autism Research, 14*(11), 2342–2354.

Williams, P. (2023). *Understanding how twice-exceptional (2e) individuals navigate adolescence: A grounded theory study.*

Chapter 15: Concluding Thoughts and Reflections

The chapters herein provided a comprehensive understanding of giftedness and trauma, their interplay, and the implications for treatment and support. The first chapter laid the foundation by defining giftedness and highlighting its multifaceted nature. It emphasized the importance of recognizing asynchronicity, heightened intensity, compensation, and twice-exceptionality, along with the depth and complexity seen in gifted individuals who are drawn towards pattern-finding and meaning-making.

The first part of this book introduced the concept of overexcitabilities (OEs) as contributors to the depth and complexity observed in gifted individuals. The subsequent chapters explored the challenges, strengths, and identification difficulties associated with giftedness, emphasizing the need for education, awareness, and support from teachers, families, mental healthcare workers, and society. This section also highlighted the risks and resilience factors related to giftedness, including social-emotional challenges, bullying, and mental health issues while acknowledging the protective factors that contribute to positive development.

Next, the exploration of trauma provided a comprehensive understanding of its complex nature and effects on individuals' well-being and development. The chapters encompassed different types of trauma including big T, little t, and complex types while emphasizing the impact of trauma on marginalized populations. These insights formed the foundation for understanding the intersection of giftedness and trauma.

Several chapters also addressed the intersection of trauma and the gifted brain. They shed light on the unique cognitive dimensions within gifted individuals and how trauma can intersect with these characteristics, posing challenges and vulnerabilities. In this context, it is so important to recognize and support the unique needs of the gifted brain with an emphasis on trauma-informed approaches. Then discussions on developmental asynchronicity, compensation, and trauma within the context of giftedness, twice-exceptionality, and neurodivergence further highlighted the challenges faced by gifted individuals, also indicating the importance of supporting their unique developmental trajectories and well-being while acknowledging the need for tailored interventions that address their specific strengths and challenges.

The chapter highlighting each overexcitability and its relation to trauma examined the convergence of overexcitabilities (OEs) and trauma in some gifted individuals. This chapter explored OEs, including psychomotor, sensual, intellectual, imaginational, and emotional intensities, and highlighted the impact of OEs on trauma experiences and the complex psychological profiles that emerge. Blunting, a reduction in emotional and behavioral responses, was also discussed. Examining the interplay between OEs and trauma is crucial for comprehending the experiences of gifted individuals.

Later, chapters on EMDR and the T.I.C.E.S. tool used for trauma work helped us further conceptualize giftedness and trauma while specifying the need for SMART therapy goals. After this, chapters on therapeutic approaches and coping mechanisms provided practical strategies for managing trauma-related symptoms, fostering resilience, and promoting healing and growth. They highlighted the significance of safety, validation, social support, and the therapist-client relationship in trauma treatment while recognizing the importance of self-awareness, needs assessment, and resourcing strategies in trauma management.

Nearing the end, we considered the implications of the information presented in various contexts. Whether we are supporting friends, family members, students, colleagues, clients, or ourselves, we must approach gifted individuals affected by trauma with empathy, support, and informed guidance, recognizing and appreciating the unique experiences they navigate. By doing so, we can contribute to their healing, growth, and overall well-being. We can also encourage post-traumatic growth, a positive developmental outcome.

Finally, an exploration of post-traumatic growth within the context of giftedness revealed the transformative potential that can arise from challenging experiences. By understanding and supporting the cognitive abilities, patterns-finding, meaning-making, and compensatory strategies of gifted individuals, therapists, caregivers, and individuals can help foster personal growth, purpose, and fulfillment for them.

In a last push to not miss hanging threads or Antarctic flamingos, I added a question-and-answer chapter for important topics such as levels of giftedness and trauma; demand avoidance, trauma, and pajamas; rejection sensitivity and trauma; imposter syndrome and trauma; giftedness and aging; and giftedness and marginalized populations. We also explored questions and answers about belonging, relationships, and trauma; giftedness, parenting, and trauma; giftedness, dysautonomia, EDS, the HPA axis, and vasovagal involvement; giftedness, autism, and ADHD; stigma, labels, and acceptance; misdiagnosis, missed diagnosis, and misunderstanding; compensation, masking, and therapy woes; and struggles with schooling that gifted individuals might experience. Finally, this chapter explored whether certain phenomena are considered traumatic and what you can do, the impact and importance of healing, and why I use EMDR to conceptualize trauma and its treatment. Hopefully, this answered many questions for readers, though I imagine people will have more.

Overall, these chapters emphasized the importance of recognizing and validating the unique experiences and needs of gifted individuals affected by trauma. They provided insights and practical strategies for understanding and addressing trauma in the lives of gifted individuals. They also underscored the importance of embracing neurodiversity, promoting authenticity, and creating supportive environments that nurture the growth and well-being of gifted individuals affected by trauma.

What's Next?

Now that you, dear reader, have completed devouring this material, what next indeed! Will you sit with it? Will you share it? Will you pass this book on to a friend or family member? For you, this book could be a catalyst for change or discovery. For others, particularly our academics, this book could act as an invitation to complete additional research into under-explored avenues such as giftedness and aging; giftedness, trauma, and unique populations; and maybe giftedness and development. For me, I intend to write another book about gifted identity development to expand on the topics herein. I also plan to relate the intersection of giftedness and trauma to marginalized populations specifically.

Regardless of how you choose to use the information in this book, my hope is that you will come away from this exploration with a deeper understanding of the different ways gifted individuals experience and encounter trauma and post-traumatic growth, and that you might have a better understanding of what to do about it while fostering compassion for self and others. This was my foremost goal. Additionally though, and at the request of yet another gifted community member, I invite you to use this information as a launching point or material for reflection and healing.

Check in and reflect.

Feel all the things.

Honor your need for rest.

Personal Reflection (My Own Check-In)

Despite the length, breadth, and depth of this book, it was my first real book writing experience. I want my readers to know this to maybe inspire them, and myself. Sometimes, I might offer such information in an attempt to bypass rejection sensitivity, impostor syndrome, demand avoidance, and fear of criticism. However, I am finishing this book with a fairly firm belief that it is super meaningful and complete. In fact, from the forward on, this entire manuscript took me less than two months to write and offer in a fantastically finished form. When I shared this progress with a mentor and friend of mine, she replied, "You wrote it so quickly. It must have been desperate to get on the page." She could not be more correct. I have presented on and studied giftedness and trauma for many years. I also teach about it and live it with my clients. The information in this book is desperately needed and begged to be written for public consumption. Being the vessel for this task was and continues to be an honor.

As I finish this final reflection, therefore, I will address a final topic that may be the antithesis of traumatic contamination, and that is flow. For this entire writing experience, I was in a ***flow state***. I was continuously inspired and consistently passionate about the topic. For those who can relate to this flow state, remember this and use it. This kind of passion fuels not only our complex lives but also our recovery from them. So this final reflection of mine is actually a final invitation to you to do what you can to find this *flow*. It is there for discovery and is fueled by our beautiful and deep complexity, pattern-finding, meaning-making, and intensity.

And, as always, be well.

A Final (Chapter 15) Check-In

Exploration: This last chapter summarized the book and major themes while offering consideration for what readers might do with the information within. A final reflection was also offered.

Conclusion: There was a breadth and depth of information in this book about giftedness and trauma. The final hope, however, was for readers to come away from these pages with a deeper understanding of the different ways gifted individuals experience and encounter trauma and post-traumatic growth. Further, it's hoped that they gain a better understanding of what to do about this intersection while fostering compassion for self and others. A final invitation to seek a flow state was also offered.

Questions to consider include:

1. What were your final takeaways from this book?
2. What information surprised or fascinated you?
3. Was there any information that you found difficult to consider?
4. Are you familiar with feeling flow as it was described?
5. What are your final reflections otherwise?

Nervous system and mental/emotional health:

1. Check in with your mind, body, heart, and energy?
2. Is there any sensation, thought, or feeling that needs attending to?
3. Sit with any thoughts, feelings, or sensations with curiosity and openness as able.
4. Consider how you feel and experience a conclusion to this weighty topic. Take a break as needed and then return to chapters that warrant an additional look.
5. As always, honor your needs for rest and regulation.

Author's Glossary of Terms

Although many of the terms used in this book are defined within the text, I find it helpful to also address them in one place for easy reference. Unlike glossaries in some books, however, this will be a list of definitions and meanings *as I use them*. That is, these are my definitions in my words so you might better understand how terms are used throughout this text. Googling and cross-referencing terms may also be helpful.

◇◇◇◇◇◇

Alexisomia:

Sometimes called introspective alexithymia, this psychological neurodivergence may present as a difficulty in identifying body sensations and somatic experiences.

Alexithymia:

A psychological neurodivergence characterized by difficulties in identifying, describing, and expressing emotions, sometimes presenting as a limited emotional vocabulary and struggle to articulate feelings or understand the emotions of others.

Antarctic Flamingos:

Atypical anomalies, not to be confused with elite entities.

Aphantasia:

The inability to create or difficulty with creating mental imagery that can also make it difficult to readily visualize or recall images in one's mind's eye. It is common for aphantasic individuals to rely on verbal or conceptual memory.

Asynchronicity:

A phenomenon where different aspects of an individual's development progress at varying rates or occur independently of each other. With asynchronous development, cognitive, emotional, social, and physical growth may progress in a way that seems out of sync. It is important to understand, however, that what is considered typical in relation to development is based on majority standards.

Asynchronous Development:

Development that is judged as uneven with seemingly rapid or precocious gains in some domains and what may seem like slower, delayed, or difficult development in others.

Autopsychotherapy:

A self-guided journey of introspection and personal development that can be a valuable tool in gaining self-awareness, achieving personal transformation, and nurturing one's unique abilities and talents.

Big T Trauma:

Events or experiences that are immediately intensive and generally more singular in nature, such as war, school shootings, a serious car crash, an injury or attack, being involved in a natural disaster, or experiencing a major loss/death.

Bilateral Stimulation:

Stimulating the left and right side of the body alternatingly. Examples of bilateral stimulation included watching an EMDR light bar, listening to tones or music that alternate in left and right ears, alternating taps on each temple, knee, or shoulder etc., galloping on a horse, knitting, and so on.

Blunting (Psychological):

A phenomenon where individuals experience a reduction in emotional responses or a dulled affective experience involving a diminished range and intensity of emotions, resulting in a decreased ability to feel and express emotions compared to what would be considered typical or expected. Psychological blunting can manifest as a decreased capacity for joy, sadness, empathy, or other emotional states. It can also present as physical in nature where people feel disconnected from their bodies or experiences.

Bottom-Up Processing:

Treatment and processing approaches that focus on the body, its sensory receptors, and psychodynamic elements such as childhood experiences and personality development.

Classical Conditioning:

A type of learning that involves pairing a neutral stimulus with an unconditioned stimulus to elicit a conditioned response such that the once-neutral stimulus causes the same response as a previously more meaningful stimulus. (Remember Pavlov's dog?)

Compensation (Gifted Compensation):

When a person uses strengths or adaptive/creative problem-solving to overcome or work around asynchronicity, presumed weaknesses, or difficulties.

Complex Trauma:

Trauma that is often identified as a mix of both big T and little t trauma or different types and combinations of little t trauma, resulting in a complex developmental profile and trauma history.

Coping Skills:

Skills that are developed or otherwise obtained to help individuals cope with distress.

cPTSD (or Complex Post-Traumatic Stress Disorder):

A type of post-traumatic stress disorder that presents when a person is significantly (and diagnosably) impacted by complex and developmental trauma.

Cumulative Relational Trauma:

Seemingly minor, inconspicuous psychic wounds that are collected gradually, eroding an individual's self-esteem, distorting their character, and compromising their ability to connect with others.

Dabrowskian:

Doing or framing something in a way that considers Dąbrowski's theory of positive disintegration, inclusive of its five levels, the five overexcitabilities, many dynamisms, and concepts such as positive maladjustment and psychoneurosis.

Developmental Trauma:

Similar to (and often used interchangeably with) complex trauma, this is trauma that impacts developmental tasks and outcomes. It generally emerges during childhood and often results in cPTSD.

Dysautonomia:

A condition characterized by imbalance in the autonomic nervous system (ANS) which regulates vital bodily functions including heart rate, blood pressure, digestion, and temperature control. Dysautonomia can manifest as a range of symptoms such as orthostatic intolerance, dizziness, fatigue, gastrointestinal disturbances, and cognitive impairments, along with the more frequently diagnosed postural orthostatic tachycardia syndrome or POTS.

Ehlers-Danlos Syndrome (EDS):

A group of genetic connective tissue disorders that affects the integrity and strength of collagen, the main structural protein in the body. EDS leads to hypermobility, joint instability, skin fragility, and other symptoms.

EMDR (Eye Movement Desensitization and Reprocessing):

A therapy modality used by highly trained mental health professionals to process trauma, triggers, other difficulties, and developmental topics. EMDR is also used in this book to conceptualize trauma and trauma treatment.

Emotional Overexcitability (*E*OE):

An overexcitability that manifests through heightened intensities of feelings and emotions, and the experiencing of extremes of both desired and difficult emotions.

Existential:

Of or relating to deep topics involving one's very existence, including life-and-death considerations, the meaning of life, personal value, and moral contemplation, action, and injury (to name just a few).

Experiencing:

The gerund form of experience, used in this book to explore a process of undergoing or encountering events, sensations, emotions, or situations. Experiencing represents the actual lived occurrences or instances of personal involvement in various aspects of life.

Experimentation (Therapy):

A therapy tool used to help clients work around perfection, extreme expectations, fear, psychological resistance, and demand avoidance by suggested skills or behaviors as experiments rather than mandates or goals.

Flow/Flow State:

A state of being where a person experiences an influx of energy related to the value of a task in relation to personal values and authentic presentation.

Folx:

An alternative spelling meant to queerify the word folks, as a way of being inclusive and gender non-conforming.

Giftedness:

A neurodivergence and measure of identity inclusive of qualities such as advanced cognitive abilities (sometimes seen as creativity or creative problem-solving), rapid pattern-finding and meaning-making, seemingly asynchronous development and compensation, and overexcitability/heightened intensity that all lend to a qualitative difference in depth and when compared to neurotypical experience and presentation. *See also Antarctic Flamingos.*

Gifted (2e) Identity Development Theory:

A theory developed by therapist, author, and researcher, Patricia Williams (2023) that originally considered the process of navigating adolescence for 2e individuals, resulting in a more broadly applicable identity development theory. This theory involves four stages, and an alternate fifth stage that explores *what just is, what happened, what I did, who I am,* and *what I do.*

Goodness of Fit:

The idea that optimal development and even behavior, processing, and healing takes place where there is an appropriate match between a person, their unique personality and needs, and their environment (ecological systems).

Grounding:

A skill used to experience a physical/somatic calming of the nervous system that is obtained by engaging with one's environment in a way that helps an individual also remain present and secure.

HPA Axis:

The hypothalamic-pituitary-adrenocortical axis is a system in the body that helps regulate the response to stress. The hypothalamus releases corticotropin-releasing hormone (CRH), which stimulates the pituitary gland to release adrenocorticotropic hormone (ACTH). ACTH then triggers the adrenal glands to release cortisol, the "stress hormone." Cortisol helps the body cope with stress and returns to normal levels once the stress is resolved. Chronic activation of the HPA axis can have negative health effects.

Imaginational Overexcitability (*Im*OE):

An overexcitability characterized by unrestricted imagination, vivid imagery, and talent for detailed visualization that can also contribute to intensifying emotional responses and anxieties.

Impostor Syndrome:

The experience of high-achieving individuals who, despite their evident accomplishments, struggle to internalize their success. They might constantly doubt themselves and fear being exposed as frauds while finding it challenging to accurately attribute their achievements to their genuine competence.

Intellectual Overexcitability (*In*OE):

An overexcitability characterized by a heightened activity of the mind and displaying intensified intellectual engagement that may include a natural curiosity, deep concentration, and an increased capacity for sustained intellectual effort.

Intensity:

Used sometimes interchangeably with overexcitability, intensity is a measure of psychological presentation that exceeds what is considered a typical level of function or experience.

Just Fine:

When a gifted, masking, or compensating individual is judged as not struggling academically, emotionally, socially, or otherwise. "Just fine" is an assertion and label used to suggest a person who may be in need of support does not require the attention and effort needed to supply it.

Levels of Giftedness:

Five levels coined in some spaces as: *mildly*, *moderately*, *highly*, *exceptionally*, and *profoundly* gifted or *moderately gifted to gifted*, *highly gifted*, *exceptionally gifted*, *exceptionally to profoundly gifted (4th form)*, and *exceptionally to profoundly gifted (5th form)* with distinct differences residing in individuals' behaviors and experiences.

Little t Trauma:

Events or experiences that can be grouped under the umbrella of adversity. The term refers more to undesirable life experiences, such as chronic criticism, shaming, neglect of emotions or physiological needs, lasting health impairments, frequent discrimination and oppressive actions, chronic harassment or bullying, and sometimes childhood difficulties that result in developmental or complex trauma.

Lived Experience:

The direct interactions, observations, and insights individuals acquire as they navigate their personal journeys and engage with the world. It encompasses the subjective dimensions of an individual's existence, including their emotions, cognitions, convictions, and recollections, all influenced by their distinct background, cultural context, identity, and environments.

Marginalized Population:

Any population that is considered atypical or a minority in relation to the typical and socially acceptable mainstream culture and population. Marginalized populations experience marginalization by governments, societies, and other structural entities, in a way that restricts their access to privilege.

Masking:

When a person conceals their traits, disguises their behaviors, or experiences some combination thereof. In relation to the neurodivergent (ND) population, masking is typically discussed as a thing ND people do to conceal something from neurotypically (NT)-normed society. Sometimes it is to conceal a behavior that seems socially unacceptable, such as a stim or excitement about non-typical interests. Gifted individuals (another type of neurodivergence) might mask overexcitability, intelligence, difficulty (disability), or otherwise. For twice-exceptional (2e) persons, sometimes the giftedness masks the disability and the disability masks the giftedness in such a way that the individual is not identified as either.

Maslow's Hierarchy of Needs:
A frequently used psychology model, often depicted as a stacked triangle, that considers a person's needs and how they motivate behavior, cognition, and development.

Meaning-Making:
A desire to ascribe a significance or purpose to something while seeking connections between it and other experiences and patterns.

Mindfulness:
A meaningful awareness, presence of mind, and state of being that can be applied purposefully.

Misdiagnosis:
When a neurodivergent or positively maladjusted individual is diagnosed with a mental health disorder or condition that they do not have. (For example, when an emotionally overexcitable individual is diagnosed with depression because they experience an injustice deeply.)

Missed Diagnosis:
When a neurodivergent or positively maladjusted individual is not diagnosed with a mental health disorder or psychological profile/label that they align with and that they could benefit from. (For example, when a gifted individual has cPTSD that is missed because they compensate and seem "just fine.")

Neurobiology:
The cross-section of a person's neurology and biology that specifically considers the brain-body connection.

Neurodivergent:

A term for those with a mind and neurology that *diverges* from what is typical in a way that is innate, acquired, or both. Neurodivergence is a way of functioning that is considered different from the norm in relation to learning, processing, feeling, interpreting information, or thinking otherwise.

Neurodivergence:

The reality of being neurodivergent.

Neurodivergences (Neurodivergencies):

More than one neurodivergence in a population or within one person. For example, I have several neurodivergences including ADHD, giftedness, dyslexia, dysgraphia, and an auditory processing disorder. As a group example, we may notice several neurodivergences in the online communities including autism, adhd, dyslexia, and communication differences.

Neurodiverse:

A term used to describe two or more people (a group) with different neurological function. This can be two neurotypical people, two neurodivergent people, a neurodivergent and neurotypical person, or a group of all sorts of people. What we need to understand is that although not all people are considered neurodivergent, every brain is different.

Neurodiversity:

The natural diversity that exists within the human population in relation to how people function neurologically.

Neurodiversity-Affirmative:

When we work, live, learn, lead, teach, parent, coach, and otherwise think, feel, and behave in a way that affirms the reality of neurodiversity and each individual's identity as valuable and valid. Being neurodiversity-affirmative generally involves using identity-first language, avoiding ableist activity, decolonizing our language, and being multiculturally competent and effective. This also involves offering unconditional positive regard to people with different neurorealities.

Neurodiversity Movement:

A social justice movement that advocates for accepting and celebrating neurological differences in individuals while rejecting the view of these differences strictly as disorders. The Neurodiversity Movement promotes inclusion and supportive environments for neurodivergent individuals (and all people) to thrive in.

Neuromajority:

The majority population in relation to neurological functioning or a term used to refer to the majority of people as having a typical neurocognitive profile, though the actual majority may be more diverse.

Neuronormative:

A term used to describe the societal norms, expectations, and attitudes that favor or are biased toward typical (non-neurodivergent) behavior and processing. Use of this concept suggests that certain neurological traits or cognitive processes are "normal" while other neurodivergent traits are marginalized or stigmatized. In a neuronormative society, neurodivergent individuals may struggle with acceptance, accommodation, and being included.

Neurotypical:

A term used to describe individuals with typical neurological development and cognitive functioning. That is, a neurotypical person's brain and cognitive patterns conform to the majority or standard neurocognitive profile in society.

Operant Conditioning:

A method of learning that uses rewards and punishment to modify behavior, based on the idea that the consequences of a behavior determine the possibility of it being repeated. (Think, B.F. Skinner.)

Overexcitabilities (OEs):

Of or related to multiple OEs and often, more specifically relating to the five identified OEs including psychomotor, imaginational, intellectual, sensual, or emotional types.

Overexcitability (OE):

The manifestation of neurological capacities or psychic tension as reactions to stimuli, sometimes referred to as increased psychic excitability, intensity, or superstimulatability. OE is also often identified as an indicator of growth potential.

Pathological Demand Avoidance or Persistent, Pervasive Drive for Autonomy (PDA):

A psychological profile initially seen as a subtype of autism that is sometimes more broadly applied as a tendency for impacted individuals to neurologically perceive a demand placed on them as a threat that launches a fight, flight, freeze, or fawn response.

Pattern-Finding:

A tendency to look for patterns both mindfully and subconsciously as a means of rapidly learning and coding new or theoretical material.

PDAer:

A person with a PDA profile or belief that they live and present with significant demand avoidance.

Post-Traumatic Growth (PTG):

The positive psychological changes that individuals can experience following a traumatic event or upbringing. It encompasses personal transformation, increased resilience, and the development of new perspectives and values.

Psychomotor Overexcitability (*Pm*OE):

An overexcitability that involves a notable surplus of energy and the psychomotor expression of emotional tension.

Radical Acceptance:

The practice of fully and completely accepting reality as it is, without judgment, resistance, or attempts to change it. It involves acknowledging and embracing the present moment, including painful or difficult experiences, without attempting to deny or avoid them. Radical acceptance also involves letting go of the struggle against what cannot be changed and finding peace within oneself. It does not mean approving of or condoning the situation. Instead, it means choosing to accept it as an undeniable reality.

Rejection-Sensitive Dysphoria (RSD):

A disruptive manifestation of emotional dysregulation (severe emotional and physical pain) experienced by individuals when faced with real or perceived rejection, criticism, or teasing.

Resourcing (Mental Health):

The process of seeking or providing individuals with tools, strategies, and support to enhance their emotional well-being, coping skills, and overall resilience. It also involves helping individuals access and utilize internal and external resources to effectively manage their mental health challenges and promote overall psychological well-being. Resourcing techniques may include relaxation techniques, self-care practices, social support networks, therapy, and other interventions aimed at building emotional strength and resilience.

Risk and Resilience Framework:

A theoretical framework that maintains that there are both risks and protective factors in one's life that can either promote or hinder resilience and growth.

Skill Building:

Learning and trying new skills that reinforce one's ability to cope with and resolve psychological distress.

SMART (Goals):

An acronym used to conceptualize effective goal setting, generally understood as goals that are specific, measurable, achievable, relevant, and timely.

Sensual Overexcitability (*S*OE):

An overexcitability that encompasses a heightened experiencing of sensory and aesthetic pleasure and a deep appreciation for various senses, such as sight, smell, taste, touch, hearing, and even sexuality. *S*OE may manifest while finding delight in beautiful objects, the melodic sounds of words, music that resonates, captivating forms, vibrant colors, and harmonious balance. Furthermore, sensual overexcitability also manifests through the sensual expression of emotional tension.

Somatic Sensations:

The sensory experiences that arise from the body's nervous system and through the tissues, that are essential for our perception of the external world and for our awareness of our bodies' internal states. The somatic sensory system allows us to feel and respond to various stimuli, providing us with information about touch, temperature, pain, and proprioception.

Stim/Stimming:

Repetitive physical actions or sounds that might form a behavioral pattern and are frequently observed in neurodivergent individuals. This phenomenon, also referred to as self-stimulation, serves various purposes like offering comfort and aiding emotional expression.

Synesthesia:

An experience where stimulation in one perceptual pathway leads to experiences in another perceptual pathway. Some synesthetes, for example, report smelling colors, seeing music, or feeling a sensation of emotion that is then pictured as a wavelength.

They/Them Pronouns:

Pronouns commonly used by gender non-conforming, two-spirit, genderqueer, nonbinary, and gender-neutral individuals, as well as by those who do not wish to align themselves with the traditional gender binary. The use of they/them pronouns allows people to express their gender identity and experience in a way that goes beyond the traditional he/him or she/her designations.

Titrate/Titration (in Trauma Processing):

A chemistry term that refers to the process of adding a substance gradually and in controlled amounts to achieve a desired effect without overwhelming the system. In trauma processing, titration involves approaching traumatic material or memories in a gradual and manageable way. Titration can take place with a slow build-up over time. It can also take place such that a trauma therapist and client move in and out of engagement with traumatic material and ground or disengage between sets or sessions. This process offers balance and a sense of safety and control to the processor.

T.I.C.E.S.:

A model used in EMDR that provides a structured way of identifying and processing the different components that contribute to a person's traumatic memory or distressing experience. Each letter in T.I.C.E.S. represents a specific aspect of an experience including the triggering stimuli or target (T), associated imagery (I), an associated negative belief or cognition (C), activated emotions (E), and bodily or somatic sensations (S).

Top-Down Processing:

Treatment and processing approaches that focus on the cognitive and logical aspects of the brain along with stabilization and affect management.

Trauma:

A pervasive problem that results from exposure to an incident or series of events that are emotionally disturbing or life-threatening with lasting adverse effects on the individual's functioning and mental, physical, social, emotional, and/or spiritual well-being

Traumatic Contamination:

When trauma informs any categories, patterns, or meanings that impact the otherwise healthy mental coding process.

Trigger:

Stimuli or reminder that elicits powerful emotional and physiological responses in individuals with past traumatic experiences. Triggers can bring forth distressing memories, intense emotions, and physical sensations connected to the original traumatic event.

Twice-Exceptional (2e):

A designation that allows a person to identify as being both gifted and neurodivergent in at least one other way. Many 2e people have several neurodivergences.

Underachievement:

A label meant to identify gifted individuals who do not meet an expected level of accomplishment, especially when they are 2e and/or experience asynchronicity with a notable disparity between their presumed abilities and actual exploits. Gifted individuals who are judged as underachieving are also often accused of not applying themselves or being lazy. Labeling someone as underachieving bases their value on an ability to produce.

Whole-Person Approach (to Giftedness):

Rather than considering a person as being gifted in one or two areas (i.e. a gifted writer who cannot understand math), a whole-person approach looks at giftedness in an identity-first manner and considers how giftedness impacts the entire person from head-to-toe (mind, body, spirit) and permeates their identity.

Wise Mind:

An integration of "emotional mind" and "rational mind" processing that allows individuals to find a middle path or balance where their emotions and logic agree. In other words, it is the capacity to acknowledge and integrate emotions while also considering logical reasoning and objective facts. When someone is in their wise mind, they can potentially make more thoughtful and effective decisions.

About the Author

Bright Insight co-founder and president, Patricia Gently, MSMHC, PhD (formerly Williams), is a trauma therapist who specializes in Eye Movement Desensitization and Reprocessing (EMDR), Neurodiversity Affirmative Dialectic Therapy (NDA-DT), and Internal Family Systems (IFS) modalities. Through Bright Insight, Dr. Patty honors the whole person(s) while working to counsel, coach, and advocate for gifted, twice-exceptional (2e), and neurodivergent (ND) persons, along with other marginalized populations. Her unique involvement with this community gives her a platform through which Dr. Patty writes, presents, and educates others. As a 2e adult, Dr. Patty is no stranger to topics impacting gifted, 2e, and neurodivergent persons and makes it her mission to connect with others, authentically. Outside of her work as a therapist and advocate, Dr. Patty teaches at various universities as an associate professor of psychology. She is also on the California BrainWaves neuroscience advisory board as a 2e specialist and is a state chapter leader for Free Mom Hugs, a group of parents, friends, and allies supporting the LGBTQIA+ community.